I0889318

The Cold War and Academic Governance

SUNY Series

FRONTIERS IN EDUCATION

Philip G. Altbach, Editor

The Frontiers in Education Series draws upon a range of disciplines and approaches in the analysis of contemporary educational issues and concerns. Books in the series help to reinterpret established fields of scholarship in education by encouraging the latest synthesis and research. A special focus highlights educational policy issues from a multidisciplinary perspective. The series is published in cooperation with the Graduate School of Education, State University of New York at Buffalo.

Class, Race, and Gender in American Education
—Lois Weis (ed.)

Excellence and Equality: A Qualitatively Different Perspective on Gifted and Talented Education
—David M. Fetterman

Change and Effectiveness in Schools: A Cultural Perspective
—Gretchen B. Rossman, H. Dickson Corbett, and William A. Firestone

The Curriculum: Problems, Politics, and Possibilities
—Landon E. Beyer and Michael W. Apple (eds.)

The Character of American Higher Education and Intercollegiate Sport
—Donald Chu

Crisis in Teaching: Perspectives on Current Reforms
—Lois Weis, Philip G. Altbach, Gail P. Kelly, Hugh G. Petrie, and Sheila Slaughter (eds.)

The High Status Track: Studies of Elite Schools and Stratification
—Paul William Kingston and Lionel S. Lewis (eds.)

The Economics of American Universities: Management, Operations, and Fiscal Environment
—Stephen A. Hoenack and Eileen L. Collins (eds.)

The Higher Learning and High Technology: Dynamics of Higher Education and Policy Formation
—Sheila Slaughter

Dropouts from Schools: Issues, Dilemmas and Solutions
—Lois Weis, Eleanor Farrar, and Hugh G. Petrie (eds.)

Religious Fundamentalism and American Education; The Battle for the Public Schools
—Eugene F. Provenzo, Jr.

Going to School: The African-American Experience
—Kofi Lomotey (ed.)

Curriculum Differentiation: Interpretive Studies in U.S. Secondary Schools
—Reba Page and Linda Valli (eds.)

The Racial Crisis in American Higher Education
—Philip G. Altbach and Kofi Lomotey (eds.)

The Great Transformation in Higher Education, 1960–1980
—Clark Kerr

College in Black and White: African-American Students in Predominantly White and in Historically Black Public Universities
—Walter R. Allen, Edgar G. Epps, and Nesha Z. Haniff (eds.)

Textbooks in American Society: Politics, Policy, and Pedagogy
—Philip G. Altbach, Gail P. Kelly, Hugh G. Petrie, and Lois Weis (eds.)

Critical Perspectives on Early Childhood Education
—Lois Weis, Philip G. Altbach, Gail P. Kelly, and Hugh G. Petrie (eds.)

Black Resistance in High School: Forging a Separatist Culture
—R. Patrick Solomon

Emergent Issues in Education: Comparative Perspectives
—Robert F. Arnove, Philip G. Altbach, and Gail P. Kelly (eds.)

Creating Community on College Campuses
—Irving J. Spitzberg and Virginia V. Thorndike

Teacher Education Policy: Narratives, Stories, and Cases
—Hendrik D. Gideonse (ed.)

Beyond Silenced Voices: Class, Race, and Gender in United States Schools
—Lois Weis and Michelle Fine (eds.)

Troubled Times for American Higher Education: The 1990s and Beyond
—Clark Kerr

Higher Education Cannot Escape History: Issues for the Twenty-First Century
—Clark Kerr

The Cold War and Academic Governance

The Lattimore Case at Johns Hopkins

Lionel S. Lewis

STATE UNIVERSITY OF NEW YORK PRESS

Production by Ruth Fisher
Marketing by Dana E. Yanulavich

Published by
State University of New York Press, Albany

Printed in the United States of America

For information, address the State University of New York Press, State University Plaza, Albany, NY 12246

Library of Congress Cataloging-in-Publication Data

Lewis, Lionel S. (Lionel Stanley)
The Cold War and academic governance : the Lattimore case at Johns Hopkins / Lionel S. Lewis.
p. cm. — (SUNY series, frontiers in education)
Includes bibliographical references and index.
ISBN 0-7914-1493-0 (ch.: acid-free paper). — ISBN 0-7914-1494-9 (pbk.: acid-free paper).
1. Academic freedom—Maryland—Baltimore—History—20th century. 2. Teaching, Freedom of—Maryland—Baltimore—History—20th century. 3. Lattimore, Owen, 1900–1989. 4. College teachers—Maryland—Baltimore—Political activity—History—20th century. 5. Johns Hopkins University—History—20th century. I. Title. II. Series.
LC72.3.M3L48 1993 92-24053
CIP

10 9 8 7 6 5 4 3 2 1

Contents

Illustrations

Preface and Acknowledgments

This book begins by examining the on-campus harassment of the Johns Hopkins University sinologist Owen Lattimore during the height of the Cold War on campus and moves from detailing specifics in a broad context to discussing the broad theme of academic governance set in a specific institution. In terms of the individual involved, the university targeted, and the political passions aroused, the Lattimore case is arguably the most notorious McCarthy-era incident in which a faculty member's career was threatened.

During the Cold War, institutions of higher learning typically sacrificed faculty in the face of political pressure. The Johns Hopkins University did not. This study considers why the university successfully resisted the assault on faculty rights, in an effort to better understand the workings of academic governance.

Although there have been other accounts of such incidents in American colleges and universities, this book is the first structural analysis of an institutional response to the Cold War on campus. Using archival and other secondary sources, it closely examines academic governance—both formal and informal processes—under the stress of Cold War political pressures, both external and internal to the campus.

Johns Hopkins' institutional authorities flinched sometimes with inaction, equivocation, and far-from-forthright statements; yet, the university's administration held its ground and Lattimore was not fired, principally because the board of trustees, contrary to popular belief, was more the captive of the administration than the reverse.

Because of its focus on the issue of academic governance, this is less a story about Lattimore than about how the Johns Hopkins University reacted to the storm around him, a major event in U. S. academic history.

In writing a book, one inevitably accumulates many debts, and I would like to acknowledge some of them here. The following organizations made materials available: Arnold & Porter, Washington, D.C.; the Special Collections Department, William R. Perkins Library, Duke University; the Federal Bureau of Investigation, Washington, D.C.; the Pusey Archives, Harvard University; Widener Library, Harvard University; the Special Collections Department, the Milton S. Eisenhower Library, the Johns Hopkins University; the Ferdinand Hamburger, Jr., Archives and archivists James Stimpert and Brian Harrington, the Johns Hopkins University; the Nevada Historical Society, Reno; the Special Collections Department, University Library, University of Nevada, Reno; the Enoch Pratt Free Library, Baltimore, Maryland; the Seeley G. Mudd Manuscript Library, Princeton University Archives; the Rockefeller Archive Center, Pocantico Hills, North Tarrytown, New York; the Franklin D. Roosevelt Library, Hyde Park, New York; and the American Heritage Center, University of Wyoming.

I am also grateful to a number of individuals who offered helpful suggestions while this book was taking shape: Ben Agger (State University of New York [SUNY]/Buffalo), Philip G. Altbach (SUNY/Buffalo), Victor Doyno (SUNY/Buffalo), Hugh Hawkins (Amherst College), Joel I. Nelson (University of Minnesota), Robert P. Newman (University of Pittsburgh), Beth Anne Shelton (SUNY/Buffalo), and C. Vann Woodward (Yale University).

Finally, I would like to express special appreciation to Ms. Nancy Komorowski for typing many drafts of the manuscript.

This book is dedicated to four friends with whom and from whom I first learned sociology: Joseph Lopreato, S. Dale McLemore, Joel I. Nelson, and Derek Phillips.

Introduction

In any society all ideas and beliefs are not considered to be of equal importance. There is general agreement about which are the most important or sacred, and which are the least important or sacred. Dogma is not casually or readily questioned; established opinions are accepted as indisputable and final. The more important ideas and beliefs are seen to be, the more they are protected from any challenge, whatever the cost. Ideas and beliefs that are accepted as final in science are called natural law. In religion they are called revelation. In government they are called the constitution.

Those who do not accept what the majority agrees are absolute truths put themselves at risk. They are labeled as heretics, and they are often pursued by moral entrepreneurs—those who take on the task of assuring conformity. Committed to enforcing absolute truths, moral entrepreneurs act, as if under compulsion, to punish heretics for insisting on other, divergent truths.

It is not uncommon for those who have taken it upon themselves to safeguard the system of beliefs to persuade others to support their efforts, no matter how extreme. Attempts to punish heretics who deny what the majority holds as absolute truth are thus sometimes overwhelming and relentless. Collective efforts to secure conformity seem to take on a life or a rhythm of their own; they do not readily subside. The thousands of documents examined in writing this book clearly show how the activities of moral entrepreneurs reverberate and gather force, even in the face of counterpressure.

This book explores what happens when moral entrepreneurs—those who are mobilized and who attempt to mobilize others to impose conformity in society—attempt to silence someone who expresses ideas contrary to generally accepted beliefs. Specifically, in the years after World War II, some Americans, alarmed by Soviet expansionism and what they believed to be the concomitant loss of American power and influence in world affairs, put pressure on the administration and board of trustees of the Johns Hopkins University to discipline a faculty member who held views that—in their eyes—were heretical. The punishment the moral entrepreneurs demanded for this political heterodoxy was the loss of employment, the loss of both a livelihood and a forum.

Owen Lattimore, the faculty member whom the moral entrepreneurs wanted punished, and a prominent sinologist with a tenured appointment at the university, had expressed ideas about events in Asia that to many Americans seemed too congruent with, and supportive of, Soviet foreign policy. What he had written in a dozen books and scores of scholarly, magazine, and newspaper articles, and said in speeches and interviews, offended the conventional definition of world events. He advised that the United States need not be as concerned by the successful Communist revolution in China as some thought it should be; he did not see changes in the government of China as a grave danger to American interests. Against the background of the Cold War, his conclusions were a good deal more than simply unpopular; many judged them to be wrong, dangerous, and un-American. A number of public figures—primarily Senator Joseph R. McCarthy, and secondarily Senator Pat McCarran—raised questions about Lattimore's loyalty. He was defamed and indicted, although, in the end, he was neither convicted nor fired.

Like Lattimore, the administration and board of trustees at the Johns Hopkins University were called to account. Those around the country who believed that Lattimore's views were a serious threat to America demanded that university authorities punish him. Between 1950 and 1955—and even after he was cleared by the courts—moral entrepreneurs used the media, correspondence, and personal contacts with great intensity to convince administrative officers and the board of trustees to apply sanctions against Lattimore. During this period the university, like Lattimore, was under constant attack. In their efforts to have Lattimore fired, the moral entrepreneurs engaged in name-calling and ridicule; they made threats, such as withholding financial support and calling in civil authorities. They questioned the integrity of the administrative officers and trustees of Johns Hopkins. They demanded considerable attention, and forced the university to consume substantial resources. They persuaded many university officials that Lattimore was an undesirable who deserved punishment. They caused dissension within and between constituencies on campus effecting considerable change.

Sanctions affect both deviants and their social worlds. Thus, to understand fully the efficacy of the moral entrepreneurs, it is necessary to consider not only what happened to Lattimore, but also what happened at Johns Hopkins during the period pressure was being exerted on university authorities to punish him. At a minimum, this examination will enable us to learn something about how the Cold War was experienced over an extended period of time at one American institution of higher learning.

After World War II, Senator Joseph R. McCarthy led a crusade against the imagined spread of Communism in the United States. Perhaps the most salient characteristic of this crusade was widely publicized, indiscriminate, and largely unsubstantiated allegations of disloyalty to the country, directed most often at government employees, labor leaders, educators, and entertainers. Indeed, this is what McCarthyism—a word that is said by some to have been added to the American vocabulary by Lattimore himself[1]—has come to mean. It has become almost a cliché to describe this zealous political movement as a witch-hunt. The materials presented in this book show how, in at least one case, the process of enforcing political orthodoxy worked in precisely this manner. Those who held unpopular views were searched out and harassed. Their freedom to believe and say what they wanted and to associate with whom they wished was challenged. Constitutional rights were challenged.

This is not, however, an examination of McCarthyism; that story has been told many times. Moreover, the perhaps unanswerable question of whether Lattimore's recommendations regarding American foreign policy in Asia were valid, is also not pursued, although certainly many of his predictions have proved to be true. To be sure, like Senator McCarthy, Lattimore has had, and continues to have, both defenders and critics. It has long been recognized that the Lattimore case was pivotal to the debate surrounding the so-called loss of China by the Nationalists to the Communists, a debate that for many years was at the heart of attacks on the Truman administration and its foreign policy. However, the impact of McCarthyism and the Cold War on the governance of institutions of higher learning, as exemplified by the Lattimore case, is the issue here, not ideology. The principles of academic freedom and tenure make Lattimore's politics and the charges against him largely irrelevant. As a tenured faculty member, his views and behavior were not subject to administrative review unless it were shown that he had acted illegally or unethically, or had been derelict in his duties. What happened to Lattimore is a well-documented piece of American history. What happened at Johns Hopkins is, by contrast, not well-known.

A close and careful look at how the governing board on one campus handled a single problem has implications for our understanding of how institutions of higher learning function. Researchers have studied who is on governing boards, but not how they go about their work. As a consequence, we know almost nothing about the process of their decision making. The disposition of the Lattimore case by the Johns Hopkins authorities thus can provide a great deal of information about the conditions and possibilities of academic governance.

In the late 1980s there was a renewed interest in academic life during the height of the Cold War. When Lattimore died in the spring of 1989, considerable commentary appeared in newspapers across the country, echoing the controversy of the 1950s;[2,3,4] he was both praised and condemned. Within a relatively brief period, four books about the effects of the Cold War on the academic careers of those on the political left were published, after nearly two decades in which the topic was barely discussed.

The first of these was Ellen W. Schrecker's *No Ivory Tower.*[5] Schrecker sets out to "explore the response of administrators and faculty members to the anti-Communist furor of the 1940s and 1950s,"[6] although her book is really about the experiences—before, during, and after the blight of McCarthyism—of a number of academics who were identified or labeled as Communists. She focuses on a few dozen individuals, in or near the Communist party before World War II, who in the 1950s defied legislative authorities investigating their earlier political activities. After interviewing these resisters, nearly all of whom were summarily fired, Schrecker recounts with more earnestness than objectivity how the onslaught of McCarthyism ruined careers and families. She describes poignantly but unreliably how her respondents saw and were affected by events.

In *Stalking the Academic Communist,*[7] David R. Holmes thoroughly examines the life of Alex Novikoff, a professor of experimental biology and associate professor of biochemistry at the University of Vermont, who was dismissed in 1953 after his political activities in 1930 had been made public. Novikoff was terminated following his refusal to reveal to the Senate Internal Security Subcommittee the names of others who had been in the Communist party with him in the 1930s.

Like Schrecker's, Holmes' account is basically from the perspective of the individual faculty member. From this point of view, established rules and principals seemed to be mindlessly sacrificed by the administration of the University of Vermont in the name of anti-communism. Academic administrators are presented as wantonly uncaring and irrational. There may well be more to the story, however. In Holmes' analysis, the experiences and perspectives of the University of Vermont's president and his colleagues are virtually absent and hence largely unknown. The assumptions that guided them, whatever they may have been, are not considered. In short, missing from Holmes' study is how matters looked to institutional authorities, the facts and pressures they confronted, and what these might have meant to them.

Notwithstanding its subtitle, Charles H. McCormick's book, *This Nest of Vipers: McCarthyism and Higher Education in the Mundel Affair, 1951–52,*[8] is mostly about the aftermath, on campus and in the local community, of an academic administrator's efforts to upgrade a backwater college (Fairmont State College in West Virginia). Against the backdrop of the Cold War, it is not surprising that one of the charges made against Luella Mundel before her dismissal was that she was a "poor security risk." But the Cold War, and questions of loyalty, political beliefs, subversive activities, and the like, are eclipsed by the intrigue, provincialism, and pettiness of faculty, administrators, board members, and citizenry. From the ensuing court case, which is described in fascinating detail, one gets the impression that the mendaciousness and narrow-mindedness of individuals explain more about events than the political climate of the institution in question. This dreadful story, attributing nonconformity, atheism and, immorality to faculty merely trying to keep their livelihood, has been retold countless times in the past 150 years.

In *Cold War on Campus,*[9] I examine the experiences of 126 faculty members from fifty eight campuses whose appointments were threatened or lost between 1947 and 1956 because of their political beliefs and activities. In my attempt to determine which faculty were most likely to become victims of the Cold War on campus, I closely examined the role played by academic administrators in the disposition of these cases. With few exceptions—whether at large or small institutions, public or private, prestigious or local—the mass of evidence indicates that academic authorities failed to afford faculty due process and to defend academic freedom. Faculty who were not fully open and cooperative with institutional committees established to inquire into their political beliefs and activities, or with institutional authorities, were invariably fired. Senior administrators seemed to act out of concern that they and their institution would be harmed by unfavorable public attention, rather than in reaction to outside pressures or the fear of communism or subversion. Institutional politics drove the Cold War on campus. Yet, as with the three other books, *Cold War on Campus* is a faculty story.

Concentrating mostly on the targets of the assault—left-wing faculty—the four books say little about the impact of events, such as congressional investigations, on academic authorities. As with earlier discussions of what was occurring on campus during the height of Cold War tensions, these analyses are primarily concerned with how the lives of individual faculty were changed during this period; the focus has been on how the Cold War affected individuals, not how it affected the structure and function of colleges and universities. There is little, for example, about how various incidents were understood or mediated by institutional authorities. Indeed, looking at academic life during the Cold War years mostly from the vantage point of faculty, the behavior of academic administrators and governing boards at times appears inexplicable. One is left with the impression that most ignored their long-term, fundamental responsibility: protecting the integrity of their college or university. They seemed neither to care about the welfare of faculty, nor to understand academic tradition. They showed almost no regard for the guarantees of academic freedom and tenure. Is it possible that the great majority of academic administrators would be so unprincipled, or are there other factors that must be considered, factors that will explain this seemingly appalling lapse? Clearly, it is necessary to learn more about the experiences of those who governed institutions of higher learning during the Cold War in order to provide a meaningful answer to this question.

On nearly every campus where the political views or activities of academics caught the attention of the administration, the suspected faculty came to grief. Faculty were dismissed, with or without the formality of a hearing, sometimes with little or no evidence that they had done anything wrong.

> Administrative responses were more often anticipatory than reactive. The habit of acquiescence appeared to be well developed among academic administrators. Of course, many responses and programs, like the introduction of loyalty oaths, were both. When pushed by anyone other than faculty or students, academic administrators were for the most part open to the most implausible assertions, timid, and quite pliant.[10]

Institutions, such as Illinois Institute of Technology, Massachusetts Institute of Technology, Antioch College, Sarah Lawrence College, the University of Rochester, and the University of Connecticut, where academic administrators showed some commitment to academic freedom or fair play, were few. The Johns Hopkins University can be added to this short list.

Because faculty were commonly victimized by the Cold War on campus, less might be learned about why American higher education responded as it did by studying yet another college or university that embraced McCarthyism than by studying one that did not. Since the institutional support given Lattimore was so different from what (with a handful of exceptions) befell faculty elsewhere, this detailed examination of the Lattimore case at Johns Hopkins has the potential to expand our understanding of what happened on American college campuses during the Cold War. Studying the deviant case should help to elucidate the common responses of acquiescence and capitulation.

Dalton Trumbo, one of the blacklisted Hollywood Ten, observed that the "dark times" of congressional investigations, the reactionary forces which gave rise to them, and blacklisting produced "only victims."[11] All the participants—tormented and tormentors—in the Cold War were bruised. There has been a great deal said and written about those individual victims, from Alger Hiss to Richard Nixon.[12] However, little has been said and written about the institutions that may have been casualties. This study addresses that imbalance, considering the Cold War on campus from the perspective of those who managed an institution of higher learning during this period.

Although most of the analysis concerns the pressures brought to bear on the administration and board of trustees at the Johns Hopkins University to fire Lattimore and the countermoves on campus, it is necessary to establish the background to the controversy. Attention is given first to Lattimore—his views, the charges against him, the congressional inquiry into his loyalty, and how the matter reached and was resolved by the courts. Chapter 2 examines the moral entrepreneurs' pursuit of Lattimore and the administration and board of trustees of the Johns Hopkins University. Drawing upon a wide array of examples, Chapter 3 details the enormous pressure on Johns Hopkins to punish Lattimore. The next three chapters are concerned with how the administration and board of trustees at Johns Hopkins responded to, and were affected by, the flood of controversy surrounding Lattimore. This, of course, is the heart of the book. Of particular interest in the analysis is the material, in large part letters and newspaper articles, that came to the attention of the authorities at Johns Hopkins, and to which they were expected to respond. Some implications to larger questions—how institutions of higher learning are governed, how decisions are made in organizations, how the Cold War on campus was driven, and the potency of academic tradition—are discussed in the final chapter.

1

Lattimore's Views and the Question of His Loyalty

Two facts make the Owen Lattimore case possibly the most celebrated and controversial incident involving an academic during the Cold War era. First, Lattimore, a recognized authority on the Far East, was one of the most visible and influential academics challenged to prove his loyalty. Second, Senator Joseph R. McCarthy, the most visible and influential anti-Communist zealot, identified Lattimore as a Soviet operative. An overview of the government's inquiry into Lattimore's views and activities, and the reasons why his loyalty came under question must first be understood before considering the involvement of the Johns Hopkins University in the case.

Lattimore's Career and Writing

Lattimore was first appointed to the faculty of Hopkins in 1938, and in 1939 was made director of its Walter Hines Page School of International Relations. During the 1930s he had established a worldwide reputation as a sinologist, with particular expertise in the economic, political, social, and cultural life of Mongolia. His extensive travel, writing, and lecturing had put him in contact with, and made his ideas known to, a wider audience than is usual, then or now, for college or university faculty. He was the sort of intellectual involved in public discourse; his writing addressed an interested public on a public issue, American foreign policy.

Over the years, Lattimore had been a consultant to a number of government officials. He had even been an advisor to Chiang Kai-shek in the months before and after America's entry into World

War II. However, after the war he had conspicuously spoken out against Chiang's autocracy, and had questioned many of the policies and actions of Chiang's Nationalist government. He had become convinced that because the corruption in Chiang's regime was so pervasive, reform was unlikely. In two books, *Solution in Asia* (1945) and *The Situation in Asia* (1949), and in a number of newspaper and magazine articles, Lattimore warned that it was a dead-end policy to back Chiang as a matter of course, and that in pursuing its interest in Asia the United States would at some point have to negotiate with the Soviet Union as an equal. Lattimore had also become convinced that due to the growth of nationalism in Asia, the West would no longer be able to control events there. It was beyond the power of the United States, even with the help of its allies, to restore the old colonial order, under any guise. Lattimore believed that world conflict, whether rooted in Asia or elsewhere, could be settled only if all the major powers made compromises; it would certainly never be settled if they ignored or confronted one another.

To many Americans, the loss of China to the Communists in 1949 was an avoidable calamity, and a calamity, in large part, because it seemed to enhance the Soviet Union's power. Lattimore disagreed. He believed that the changes in China could not have been prevented. In a quite controversial and widely read article in the January 1950 *Atlantic Monthly*,[1] Lattimore pointed out that although Chiang Kai-shek had been an effective leader during World War II, in the postwar years he had failed to hold his people's confidence as an architect of a new and viable social and political structure. Largely due to this fact, the United States policy backing Chiang was a failure, and this reality had to be acknowledged. Lattimore was convinced that a State Department policy of determined support for Chiang had done, and would continue to do, more harm than good to American interests. It seemed self-evident to Lattimore that the fall of Chiang had damaged American prestige. The Nationalist cause may have been good and just and for that reason should have been won. However, it had been poorly defended, and it had failed. Given the incompetence of the Nationalists, it could not possibly have succeeded.

Lattimore argued that neither India nor Japan could become satisfactory instruments of American policy. He reviewed the reasons that he believed also made it unlikely that Southeast Asia, the Philippines, or Korea would end up as major bases of American action. Lattimore went on to express the view that the Communist regime of Mao Tse-tung could not be brought into line by economic coercion. He predicted that it had only to achieve a minimum level of economic stability to make itself politically tolerable to the majority of the Chinese people. He believed that it would win popular support, that it could feed the masses.

Contrary to almost everyone else's expectation, Lattimore doubted that the Soviet Union could easily move in and take over direct control in China. The matter was much more complex; the Soviet Union's primary interests were in Europe. On the other hand, American interests could only be advanced with a more positive approach to Communist China. As a start, he suggested that if the United States did not directly want to recognize the legitimacy of the Communist government in China, it should at least not block the United Nations' efforts to do so.

In looking toward the future, Lattimore argued that Asian nondependence on the Soviet Union should become a central tenet of American foreign policy. Toward this end, the United States could encourage the nations of Asia to do without the Soviet Union through improving the three-way economic relationship between Asia, Europe, and America.

Peace around the world, Lattimore again argued, could come about only if there was stability in the relationship between the United States and the Soviet Union.

> The grounds for compromise therefore exist. They are: less control over Asia than Europe wants; less political independence in some countries, and less economic independence in most countries, than Asia wants; more socialism, more state enterprise, and more neighborly relations with Russia than America wants.
>
> On these grounds of compromise, United States policy in Asia can be rebuilt successfully enough not only to stabilize Asia, but to contribute to the stabilization of the world.[2]

These views were not part of the main current of American thought in 1950, or for many years after, although in the end they proved, in large measure, to be correct.

A few months after the *Atlantic Monthly* article appeared, Lattimore began yet another magazine article, "Asia Reconquers Asia,"[3] with the assertion that the change in power in China was not a victory for the Communist armies or Communist ideas:

> The chief phenomenon has been the moral and political bankruptcy of the National government of China, whose "ability" to

> collapse greatly exceeded the ability of the Communists to push it over.

He again expressed the view that the new Asia was controlled neither by the Western powers nor the Soviet Union. He wrote that Russia's role in the Communist victory in China was insignificant: "Whatever the Russian strength [in Asia], it remains behind the Russian frontier—undeployed, unexposed, a card unplayed."

> The importance of this relative absence of Russian intervention in China has been overlooked partly because of the human tendency toward wishful thinking.
>
> The American policy in China costs a great deal. It is somehow more comforting to provide an alibi by claiming that the American intervention failed because of a stronger Russian intervention than to confess that the effort failed of its own ineptness.[4]

It was Lattimore's contention that the Communist ascendancy in China meant that for the first time in a hundred years the country was beyond the control of the most powerful of the Western nations. He predicted that Europe would never again regain its old power over Asia, and would probably lose most of the power it still retained. Moreover, he believed that "experience in China is a warning that very little of Europe's former power over Asia has passed into the hands of the United States."[5]

Lattimore was adamant in his belief that the security of the United States would be enhanced if it helped to promote the evolution of democracy in Asia by the peoples of Asia. America should not attempt to subordinate Asia to the defense of its interests, Lattimore concluded, but should link American and Asian interests in a common cause. Again, this line of thinking was clearly a minority view, and, because of who Lattimore was, it generated considerable criticism.

In the months before the United States became involved in World War II, Lattimore was closely involved in the U.S. government's attempts to make peace between Chiang's Nationalists and the Communist forces. The Roosevelt administration was determined to prevent American military aid to China from being dissipated in a civil war. Thus, when he was appointed as the political advisor of Chiang Kai-shek, it was hoped that Lattimore would effect some compromises between the hostile factions. President Roosevelt was convinced that Lattimore could be successful, and gave him considerable latitude. In a letter to Chiang Kai-shek, Roosevelt stated:

> My dear Generalissimo:
>
> I take great pleasure in introducing to you Mr. Owen Lattimore. I have the highest opinion of his capabilities and I know that he is intimate with and in complete accord with my basic political attitudes. I trust that you will find his advice helpful. I fully appreciate, as does he, that while serving as your political advisor he will be working solely in China's interests and that his complete loyalty will be to you.
>
> It has taken some time to work up a comprehensive and detailed lease-lend aid program for China and to fit it in with our own and the British programs.
>
> Mrs. Roosevelt joins me in extending to you and Madame Chiang our heartiest wishes for your personal health and prosperity.[6]

On their face, Lattimore's efforts to minimize conflict between competing political forces in China acknowledged the legitimacy of the Communist cause. Given his views and the role it was believed he had played in implementing policies that seemed to work to Chiang's disadvantage, it is hardly surprising that Lattimore was very much out of favor with those friendly to the Nationalist Chinese cause and opposed to all Communist governments. In the months after the forces of Mao Tse-tung overthrew Chiang's regime and forced him from the mainland to Formosa, this annoyance turned to acute and open antipathy. The climate of the Cold War insured that Lattimore and his ideas of coexistence would be forcefully attacked.

The 1940s: Before the Cold War

Actually, doubts about Lattimore's political sympathies were voiced even before the Cold War. A few months after he was appointed as liaison between Chiang Kai-shek and President Roosevelt, it was reported that even the Nationalist government had some concerns:

> He is likewise suspected of leaning rather toward left-wing causes, and there was the feeling in some quarters that the recent announcement by the official Chinese Central News Agency of the outbreak of new fighting between the Kuomintang (Nationalists) and Red forces, the first of such press

> announcements ever to be made, was synchronized with the arrival in Chungking of Mr. Lattimore to impress him with the wickedness of the Chinese Communists.
>
> Advocates of this interpretation pointed out that the clashes apparently were not of any great seriousness and that in the past even larger outbreaks had been regarded with no great alarm.[7]

Questions were again raised about Lattimore not long after he was appointed as the chief economist of the Reparations Commission in Japan in 1945. The congressional committee investigating the delivery of government secrets to the magazine *Amerasia* made formal inquiries into why he, having been a member of the magazine's editorial board, was an instructor at a training school for diplomats run by the State Department. It was made public that he had five listings in an index of Communist-front organizations previously issued by the House Committee on Un-American Activities, that he lectured jointly with someone who had twenty-three such listings, and that he was "one of the principal writers for the Institute of Pacific Relations, a veritable mill of Russian propaganda."[8] In the October 1945 issue of the *China Monthly,*[9] Alfred Kohlberg, a virulent and early critic of Lattimore and State Department policy in the Far East, quotes unidentified Chinese as having "asked their American friends why, if President Roosevelt wanted to send an advisor [to Chiang Kai-shek], did he have to pick a Red?"[10] He went on to assert that under Lattimore's editorship, the tenor of articles in *Pacific Affairs* largely followed the Communist line, particularly refraining from any criticism of the government of China between the United Front agreement of February 1937 and the Hitler-Stalin pact of August 23, 1939. "During the seven years of Mr. Lattimore's editorship, *Pacific Affairs* featured numerous articles by well-known pro-Soviet and Communist writers."[11] He accused Lattimore of wanting to "lock China into the Communist world system."[12] In a lengthy reply,[13] Lattimore took issue with many of Kohlberg's statements, and angrily dismissed as ridiculous the charges that he was a Communist or had Communist sympathies. He, in turn, accused Kohlberg of drawing unjustified conclusions "from a mass of incorrect statements and unwarranted imputations." He called the allegation that he was a Communist "slanderous."[14]

In a 1945 article in *Reader's Digest,*[15] "The Fate of the World Is at Stake in China," Max Eastman and J. B. Powell described Lattimore as "perhaps the most subtle evangelist" in promulgating the "deception" that "Russia is a democracy," and that it is therefore safe to leave China to its influence. Not only had Lattimore irresponsibly not condemned Stalin's reign of terror in the 1930s, but, Eastman and Powell argued, in the 1940s he had been urging the U.S. government and people "to accept cheerfully the spread of 'the Soviet form of democracy' in Central Asia."[16] This sort of thinking would surely bring nearly one-half billion people under totalitarian regimentation. Eastman and Powell concluded that this number, added to the 200 million enslaved in the Soviet Union, was a threat to any hope for a truly democratic world and would ensure that Iran and India would follow the same path as China. Lattimore's thinking was contradictory to the "clear-headed, informed and resolute campaign" needed to promote popular forms of government.[17]

Individuals in the government joined in condemning Lattimore and his work in China. Senator Kenneth S. Wherry, a Republican from Nebraska, took up the theme that because of his Communist sympathies, Lattimore had worked against American interests.

> But when that plan [to avert the attack on Pearl Harbor] reached Chiang Kai-shek, in that momentous hour when the fate of America was hanging between peace and war, there stood at Chiang Kai-shek's elbow another one of the Communist fellow travelers, Owen Lattimore, a notorious champion of Communist revolutionary tactics and philosophy. There he stood in that critical moment, as the agent of the United States government, the State Department, not only did Chiang Kai-shek turn this plan down, but Owen Lattimore wrote to the President's representative . . . a passionate appeal against the sending of that note to the Japanese. How does it come about that Communists or Communist sympathizers in this country and worshippers of Soviet Russia managed to find themselves so often at the very point where the switch must be turned one way or the other to determine the course of our government?[18]

In 1947, Lattimore was one of 102 artists, writers, actors, and others named by the American Legion's National Americanism Commission as unsuitable for sponsorship as speakers or entertainers. According to the American Legion, those placed on the list "do not adhere to the same beliefs that we adhere to," and therefore it would be inappropriate to invite them to functions or meetings.

Lattimore barely reacted to the publication of the list, claiming that the only other person named with whom he was acquainted was William L. Shirer (he did not know any of the others—e.g., Margaret Bourke-White, Lee J. Cobb, José Ferrer, John Garfield, Dashiell Hammett, Burl Ives, Gene Kelly, Ring Lardner, Jr., Frederick March, Arthur Miller, Zero Mostel, Clifford Odets, Artie Shaw, Kurt Weill), and that he would "always be glad to be on any list with him."[19]

In the late 1940s, the charge was frequently made that Lattimore had secretly written Henry Wallace's report on China, following his 1944 mission there, which purportedly advocated shifting support away from the Nationalist government to the Communists. Many, in and out of government, were convinced that Lattimore had been central in a clique working on behalf of the Communists to destroy the Nationalists. In the October 1948 issue of the *China Monthly,*[20] Kohlberg charged that Lattimore was part of a "plot [which] developed in May, 1943 . . . [that] planned to slowly choke to death and destroy the government of the Republic of China and build up the Chinese Communists for post-war success."[21]

In the fall of 1949, a memorandum was prepared for J. Edgar Hoover, director of the Federal Bureau of Investigation (FBI), reviewing intelligence that Lattimore was a spy or foreign agent.[22] Lattimore had been placed "under investigation by the Bureau as a Soviet espionage agent" primarily because of his contacts with suspected subversives. The FBI believed what it had learned

> coincides with the belief expressed by—admitted Soviet agents who expressed the belief that Lattimore is a Russian agent . . . . advised that he considered Lattimore to be an unswerving devotee to Communist ideology and that as a member of the State Department during World War II, Lattimore was a disrupting and disloyal influence. . . . Undoubtedly Lattimore is not a card carrying member of the Communist party as he is too useful to them otherwise and that his membership and affiliation could only be proved by a comparison of Lattimore's writings and expressions with the Communist party line.

The FBI was especially concerned about Lattimore's appointment by the secretary of state to a three-person advisory committee charged with reviewing the situation in China and Central Asia in order to determine American foreign policy.

> Assuming Owen Lattimore is a Soviet agent as alleged, a fact which has not been proved or disproved, it is reasonable

> that Lattimore could be of immense importance to the Russians both as an advisor to this committee in that it will formulate United States foreign policy with relation to the Far East and also because of the authoritativeness with which his writings are accepted by the American public.

At the bottom of the memorandum, Hoover responded: "This is shocking. Press vigorously investigation of Lattimore."

The criticism of the State Department over the loss of China to the Communists was particularly virulent. Public figures representing a variety of political views, but most particularly Republican members of Congress, were relentless in their attacks on policy and personnel. "Who lost China?" was asked repeatedly. Asking the question presupposed an answer, and people expected one. Purely by personalizing the issue of subversion, Senator Joseph R. McCarthy was becoming a national political figure. Featured in the conservative press, the denunciations helped foster the widespread public perception that a number of career diplomats had sold out China, had betrayed American interests, had actually abetted the Communist takeover of a wartime ally and friend. From the first, Lattimore became enmeshed in the attack on the State Department and its China policy.

Senator McCarthy's Attack

Against the backdrop of Alger Hiss's conviction for perjury (which to many simply meant that he was guilty of treason) two and a half weeks earlier, Senator Joseph R. McCarthy galvanized the assault with his often-quoted and controversial speech to the Republican Women's Club in Wheeling, West Virginia, on February 9, 1950. In that address, he asserted that he had a list of 205 individuals involved in "a spy ring" known to the secretary of state as "members of the Communist party and who nevertheless are still working and shaping policy in the State Department." Senator McCarthy more than once modified his charges (e.g., "Last night I discussed the Communists in the State Department. I stated that I had the names of fifty-seven card-carrying members of the Communist party"), but most Americans hardly noticed the inconsistencies.[23] The charges readily captured the public's imagination. It did not much matter how true McCarthy's allegations were; the speech and what was to follow were hardly about truth.

While in Afghanistan with a United Nations technical assistance mission in late March 1950, Lattimore received word that he had been accused by Senator McCarthy of being the "top Soviet [Russian] espionage agent" in the United States.[24] Earlier in the month (on March 13), Senator McCarthy had told a senate committee that Lattimore had Communist sympathies and that his record as a pro-Communist went back many years. When he initially gave his testimony about Lattimore, Senator McCarthy referred to him as "a policy-making State Department attaché collaborating with those who have sworn to destroy the Nation by force of violence."[25]

Almost daily, it seemed, there were leaks to the press linking Lattimore to a variety of improprieties. Lattimore's was called the "No. 1 case";[26] what followed would rival the Hiss case and rock the country. Although Senator McCarthy downgraded his original charge, first to "one of the top Communist agents" in the country, and finally to a "bad policy risk,"[27] few seemed to notice the difference.

Senator McCarthy asserted that Lattimore, who was without question "a Soviet agent,"[28] had taken the opportunity during those times when he was employed by, and was an advisor to, the State Department to infect America's foreign policy toward China. Lattimore was described as the chief or principal "architect" of American Far Eastern policy. McCarthy expressed concern about Ambassador-at-Large Philip C. Jessup's "apparent wholehearted trust in and reliance on" Lattimore's judgment, which made him the "voice of Lattimore"—"a dangerously efficient Lattimore front."[29] He stated that U.S. Far Eastern policy, and especially China policy, followed Lattimore's recommendations "step for step."[30] Since, the accusation continued, Lattimore was the "former boss of Alger Hiss" in an "espionage ring in the Department,"[31] it was hardly surprising that official government policy had become pro-Communist. The charge that Lattimore was instrumental in formulating American foreign policy was partly based on a memorandum that he had submitted to the State Department Round Table on Far Eastern Policy the previous October. His central theme was that

> the aim of the United States policy should be to enable the countries of the Far East to do without Russia to the maximum extent. This is a much more modest aim than insistence on an organization of hostility to Russia; but it is an attainable aim, and the other is not.[32]

In a four-hour speech in the Senate at the end of March, Senator McCarthy asserted that he had an important witness who would swear that for years Lattimore had been a member of the

Communist party. He accused the secretary of state of being "the voice for the mind of Lattimore," and charged that every major aspect of the State Department's Far Eastern policy had followed a line welcomed by the Soviet Union and recommended by Lattimore. He promised that he would "give some documentation to show that [Lattimore] is a Soviet agent and also that he either is, or at least has been, a member of the Communist party." He said that he possessed a deposition in which it was sworn that Lattimore had acknowledged that he was "declassifying [removing the restrictions on] secret documents in favor of some friends."[33] Senator McCarthy added that he was less interested in whether Lattimore was a paid espionage agent than in seeking to prove that he was a dominant influence in the development and implementation of the policy which delivered China to the Communists.

Establishing Lattimore's culpability was clearly important to McCarthy. It was to be a test case upon which he would risk his reputation. He stated that he would stake his case that the government had been penetrated by Communists on proving Lattimore guilty. He told the press:

> I am willing to stand or fall on this one. If I am shown to be wrong on this I think the subcommittee would be justified in not taking my other cases too seriously. If they find I am 100 percent right—as they will—it should convince them of the seriousness of the situation.[34]

This attention and offensive by Senator McCarthy was of grave significance. McCarthy was a great deal more than a powerful politician; he was to become towering. As Richard Rovere observed, "He held two presidents captive—or as nearly captive as any presidents of the United States had ever been held. . . ."[35]

On returning to the United States, Lattimore called Senator McCarthy's charges "base and contemptible lies." He referred to him as a "madman," a "base and miserable creature," and a "hit-and-run politician." He said that Senator McCarthy's charges against him had been made "falsely, irresponsibly and libelously." He added that the Soviet Union should decorate Senator McCarthy for "telling the kind of lies about the United States that Russian propagandists could not invent."[36]

The principal witness supporting Senator McCarthy's charges was Louis F. Budenz, former managing editor of the *Daily Worker* and member of the national committee of the Communist party. Senator McCarthy promised that Budenz would testify that Lattimore "was known to him to be a member of the Communist party, a member over whom they had disciplinary powers."[37] When he later gave public testimony, Budenz recounted how he had been told by high-ranking party officials Earl Browder and Frederick V. Field that Lattimore's assignment was to organize writers to put out stories to lull the American public into believing that the Chinese Communists were merely reformers and not dangerous revolutionaries.

The Tydings Committee

On February 22, 1950, the U.S. Senate adopted a resolution authorizing the Committee on Foreign Relations to conduct an investigation into the loyalty of employees of the State Department. A subcommittee of the Committee on Foreign Relations (the Tydings committee) was appointed, and between March 8 and July 7 it called thirty-five witnesses over thirty-one days to give testimony in public or executive session. Among those who gave evidence to the committee were Senator McCarthy and Lattimore.

When Senator McCarthy appeared before the committee in open session, he testified that Lattimore had held numerous positions with the State Department, and had been one of its most regular consultants. He told the committee in executive session that it was his understanding that Lattimore had free access to a desk and all of the files in the State Department. McCarthy insisted that Lattimore's FBI file would show "in detail not the case merely of a man who appears to favor Russia, not the case of a man who might disagree with what we think about Russia, but a man who is definitely an espionage agent."[38]

In addition to Budenz, Freda Utley, a former member of the British Communist party, appeared as a witness and made a determined effort to tie Lattimore to the cause of communism. In her testimony, Utley attempted to demonstrate that by the early 1940s Lattimore's writings consistently followed the Communist party line; he had become a defender of Communists and communism. She did disagree with Senator McCarthy that Lattimore worked as an operative for the Soviet Union, but this was not really to defend him, as in her mind McCarthy erred by understatement:

> I think that Senator McCarthy was wrong in his original statement that Owen Lattimore is the Soviet government's top

espionage agent in America. I think the senator underestimated Lattimore. Mr. Lattimore is such a renowned scholar, such an excellent writer, so adept at teaching the American people that they ought to stop opposing the great, good and progressive Soviet government, that it is impossible to believe that Moscow would regard him as expendable, as all spies are. To suggest that Mr. Lattimore's great talents have been utilized in espionage seems to me as absurd as to suggest that Mr. Gromyko or Mr. Molotov employ their leisure hours at Lake Success, or at international conferences, in snitching documents.

I do not know whether Mr. Lattimore is a member of the Communist party or know the influence he has devoted to the detriment of America, but, as I say, his function has been to lead us to destruction.

Although Utley conceded that she had no concrete proof or personal knowledge that Lattimore had Communist ties, she compared him to a "Judas cow" that in a stockyard leads other animals to slaughter. She was convinced that he knew that what he was writing and saying was false. He cleverly hid his intent.[39]

Lattimore had been openly and plainly labeled; there seemed to be a good deal to which he needed to respond. In early April, he was given an opportunity to defend himself. Appearing before the Tydings committee with his principal attorney, Abe Fortas, of the prestigious Washington law firm of [Thurman] Arnold, Fortas & [Paul] Porter, Lattimore denied the charges, and in a forty-two page prepared statement, directly and aggressively counterattacked Senator McCarthy. He questioned McCarthy's methods and probity, repeating his contention that the charges were "base and contemptible lies."[40] (For the temper of this testimony, see Appendix B.) He was most concerned that Senator McCarthy ultimately would silence those whose views were contrary to his and who were opposed to further military or economic aid to the Chinese Nationalists' cause.

Now it is obvious that Senator McCarthy and I differ on each of these points. Judging from his unquestioning acceptance and extensive use of the propaganda of the so-called China Lobby, he is at least its willing tool. The senator seems to feel that everyone is disloyal whose opinions do not agree

> with those of himself and the China Lobby with respect to total and complete commitment of the United States to the Nationalist government of China. Some of his denunciations are understandable only on the theory that he believes that anyone is disloyal whose opinions on China policy during the last 9 or 10 years parallel or support those of the government of the United States. In the latter category the senator would have to include General George C. Marshall, General Stilwell and presumably the various Secretaries of State, Messrs. Hull, Stettinius, Byrnes and Acheson.[41]

He vigorously denied the charge that he was a Communist:

> I am not and never have been a member of the Communist party. I have never been affiliated or associated with the Communist party. I have never believed in the principles of communism nor subscribed to nor advocated the Communist or Soviet form of government either within the United States, in China, in the Far East, or anywhere in the world. I have never consciously or deliberately advocated or participated in promoting the cause of communism anywhere in the world.[42]

The Democratic majority on the Tydings committee was predisposed to believe Lattimore. During Lattimore's testimony, Senator Tydings informed him:

> I think as chairman of this committee that I owe it to you and to the country to tell you that four of the five members of this committee, in the presence of Mr. J. Edgar Hoover, the head of the FBI, had a complete summary of your file made available to them. Mr. Hoover himself prepared those data. It was quite lengthy. And at the conclusion of the reading of that summary in great detail, it was the universal opinion of all of the members of the committee present, and all others in the room, of which there were two more [the attorney general and the first assistant attorney general], that there was nothing in that file to show that you were a Communist or had ever been a Communist, or that you were in any way connected with any espionage information or charges, so that the FBI file puts you completely, up to this moment, at least, in the clear.[43]

Even after these encouraging words, Lattimore's attorneys were not sanguine. There was a danger that Lattimore could be overwhelmed by the political climate, or worse.

> Washington today is in a state of hysteria which you wouldn't believe unless you were here. The fantastic cloak and dagger intrigue, the bribery which we suspect surrounds the Lattimore case, is unthinkable.[44]

In July, the Tydings committee concluded that there was no basis for Senator McCarthy's accusations. The Democratic members on the committee denounced his charges of communism in the State Department as false and "contemptible." They accused their colleague of conscious falsehoods and of serving the interests of communism by raising baseless suspicions. In the most blistering terms, the report characterized Senator McCarthy's charges and methods as a "fraud and a hoax perpetuated on the Senate of the United States and the American people."[45]

It is not surprising, then, that Lattimore was exonerated: "From the foregoing we are left with no alternative but to believe that every possible unfavorable twist has been applied to the information concerning Mr. Lattimore by those presenting it against him. The misrepresentations are clear and demonstrable." The committee did not believe that Lattimore had been, as Senator McCarthy had charged, the "architect of our Far Eastern policy." It left no question of where it stood with regard to Senator McCarthy's basic accusation.

> We find no evidence to support the charge that Owen Lattimore is the "top Russian spy" or, for that matter, any other sort of spy. . . . We have every confidence that were Mr. Lattimore an espionage agent the efficient FBI would long since have taken action against him. . . .
>
> We do not find that Mr. Lattimore's writings follow the Communist or any other line, save as his very consistent position on the Far East may be called the Lattimore line.

The committee's majority found that Budenz's testimony against Lattimore could establish no more than that the Communists used him "to project a propaganda line anent China."[46] It concluded that Lattimore had never been connected in any proper sense with the State Department except as a one-time advisor. The committee did suggest that perhaps Lattimore was not always discreet in his associations.

Many critics of the State Department saw the Tydings committee's work as little more than a whitewash. Senator McCarthy called the committee report "an evil fraud" giving a "clean bill of health to Stalin's fifth column in this country." He predicted that it would give "a green light to the Red fifth column in the United States." He added that it would be a signal to the "traitors, Communists and fellow travelers" in government that they need have no fear of exposure from the Truman administration.[47]

In his capacity as an official of the American China Policy Association, Alfred Kohlberg, the long-time and committed adversary of Lattimore, sent an open letter to Senator Tydings charging that the report had made numerous factual statements "in large part not taken from the testimony." Kohlberg suggested that some outside source may have been drawn upon in drafting the report, and asked Senator Tydings if Lattimore or his attorney had helped write it. As far as Kohlberg was concerned, Lattimore was not peripheral to what many saw as the problems in the State Department.

> You left the real question unanswered. Who so advised President Truman that though he stepped into office as commander of the most powerful armed forces in the history of the world heading an alliance of 1,890,000,000 people, he is today the commander of skeletonized forces fighting the armies of a satellite of Red China, which is in turn a satellite of the Soviet Union?
>
> Professor Lattimore may claim "clearance" by you; the administration that permits Communist meetings and the Communist press to cheer North Korea and blackguard Americans who are dying tonight for liberty in that far-off country may claim "clearance" by you; the 1,700 *Amerasia* documents may be "cleared": but who will do the "clearing" when the bill is paid in "blood, sweat and tears?"[48]

In spite of the Tydings committee conclusions, the attacks on Lattimore were far from over. Even before the committee issued its report, Senator McCarthy had asked President Truman to "silence" Lattimore. Speaking at a convention of the Sons of the American Revolution in May, McCarthy asserted that Secretary of State Dean Acheson "bought" a plan for the Far East, masterminded by Lattimore, that was "gigantic in its fraud and complete in its deceit." The plan, which McCarthy had characterized as the "Acheson-Lattimore axis," would enslave Asia as it involved "hitting Communists at the front door with a silk handkerchief while they beat the brains out of your friends at the back door". . . . "That was the plan for China; that is Lattimore's plan for South Korea." McCarthy argued that by their actions, Secretary Acheson and Lattimore had forfeited their right to speak for America.[49]

There was no pause in Senator McCarthy's attacks on Lattimore even after the Tydings committee report had been made public in July. Ten days after its release, McCarthy told his colleagues in the Senate that Lattimore had sold his summer home in Vermont to an "avowed" Communist for a $3,000 profit, and suggested that the transaction might have been a "pay-off" by the Communists. McCarthy added that Alger Hiss, the former State Department official convicted of perjury for denying Communist ties, had a summer home near Lattimore's.[50] Lattimore continued to repay in kind, calling McCarthy a publicity-seeking demagogue who was prompted by pro-fascists, ex-Communists, anti-Semites, and "similar fringe fanatics of the political underworld."[51]

The McCarran Committee

In November 1950, the Senate Committee on the Judiciary was authorized to make an investigation and study of the Internal Security Act of 1950; of the administration, operation, and enforcement of other laws relating to espionage, sabotage, and the protection of the internal security of the country; and of the extent, nature, and effects of subversive activities in the United States.

In part due to a dissatisfaction with the work of the Tydings committee, as well as to specific charges made by Senator McCarthy, it was decided to investigate the Institute of Pacific Relations, an international body organized in Honolulu in 1923 under the auspices of the Young Men's Christian Association (YMCA) as a clearinghouse for information about the Far East, and composed of countries with interests in the region. Its founders hoped to promote understanding of the area and its problems. The Soviet Union had long been a member. The purpose of this specific inquiry was to determine the extent to which the institute may have been infiltrated or controlled by Communists and dominated by Communist ideology, and—whatever the influence of communism—what effect the institute may have had on American foreign policy and public opinion in the 1930s and 1940s. The investigation was designed to determine whether subversive influences softened the policy of the United States toward Mao Tse-tung's Communist forces in China, and as a consequence harmed Chiang Kai-shek's Nationalists. When it held its hearings between July 1951 and June 1952, this second investigatory body, the Internal Security Subcommittee of the Senate Committee on the Judiciary, chaired by Pat McCarran of Nevada (the McCarran committee), was considerably less friendly toward Lattimore than the Tydings committee.

As far as the inquiry into the Institute of Pacific Relations was concerned, the McCarran committee narrowed its focus to determine whether or to what extent the institute was part of the Communist world conspiracy and how it may have exerted an influence on U.S. foreign policy. The investigation was informed by the premise that a number of officials and staff of the institute had disseminated pro-Communist propaganda about economic, political, and social conditions in the Far East, and had successfully oriented American foreign policy toward Communist objectives. The inquiry was to unravel who was involved and how the goal had been achieved.

The Institute of Pacific Relations was believed to have had a substantial influence on American foreign policy in the Far East in the 1930s and 1940s, the years that the country's power in that region declined. Some in and out of government had come to believe that this was because the Institute of Pacific Relations, and particularly its leadership, was secretly under Communist control and for many years had been used as an instrument of Soviet foreign policy.

Lattimore's long-standing relationship with the Institute of Pacific Relations put him again directly in the spotlight. As had become apparent when the Tydings committee had investigated him, Lattimore was indeed visible and had a following, actually, more than he was willing to acknowledge. He claimed he was merely a writer, reporting on what he had observed, and that he did not try to impose his ideas on others. Indeed, he contended his views had had virtually no effect on government policy. His work and ideas were known to government officials. Among other things, he was known to some in the State Department, had been a presidential appointee to the Chinese Nationalist government when he was serving as the political advisor to Chiang Kai-shek, had been the deputy director of the Office of War Information in the Pacific area during World War II, and was a member of Henry Wallace's mission to Siberia and China. He had also been a member of the board of trustees and for a short time a member of the executive committee of the Institute of Pacific Relations. Moreover, for seven years, from 1934 until 1941, he had been the editor of *Pacific Affairs,* a quarterly published by the institute and taken quite seriously by policy makers and in the academic community. The charge had been made that under the editorship of Lattimore, *Pacific Affairs* had become a vehicle for Soviet propaganda, and like Lattimore had had considerable influence on the thinking of those in the State Department who determined and carried out American foreign policy. Instead of preventing the fall of China to the Communists, American foreign policy, badly distorted by *Pacific Affairs,* Lattimore, and those whom he had published, contributed to the process. Thus, in the eyes of some, Lattimore was seen as having a major responsibility for the defeat of the Nationalists by the Communists.

Few doubted that Lattimore was one of the half dozen or so experts on Asia—nearly all in one way or another affiliated with the Institute of Pacific Relations—who, as World War II came to an end, had attempted to move American foreign policy with respect to China away from full and unqualified support of Chiang Kai-shek's Nationalist government. He was seen as being instrumental when after the war the United States seemed to adopt a policy less favorable to the Nationalists. Once more it was alleged Lattimore had argued that Mao Tse-tung and his followers were basically reformers who would bring about democratic changes, that their real goal was agrarian reform, and that their movement had no connection with communism in the Soviet Union. When the McCarran committee decided to look into the activities of the Institute of Pacific Relations, it was hardly surprising that Lattimore became a central figure to the inquiry.

Although in his testimony Lattimore adamantly denied most of the allegations made against him ("I never believed that the Chinese Communists were merely agrarian reformers. I have always believed that they were right straight down-the-line Communists"[52]), the proceeding did not go well for him. The head of the Russian Department of the Voice of America in the State Department who had been a general in the Russian army testified that Lattimore and a friend were designated in the mid-1930s by another general, the chief of the Soviet military intelligence, as "our men" who could be depended on to use the Institute of Pacific Relations to work with Soviet military intelligence. The generals were discussing individuals who might help in a Russian scheme to build up secret caches of arms in China. He further stated that this information had been repeated—"they are still our men"[53]—by another general, the underground leader of Soviet military intelligence, some years later. Lattimore denied these accusations, stating that in 1934, he had no contact with Russia and had never been in Russia. (For relevant testimony, see Appendix C.)

As he did before the Tydings committee, Louis F. Budenz again claimed he had been told by party officials that Lattimore was a member of the Communist party.

> **Mr. Budenz.** He was specifically mentioned as a member of the Communist cell under instructions. There was no loose mention of his name.
>
> **Senator Ferguson.** Was it ever discussed in these [Politburo] meetings that Owen Lattimore was a man who could put out propaganda and conceal the Communist activity, but still have it carry out the policy of the Communists?
>
> **Mr. Budenz.** That was precisely the estimate given, that the weight of his discussions was always along the lines of the Soviet policy, but that they were expressed in that language which was non-Soviet in character.[54]

An Asia specialist from Yale University, David Rowe, told the committee: "As of today, among Far East specialists in the United States, Lattimore is probably the principal agent of Stalinism. . . ."[55] It was also said that Lattimore made trips to Communist China and the Soviet Union, "receiving extensive privileges there. . . ."[56] He was accused of "trying to advocate the Stalinist approach"[57] in *Pacific Affairs.* His book, *Solution in Asia,* was described by an employee of a Communist bookstore as a publication used to give the party viewpoint. (For relevant testimony, see Appendix D.)

Lattimore engaged in a protracted *pas de deux* with one or another of the senators on the McCarran committee. Not counting his testimony in executive session, he appeared publicly before the committee for twelve days between February 26 and March 21, 1952.[58] His testimony was the high point of the committee's hearing. From the beginning, Lattimore vigorously assailed the committee as being deliberately unfair, determined to find Communist designs even where none existed. In language forceful and unequivocal, he argued that the committee was so intent to find evil that it had given undue credence to "a nightmare of outrageous lies, shady hearsay and undisguised personal spite."[59] He bitterly accused the committee of suppression and distortion of evidence and of welcoming "stacked"[60] testimony that was harming individuals and the Nation.

> All kinds of attempts have been made to depict me as a Communist or a Soviet agent. I have in fact been falsely iden-

tified as a fellow traveler, sympathizer, or follower of the Communist line or promoter of Communist interests. Now I want to make my position clear. I am not interested in fine or technical distinctions. I am not interested in graduations or degrees of disloyalty. I have no use for fancy, legalistic distinctions. I am none of these things and have never been. I am not and have never been a Communist, a Soviet agent, a sympathizer, or any other kind of promoter of communism or Communist interests, and all of these are nonsense. I so testified long ago, under oath, before the Tydings committee, and I do so again.[61]

Lattimore's defense was to no avail; he had stumbled into a net. At least the majority of the committee had made up their minds about him.

Senator Eastland. You have always read what Owen Lattimore wrote?

Mr. McGovern. I will not say I have read every word he has written, but I have read several of his books.

Senator Eastland. What kind of a Communist did you think he was?[62]

The obvious bias further inflamed Lattimore and frustrated his allies. As one of his attorneys (Thurman Arnold) saw it:

Never in my life have I seen anything more vicious or contemptible than the way the committee is trying to break Lattimore. They are crookedly and dishonestly attempting to spring traps on him. So far they have not succeeded, in spite of day after day of constant hammering by at least four or five people. McCarran threatened to throw Abe out of the hearing room. He also threatened to throw me out for attempting to protect our client against this sort of unfair questioning. They let Lattimore go on Friday, to be called back again. There seems to be no end to it.[63]

The McCarran committee long ago gave up all idea of proving Lattimore was a Communist. Instead they spend weeks of time in trying to catch him up in contradictions and give the impression that he is an evasive and untruthful witness.[64]

Senator McCarran in turn immediately counterattacked Lattimore, characterizing his defiant challenge as not being out of line with the general procedures of the Communist party. The exchange between Lattimore and various committee members was so spirited and prolonged that in his first two and a half hours of testimony he was able to complete only the first eight sentences of his prepared eighty-page, 17,500-word statement. In his testimony, Lattimore was unwilling to retract or modify the attack on the committee and its witnesses that he had written and circulated to the press. Some committee members were offended by Lattimore's aggressiveness and disrespect; others were incensed.

After he completed his testimony, which Arnold characterized as "the longest congressional interrogation of one man ever conducted,"[65] Senator McCarran soundly rebuked Lattimore for his attitude and deportment. His conclusions were described as "insulting"; he was described as "flagrantly defiant of the United States Senate" and "evasive, contentious, and belligerent"; and his language was described as "insolent, overbearing, arrogant and disdainful."

> He flouted the committee, he scoffed at the committee's efforts, he impugned the committee's methods and he slandered the committee's staff. His language was frequently such as to outrage and offend both the committee as a whole, and its members individually; and, apparently, with intent to do so.
>
> Few witnesses within the memory of the members of this committee have been permitted to use language as intemperate, provocative and abusive of the committee, as Mr. Lattimore used in his prepared statement, which he was permitted to read. No witness, so far as any member of the subcommittee can recall, ever before was given free rein to read, before a senate committee, a prepared statement so clearly contemptuous of the committee of the senate.

In sum, Lattimore's behavior was characterized as "an affront to the people of this Nation." So that his observations would have the maximum impact, Senator McCarran had Senator Herman Welker of Idaho place them in the *Congressional Record*.

Not only was Lattimore accused of being offensive and of attributing bad faith to the members of the committee, but also of making assertions that he could not substantiate.

Beyond Lattimore's discourtesy ("fusillade of invective"), the senators were offended by "his efforts to confuse and obscure the facts." Senator McCarran also pointed to "patent" and "flagrant" untruths in the record, mostly with regard to the timing and details of events and what Lattimore knew or did not know about the politics of others.[66]

Indeed, Lattimore was at times confused, vague, or imprecise on a number of points, and the committee members were persuaded that his misstatements had material implications.

> **Mr. Morris.** Will you read the first paragraph of that letter, please?
>
> **Mr. Lattimore.** Yes.
>
> Dear Carter: Currie asked me to take care of his correspondence while he is away and in view of your telegram of today, I think I had better tell you that he has gone to China on a special trip. This news is absolutely confidential until released in the press.
>
> **Mr. Lattimore.** Mr. Morris, I should like to add to what I have just said that this refreshes my recollection and that I believe that Currie told his secretary to open his mail and to pass on to me anything that might be of concern to me.
>
> **Mr. Morris.** Mr. Lattimore, I am asking you if you can reconcile the statement you have just made with your testimony in executive session which reads as follows—
>
> **The Chairman.** The page?
>
> **Mr. Morris.** Page 26.
>
> **Mr. Morris.** Mr. Lattimore, isn't it a fact that when Currie went away for a period of time he would ask you to take care of his mail at the White House?
>
> **Mr. Lattimore.** No. When I was back on leave from China in the summer of 1942 Mr. Currie allowed me to use an outer office attached to his office.
>
> **Mr. Morris.** What do you mean allowed you to use it?
>
> **Mr. Lattimore.** He said there was an empty office there with a desk and a chair in it, and I was living in Ruxton and when I came over to Washington and had appointments to see people, and so forth, I used that as the place where I hung my hat.
>
> **Mr. Morris.** Tell me this, Mr. Lattimore. Is it your testimony that you did not at the request of Lauchlin Currie take care of his mail at the White House when he was away?

Mr. Lattimore. That certainly is my statement.

Mr. Chairman. Again, will you please read that paragraph that you read in that letter? Read it out loud.

Mr. Lattimore (reading): Currie asked me to take care of his correspondence while he is away and in view of your telegram of today, I think I had better tell you that he has gone to China on a special trip. This news is absolutely confidential until released in the press.

Obviously my memory was inaccurate.

Mr. Morris. That is written on White House stationery, is it Mr. Lattimore?

Mr. Lattimore. Yes, dictated to Lauchlin Currie's secretary.

Mr. Morris. Are you acquainted with the testimony before this committee that Lauchlin Currie aided an espionage ring in Washington during the war?

Mr. Lattimore. No, I don't remember seeing that.

Mr. Morris. Did you read Miss Bentley's testimony to that effect?

Mr. Lattimore. No, I didn't.

Mr. Morris. Is it your testimony you have not read all of the published hearings of this committee, Mr. Lattimore?

Mr. Lattimore. No, I haven't read all of them.

Mr. Morris. Are you acquainted with the testimony before this committee that Lauchlin Currie had informed agents of an espionage ring that the United States was about to break the Soviet code?

Mr. Lattimore. No, I don't remember reading that. Oh, I think I have read that in the press, but I don't remember reading it in the transcript.[67]

The heading of one section of the McCarran committee's lengthy report was "Owen Lattimore was from some time in the middle 1930s a conscious, articulate instrument of the Soviet conspiracy."[68] The conclusion of the report reiterated this judgment. It specifically charged that he had testified falsely "with reference to at least five separate matters that were relevant to the inquiry and substantial in import."[69] The senators seemed convinced that in the main Lattimore's activities had had an adverse effect on American foreign policy interests.

There was no evidence from the committee's investigation or from the verifiable testimony of other witnesses that Lattimore had lied when he denied being a Communist, a member of the Communist party, a Soviet spy, or a fellow traveler. Nonetheless, the committee recommended that the Justice Department have a grand jury determine whether Lattimore had made deliberate misstatements on other matters when he gave testimony to them. Roy Cohn, the assistant U.S. attorney for New York, was called upon to lead in the preparation of the government's case to a grand jury.

The Indictment for Perjury

After deliberating for more than two weeks, the grand jury was convinced that Lattimore had indeed perjured himself and in December 1952 voted to indict him on seven counts of perjury, as to his sympathies with communism or Communist interests, whether he had been told or knew certain persons were Communists, whether when he was editor of *Pacific Affairs* he had published articles by individuals he knew were Communists, whether he had had a luncheon engagement with the Soviet ambassador to the United States after Germany invaded Russia in 1941, whether he deliberately lied when he told the senators that he did not take care of Lauchlin Currie's mail at the White House, and whether he had made prearrangements with the Communist party to travel to Yenan. The key issue was whether or not Lattimore had lied when he denied promoting Communist interests. The maximum penalty for each count was ten years' imprisonment. Not unexpectedly, the Johns Hopkins University immediately placed Lattimore on a leave of absence with pay. Three days after the indictment was made public, Lattimore entered a plea of not guilty. Senator McCarran was dogged in pressing the government to pursue the case against Lattimore. He demanded the removal of the attorney the Justice Department had assigned to prosecute the case because he did not appear to be vigorously committed to the task. At a Senate Judiciary Committee hearing he extracted a promise from the attorney general–elect that the case would expeditiously go forward.

During the expected and usual legal skirmishing and delay in moving the case to trial, Lattimore and his attorneys filed ten motions and exhaustive written briefs. Then, in the late spring of 1953, a federal district court judge, Luther W. Youngdahl, former Republican governor of Minnesota, held that four of the counts (including the main count, which he found to be "fatally defective") were so "nebulous and indefinite" as to be invalid, and that the other three were indefinite enough that Lattimore was entitled to a bill of particulars giving him certain information so that he could defend himself. He recognized that constitutional rights—freedom of belief, of speech, of association—were at issue.

> The arguments against the validity of count one are even stronger when applied to counts three and four. Counts three and four must also be stricken down as violative of the First and Sixth Amendments. . . .
>
> Count seven is clearly defective in its plain inconsistency and indefiniteness. . . .
>
> As the Court previously indicated there is serious doubt whether the remaining counts two, five and six can ultimately pass the test of materiality so as to present a jury issue. But this must await the trial.[70]

On review, the court of appeals in part agreed that there was too much "vagueness" in the indictment and concurred by a vote of eight to one that two of the charges (including the main count) were invalid and should be dismissed.

> We are of the opinion that this first count of the indictment is void for vagueness.
>
> The word sympathizer is not of sufficiently certain meaning to sustain a charge of perjury. The count is that Lattimore said he had never been a sympathizer whereas he had been a sympathizer. There is no definition of the term: "sympathizer" or any concrete specification of its content in the indictment or in the statute. Without such definition or specification the term has no certain meaning.[71]

The U.S. attorney next filed an affidavit of bias and prejudice against Judge Youngdahl:

> while your affiant has the greatest respect for the honor and integrity of Honorable Luther W. Youngdahl, who is presently assigned to preside at the trial of the above-entitled case, he is convinced that the said judge has a fixed opinion that the defendant herein is innocent of the charges set forth in the in-

> dictment and has such a fixed, personal bias and prejudice in favor of the defendant, that affiant would be recreant in his duty to insure for his client a fair and impartial trial if he did not respectfully request the said judge to disqualify himself from any further official connection with this case. . . . [72]

Youngdahl not only refused to disqualify himself, but in response made a vigorous counterclaim against the government:

> The affidavit is therefore so patently and grossly insufficient that I cannot escape from the conclusion that the purpose of the affidavit is to discredit, in the public mind, the final action of our courts, or else to intimidate the courts themselves. It follows that those who made or authorized the certificate that the affidavit was made in good faith acted irresponsibly and recklessly as lawyers and officers of the government.
>
> Under my oath to preserve sacred constitutional principles, I can properly do no less than to strike the affidavit as scandalous.[73]

The Justice Department was not ready to abandon the case, and announced that it would prepare new indictments. Lattimore and his attorneys hoped that the government would instead drop the matter, and its persistence was disconcerting. While offering some advice, Abe Fortas wrote Lattimore describing his own reaction and expressing his misgivings.

> When you were in the office the day of Rover's announcement, I am rather confident that all of us successfully concealed from you our own distress at his announcement. In part this was because we had proceeded from the morning's explosion of indignation to the consideration of what should be done. In part it was due to the lawyer's habitual behavior: the effort to "spare the client" and the effort to be or appear dispassionate. The fact, however, is that we *were* distressed—not so much because of the additional hazards threatened by Rover's action, which are not measurable in advance of the indictment, as because of the added trouble and disturbance for you that are involved.
>
> Rover's announcement of impending reindictment should not have come as a surprise. It was one of the possibilities that we envisaged from the start, as you will remember. Indeed, it is somewhat remarkable that he does not completely abandon

the old indictment and seek an entirely new one. If he did this, he might have some chance of getting a judge assigned other than Youngdahl, and he could certainly improve the technical framing of the indictment as a whole.

Thurman and I have talked about your idea that you might go before the grand jury, and also about your suggestion of a press conference after the indictment. I am not prepared to advise you as to these, and I doubt if Thurman is yet ready. But I think that there are some factors that you ought to take into account.

I think that if this were an ordinary case, which I could view dispassionately, I would almost certainly believe that there are only two possibilities:

1. A complete, thoroughgoing dedication to the effort to win the case on the merits of the law and the facts, without an attempt to deal with it through publicity, whether for its own sake or for the sake of the values to democracy and decency that are involved in it; or

2. To handle the case on the basis of a slashing counterattack, in which the monstrous nature of the prosecution would be dramatized and the fundamental values at stake would be pointed up.

I think there is no middle course. By this I mean that a one-shot effort to criticize Rover or to attack the proceeding would result in all of the disadvantages and practically none of the possible advantages of the second alternative.

Thurman, being of an optimistic turn of mind and being full of good red blood, strongly asserts that the case against you cannot prevail. I think that the outcome is entirely unpredictable and that it depends to a substantial extent upon the state of the world and the state of the Nation at the time that the case goes to jury.

However, as you undoubtedly know by now, although lawyers are people—and sometimes excessively so—they are also lawyers, confined and restricted by their odd art. As the years of law practice go by, lawyers develop an attitude and a routine which is somewhat comparable to surgeons in an operating room. I think that it is practically impossible for seasoned lawyers—perhaps I mean successful lawyers—like us to operate, with respect to a case in the courts, except in the framework of

> conventional legal rules. In a free-wheeling proceeding before a committee of the congress, or even before an administrative agency, we seem to be able to use a combination of the instruments of persuasion—which often include publicity; but this does not seem to be true as to a case in the courts.[74]

In reformulating its case, the government made an attempt to be more specific in its charges. In October 1954, Lattimore was indicted on two additional counts of perjury, namely that he had not told the truth when he denied that he was a "follower of the Communist line" and when he testified he had never been a "promoter of Communist interests." The new indictment cited scores of public and private statements made by Lattimore in conversations, correspondence, and writing that allegedly proved that he had testified falsely before the McCarran committee. The government had examined some of Lattimore's published work in its attempt to show that he was a sympathizer and promoter of communism. For example, the quotation "my own opinion is that now and for a long time to come the Chinese Communists will have great defensive strength if attacked, but little offensive strength beyond their own frontier" was used as evidence that Lattimore sought to further Communist interests. Editorial decisions Lattimore had made as editor of *Pacific Affairs* were to the government evidence that he promoted Communist positions.

In brief, the case against Lattimore was that he had meant to tell the McCarran committee that he had never done anything, written anything, or said anything to encourage any objectives of the Communist party or a Communist country. The government charged that to forward the Communist cause, Lattimore "did make use of his position to engage directly and indirectly in the placing and disseminating within the United States and other countries throughout the world, of oral and written statements containing the positions taken, the policies expressed and the propaganda issued on political, diplomatic, military, economic and social matters" by the Soviet Union.[75] However, in January 1955, Judge Youngdahl, for the same reasons as before, dismissed both of the new counts of the indictment, holding that the phrase "follower of the Communist line" had no "meaning about which men of ordinary intellect could agree, nor one which could be used with mutual understanding by a questioner and answerer," and that "promoter of Communist interests" might be more definite but it was also too vague.

Judge Youngdahl noted that

> the charges here serve only to inform the defendant that his sworn statements are to be tested against all his writings for chance parallelism with, or indirect support of, communism regardless of any deliberate intent on his part. They demonstrate that the government seeks to establish that at some time, in some way, in some places, in all of his vast writings, over a fifteen-year period, Lattimore agreed with something that it calls and personally defines as following the Communist line and promoting Communist interests.

He concluded:

> To require defendant to go to trial for perjury under charges so formless and obscure as those before the court would be unprecedented and would make a sham of the Sixth Amendment and the federal rule requiring specificity of charges.[76]

Judge Youngdahl left standing five counts of the original indictment.

The government appealed, but Judge Youngdahl's dismissal of the indictment was upheld by a higher court.[77] In June 1955, more than five years after his loyalty became a public issue and after Attorney General Herbert Brownell decided not to apply to the Supreme Court for review since "there is no reasonable likelihood of a successful prosecution on the five counts remaining," the government dropped all charges against Lattimore.[78]

Not surprisingly, in the minds of a good many people the end of Lattimore's legal problems did not settle the question of his guilt. Lattimore's documented defense convinced those who were disposed to believe him, but not those who could not believe he might be only an innocent liberal. Even some who were sure he had not engaged in anything illicit could not believe that he was blameless. In the study "initiated . . . as a public service"[79] by the American Committee for Cultural Freedom, which spoke for many who called themselves liberals, Rorty and Decter characterized him as a "skillful, effective and influential party-lining propagandist."[80] The moral entrepreneurs would not let matters rest; the fact that Lattimore was cleared was taken as more evidence of the pervasiveness of the Communist conspiracy. They were persuaded of his perfidy and would not be convinced otherwise by what they saw as legal technicalities and a lack of will on the part of the government to pursue the issue. They would not acquit Lattimore, as they were satisfied that his guilt had been vividly demonstrated. As we learn more about them in the next chapter, this reaction becomes more understandable.

2

Pursuit by the Moral Entrepreneurs

It is essential to give some attention to the nemeses of Lattimore, moral entrepreneurs who set about to expose him and make sure that he was accordingly punished. In taking it upon themselves to establish what is proper and what is not, moral entrepreneurs affect not only individuals but the larger culture and institutions. The Lattimore case shows their potency.

The exceptional interest they took in prosecuting ideological deviants on the Left during the height of the Cold War is to be expected; moral entrepreneurs are always most active in times of great social tension. (The lack of consensus by the public and politicians about the direction of American foreign policy after military successes in Europe and Asia contributed much to the uncertainty. It also contributed to voter dissatisfaction and to election victories by Republican candidates in the 1946 elections that gave the party control of Congress for the first time in eighteen years.) Working through pressure groups, moral entrepreneurs zealously try to make others conform to their ideas. Driven by the conviction that the only way to stop their opponents is to purge them, they are as much a part of social life as are deviants. They are energized by the belief that when consensus is lacking, social control will reestablish it. As they see it, their goal to establish an orthodoxy can be advanced by working to eliminate differences. By trying to organize and manage the social conscience they become entrepreneurs. Only a few are instigators or innovators; most are followers.

That moral entrepreneurs pursued Lattimore unmercifully was not exceptional. Throughout history they have pursued many, often concerned about books in schools and libraries, speakers at public events, the perfidy of government employees, the sermons of liberal theologians, disloyal ideas in the media, and all forms of expression of opinion. They are as keen in proscribing intellectual dissent as deviant behavior; both are antisocial. Some of the time they are most interested in how others behave on the sabbath, in their bedrooms, or during their leisure. At other times they are more interested in what others think about social, economic, or political questions. Their quarry are often viewed, as were witches in colonial America, as "powerful, resourceful [and] devious."[1]

In the years after World War II some who were convinced that Communists had infiltrated the federal government, the labor unions, the schools, and the entertainment industry and had corrupted the values of American society felt impelled to alert others and effectuate change. They saw the influence of communism everywhere, and they organized or joined movements to eradicate it in America and beyond. They were leaders and followers in a crusade—"a remedial enterprise undertaken with zeal and enthusiasm." A foreign policy that did not further American interests was thought to be the result of conspiracy. There was a widespread feeling that the Cold War was going badly, that the Communist takeover of China was preventable, and that there were security leaks in the government. Communist successes in China and elsewhere were attributed more to the machinations of bureaucrats, diplomats, and foreign influences than to world economic and social conditions. They were able to convince many with very little idea of what the term meant that communism posed a great danger to America. Their collective efforts could not be ignored.

In describing the moral entrepreneur, Becker says, "he operates with an absolute ethic; what he sees is truly and totally evil with no qualification. Any means is justified to do away with it. The crusader is fervent and righteous, often self-righteous."[2] In action, moral entrepreneurs are enterprising:

> People must be made to feel that something ought to be done about it [a harmful practice]. Someone must call the public's attention to these matters, supply the push necessary to get things done. . . . Offenders must be discovered, identified, apprehended and convicted (or noted as "different" and stigmatized for their nonconformity . . .).[3]

Such rule-creating moral entrepreneurs were in the forefront in enforcing political orthodoxy during the whole of the Cold War years.

After World War II, rules were being made in America that placed limits on how much sympathy citizens could show towards

Communists, communism, and Communist countries. There was a growing consensus that all were dangerous, and that intercourse with communism or those who practiced it should be restricted. One could not compromise with evil. Communism was seen as a deadly, rapidly spreading virus, infecting anyone it touched. The Alger Hiss case, the revelation that atomic secrets had been delivered to Soviet agents, the outbreak of the Korean War, "the loss of China" to the Communists, all within a very short period, gave the claims of the moral entrepreneurs considerable credence.

Many took it upon themselves to see that Americans did not traffic with Communists. They spread the word about its evils, they identified those suspected of doing what was forbidden, and they set about to punish those who broke the rules. These enforcers—these moral entrepreneurs—were everywhere. They held official positions in the government, they worked through voluntary organizations, they wrote for newspapers and magazines and to newspapers and magazines, they preached from pulpits, and they were in business and commerce. Much of their effort was directed toward bringing infractions of the new standards to the attention of others. As Becker has pointed out, "an infraction cannot be ignored once it is made public."[4]

Owen Lattimore became the focus of initiatives of moral entrepreneurs troubled by communism. His conclusion that the Communist victory in China was inevitable enraged them. They were fervent to call attention to the folly of his thinking and to his treachery and guilt. Their generalized concern about the vulnerability of the country, the decline of patriotism, and the decay of morality was unbounded and a catalyst.

Without exception the moral entrepreneurs were unyielding, unforgiving of those less dogged. Like vigilantes, they energized and drove each other with their commitment and a miscellany of fact, half-truths, and fiction. None had any doubts about Lattimore's involvement with communism, the evil he represented, and the need to disempower him at all costs. All the time there was an appeal to the highest motives—the love of God, a fervent devotion to the country (Americanism), and the protection of youth. The attacks on Lattimore were well within a long-standing American tradition and were assured widespread support. Americans have never hidden a deep-seated resentment toward authority, especially intellectual authority. As Richard Hofstadter has noted, in America

> the citizen . . . can achieve a kind of revenge by ridiculing the wild-eyed professor, the irresponsible brain truster or the mad

> scientist, and by applauding the politicians as they pursue the subversive teacher, the suspect scientist or the allegedly treacherous foreign-policy advisor. There has always been in our national experience a type of mind which elevates hatred to a kind of creed; for this mind, group hatreds take a place in politics similar to the class struggle in some other modern societies. Filled with obscure and ill-directed grievances and frustrations, with elaborate hallucinations about secrets and conspiracies, groups of malcontents have found scapegoats at various times. . . . [5]

The thinking, the reasoning, the arguments of the moral entrepreneurs would fall under what Hofstadter has called the "paranoid style" of mind which is marked by "heated exaggeration, suspiciousness and conspiratorial fantasy."[6] Those with this paranoid style have intense feelings of righteousness and moral indignation. Hofstadter uses the following words of Senator McCarthy to illustrate this style.

> How can we account for our present situation unless we believe that men high in this government are concerting to deliver us to disaster? This must be the product of a great conspiracy, a conspiracy on a scale so immense as to dwarf any previous such venture in the history of man. A conspiracy of infamy so black that, when it is finally exposed, its principals shall be forever deserving of the maledictions of all honest men. . . . What can be made of this unbroken series of decisions and acts contributing to the strategy of defeat? They cannot be attributed to incompetence. . . . The laws of probability would dictate that part of . . . [the] decisions would serve this country's interest.[7]

In effect, Senator McCarthy has given his name to describe the thinking, reasoning, and arguments of the moral entrepreneurs of the 1950s.

As a result of the activities of moral entrepreneurs, between 1945 and 1955 there were what John Lord O'Brian described as "conspicuous governmental developments which seem to provide unmistakable evidence of an expanding trend of policies at variance with the American conception of fair play."[8] Of the eleven notable changes that gained public acceptance during these Cold War years specified by O'Brian, six were manifest in the Lattimore case: the establishment in jurisprudence of the doctrine of guilt by association; "adjudging men to be untrustworthy, not because of wrongful acts, but because of their ideas, because of motives attributed to them or because of suspicion as to their future conduct"; the compiling of lists of organizations thought to be subversive and the use of these lists to determine fitness for employment; the use of secret information from anonymous accusers; the denial of the right of cross examination to the accused; and the supervision and limitation of freedom to travel abroad.[9] All six had a direct bearing on what happened to Lattimore and Johns Hopkins.

Lattimore's career put him at a confluence where at the height of the Cold War he was a likely target for the moral entrepreneurs. For at least the entire decade of the 1950s their misgivings over the Communist victory in China had helped move the question to the center of political debate in America. Lattimore had written on the subject and his work was studied by them to see where he stood. His views were hardly extreme, but he had obviously sided with their opponents. Those who attacked him in books and letters, in newspapers and magazines, and before congressional committees thought that he should answer for this. He was an unbeliever; he was distrusted. In the atmosphere of the Cold War years a degree of guilt was imputed to anyone under suspicion.

Most of the efforts by the moral entrepreneurs to have Lattimore dismissed from Johns Hopkins were directed at the university's administration. The office of the president received the brunt, but certainly not all, of the pressure. Members of the board of trustees, other administrative officers, and senior faculty were also contacted from time to time. Between 1950 and 1955 the pressure was continuous; later it was more sporadic.

Alfred Kohlberg, of the American China Policy Association and a highly visible member of the so-called China Lobby, continued to make claims designed to harm the university and in the end Lattimore. Kohlberg, a wealthy New York textile importer with business interests in China, had been highly critical of Lattimore and his colleagues in the Institute of Pacific Relations for about ten years prior to the Nationalists' defeat in China, having become convinced that almost every position they took was designed to undermine America's interests in world affairs and that they had done much to harm Chiang. He had come to believe that the Institute of Pacific Relations had not only helped engineer the overthrow of Chiang, but at least since the end of World War II had been working with traitors in the government to direct American foreign policy toward Soviet ends.

From the facts that Johns Hopkins managed the Operations Research Office (ORO) of the Department of Defense in Chevy Chase, Maryland, and that a small, unclassified project concerned with various aspects of Russian economics sponsored by it had an office on campus adjacent to the Page School of International Relations, Kohlberg raised the specter that Johns Hopkins was a party to arrangements that compromised national security.

> So the ORO gets all the information on the secret weapons—when they are being planned, projected. Now, that contract, and I haven't seen the contract, the contract is being carried out, that I know, but I understand that it is being carried out by the Page School of International Studies [*sic*]. Now, I don't know what personnel of the Page School are carrying out that contract; that's all secret. But it's the Page School and I don't think that that's the kind of contract that I would let out to the Page School of International Studies until I knew a lot more about Owen Lattimore than those people seem to know.[10]

Such charges found their way into the *Congressional Record,* and to the Right they became unimpeachable proof of chicanery. They were continually repeated in newspapers as if they were fact.

> Everybody from Acheson on down, including Secretary of Defense George C. Marshall, will deny that the Baltimore bugle [derogatory reference to Owen Lattimore] is on any official administration payroll. Take a look at this, however.
>
> The Operations Research Office of the Department of the Army, which handles super-secret research and weapons evaluation work, decided last year to turn over its functions to the Johns Hopkins University. It signed a contract with the Johns Hopkins School of International Studies [*sic*], of all things, and now funnels its secret data to that institution. Guess who runs the school of International Studies? You couldn't guess wrong, it's the Baltimore bugle, Mr. Lattimore.[11]

In another well-publicized accusation, Kohlberg charged that the board of trustees was acting irresponsibly in not warning students of the Page School that they would be discriminated against for government employment because Lattimore was on the faculty. Since, Kohlberg stated, Lattimore was "not a scholar" and "didn't have the proper degrees," the university's graduates in international studies "have a black mark against them, perhaps for life, because they studied there."

> The trustees of the Johns Hopkins University have for many years committed a crime against the students there—that of taking money under false pretenses.

The trustees should have told students of the great risk associated with studying under Lattimore. In case the message was lost on someone, Kohlberg added that one of the causes of Communist supremacy in the Cold War was that universities which keep "proven Communists and fellow travelers" on their faculties continue to be supported.[12]

University authorities took the agitation of some moral entrepreneurs quite seriously. They were sensitive to anything in the media that maligned the university for not having terminated Lattimore. Those administrators and trustees most suspicious of Lattimore were hypersensitive and felt the most harassed by criticism.

The moral entrepreneurs were unrelenting in their advice to university authorities. Many of their suggestions as to what steps the university should take to ensure that the faculty was above reproach were farfetched and unsound. Some were quite irrational. How reasonable or even how persistent moral entrepreneurs were had less to do with how seriously university authorities took them than how influential they appeared to be. Some very befuddled observations were given careful consideration by administrative officers and the board. Some valid criticisms of Lattimore—that he had not always been a neutral editor or unbiased observer or that his assessment of the people and politics of Asia were sometimes quite inaccurate—were ignored.

Acting as megaphones for the charges against him, the moral entrepreneurs most often worked through government agencies and newspapers to coerce those in the university who they believed were in a position to punish Lattimore. From the beginning, the media were their voice. Local politicians, congressmen, bureaucrats in the state and federal government, and the Federal Bureau of Investigation were regularly written to or telephoned, given information, and urged to use their authority to make Lattimore's misdeeds public so that sanctions—from dismissal from the university to standing trial for treason—could be applied.

The FBI's Activities

The FBI was the repository for accusations by the moral entrepreneurs, and its file of his activities is extensive, amounting to thousands of pages. In it there are letters, telegrams, teletype messages, memoranda, reports, clippings, and the like. Little of Lattimore's professional and private life escaped notice. Rumors and factual materials are intermixed. There is considerable redundancy. The moral entrepreneurs were determined to affect Lattimore's credibility; they were determined in their pursuit of him. The information they supplied is voluminous; they were unyielding in their efforts. They were instrumental in keeping the FBI abreast of Lattimore's activities.

> ... [T]he informant advised she had undertaken a campaign to "get" Lattimore. She outlined her program as follows: The matter was discussed with officials of the Maryland Committee of Representative Government, and it was decided that it would be better for the informant to undertake the project without it being an official function of the committee. The informant stated her first objective is to have Lattimore discredited and discharged from the faculty at the Johns Hopkins University in order to strike an initial blow at his prestige. After that is accomplished she intends to endeavor to remove Lattimore from his present position of prominence as an advisor to the State Department, where she feels he wields an unusual influence on United States policy in the Far East.
>
> The informant has talked with many people regarding Lattimore. She claims to have read practically everything Lattimore has written in newspapers, magazines and books since 1930. At the present time, she advised she has a project underway whereby she plans to trace the writings and utterances of Lattimore since 1930 up to the present time and to compare such utterances and writings with the known Communist party line during this same period.
>
> To implement her project of "getting" Lattimore, the informant stated that when she has accumulated all the information she can obtain regarding Lattimore and has completed her personal investigation she intends to take the information to Mr. Carlyle Barton, President of the Board of Trustees of the Johns Hopkins University, who is reported to be a prominent Baltimore attorney and a wealthy individual. The informant stated that if Mr. Barton fails to take any action in regard to removing Lattimore from the Johns Hopkins University campus, then she and her associates intend to release everything to the newspapers and the press generally in order to force action of the Johns Hopkins University. If successful in

> having Lattimore removed at the Johns Hopkins University, the informant intends to continue the campaign to remove Lattimore from influence in the State Department by dealing with the House Committee on Un-American Activities.
>
> Through her Congressman, the Honorable William C. Bolton, Second Maryland Congressional District, she has already had herself introduced to Congressman Velde of Illinois who is a member of the House Committee on Un-American Activities. The informant has already talked to both Congressmen Bolton and Velde regarding Lattimore but has not revealed the information she has accumulated to them as yet. . . . [13]

Other moral entrepreneurs were just as busy.

What was not initially directed to the FBI was often forwarded to it. Some public officials were convinced that the charges against Lattimore were so serious they could be ignored only at the greatest risk to national security.

> Dear Mr. Hoover:
>
> I am in receipt of a communication, dated January 5, 1953, from . . . addressed to the Honorable Frank L. Chelf. This communication sets out certain information regarding the Walter Hines Page School of International Studies [*sic*] at the Johns Hopkins University and Owen Lattimore.
>
> I am attaching the original of . . . letter, as well as a copy of my communication to him. This matter is referred for such action as you deem appropriate.
>
> With best regards.
>
> Sincerely,
> Robert A. Collier
>
> Chief Counsel[14]

> Hon. Frank L. Chelf
> House Office Building
> Washington, D.C.
>
> Investigation Johns Hopkins
>
> Dear Sir:
>
> In your investigation of the above, you should not overlook some things in connection with the Walter Hines Page

> School of International Studies [*sic*] at Hopkins—headed by Prof(?) Lattimore.
>
> This fellow Lattimore has had as his house guest here, one Prince Abdul Baraba Baha (alias Diluwa Hutuktu)—supposed to be the living Buddha, and brought into this country by Lattimore.
>
> This Hutuktu is a Mongolian Jew, supposedly the King Communist and who had his headquarters in Tibet before Lattimore got him in here. He is supposed at least to be the top man even over Stalin in this oriental Communist conspiracy.
>
> In addition, he was the boss of Nicholas Roerich, the mystic that had Henry Wallace in his clutches and whom Wallace referred to in the famous letters exposed by Pegler—as the Guru or teacher. Roerich's trips to Asia on the behalf of Wallace and his pals was to contact Hutuktu the kingpin. Evidently Wallace was not crazy as claimed—but was simply dealing with the "head man." Understand that Naval Intelligence has the dope on this chap—if you can pry it loose from Harry [Truman].
>
> If what we have developed so far is true, this fellow Lattimore is just what McCarthy called him—the leading Soviet espionage agent, and his boss Hutuktu living in the same house. How did Lattimore get him by the immigration authorities? We hear he was smuggled in.
>
> No doubt all this sounds crazy to Americans. But you must remember that you are dealing with oriental communism and conspiracy. This is the way they do things. . . . Fantastic? Sure—as fantastic as Hiss standing alongside FDR at Yalta—Stalin knowing all the time that Hiss was his man.[15]

The FBI dutifully collected and filed everything passed to it. Every whisper about him, no matter how much it stretched credulity, no matter how bizarre, found its way into Lattimore's dossier.

Even before Lattimore's name was publicly linked to Communist activities by Senator McCarthy, the FBI had received a report that he was part of a "regular 'Red' apparatus operating at the Johns Hopkins University, consisting of six or seven professors." Among those identified, besides Lattimore, was President Detlev Bronk. There were indications, the FBI in Baltimore had come to believe, that Bronk "may have been affiliated with some front organizations."

In February 1950, Lattimore was described in an FBI internal memorandum as a "pro-Soviet propagandist and apologist on matters relating to China and the Far East." The FBI had been told that Lattimore had possibly served as a Soviet agent, but these reports had not been corroborated, and this lead could not be developed.[16]

The early records show that one informant had led the FBI to believe that Lattimore had converted at least 50 percent of his students to communism, that he tried to convince audiences that Mao Tse-tung and his followers were not "Russian type Communists, but . . . agrarian reformers," and that, although there are no indications that he was engaged in espionage activities, he was in an excellent position to do so. Such reports caused from moderate amounts to a great deal of official apprehension. There were additional concerns that "over the years various Oriental individuals" who had visited the United States and the Johns Hopkins University were sponsored by Lattimore and had been his house guests.[17]

Apparently some in its Washington headquarters gave credence to most of the information the FBI received. As late as 1954, over four years after agents first heard that Lattimore had influenced about fifty percent of his students to become Communists, there were urgent messages from Director J. Edgar Hoover to locate the informant so he could "be asked to state whether he can name any of those students and furnish any leads re: their whereabouts so that they can be interviewed by [the] Bureau concerning truth or falsity of this statement."[18] The reply from a field agent to the FBI's Washington office to this message was felt not to be specific enough and not useful, and Director Hoover immediately responded that the informant should be reinterviewed for the "purpose of pinning him down."[19]

Almost no charge was too tenuous or farfetched. Most of the intelligence received by the FBI regarding Lattimore was thought to merit serious attention, as he was seen as a serious threat.

> Informant stated that one of the vicious effects of Lattimore's activities is the subversion of students at the Johns Hopkins University, practically all of whom, informant states, Lattimore eventually converts to disciples of Lattimore. It is informant's opinion that subject in the training and indoctrination of some of his students and associates in the Page School of International Relations, is, in fact, grooming them for subsequent roles with the State Department in definite fields of international relations. It is informant's opinion that subject, in so doing, intends to continue thereby his control and influence over the policy of the United States State Department. In support of this theory, informant advised that

> Lattimore is deliberately specializing his associates, as follows, at the Page School of International Relations on the following subjects. . . .

There is no telling what senior officials of the FBI had come to believe; many must have been persuaded by a great deal of what field agents had been told as their communications expressed grave misgivings about Lattimore.

The accounts heard by the FBI varied from the trivial to the serious, and from the vague to the concrete.

> . . . advised that subject Lattimore evidently exerted some pressure on Dr. Isaiah Bowman, formerly president of the Johns Hopkins University, Baltimore. . . . Facilities were available for subject to maintain pressure on Dr. Bowman because of the following alleged facts:
>
> Dr. Bowman's only son, Robert Bowman, when studying at the University of California at Berkeley, California, is alleged to have become associated with Communists and to either have played on the fringe of the Communist party, or to have actually joined the Communist party. It is alleged that probably subject learned of the above facts and held this over the head of Dr. Bowman as a stick used by the subject in self-protection. It is noted that she arrived at the above conclusion through a rather tenuous line of reasoning, with practically no facts to support her allegations. . . . that Robert Bowman is presently on the staff of the School of Geography at the University of Nebraska.[20]

It is recorded that Lattimore and another man "were observed by confidential informant T-53, of known reliability, to be engaged in a brief personal conversation with Mrs. Paul Robeson [wife of the dissident activist]."[21] The FBI was told that Lattimore was "highly impractical" in having urged that Chiang Kai-shek's Nationalists bring Communists into the government, and that they could have a working agreement with the Communists.[22] One "informant also stated that Lattimore has several cameras, among them a Leica, which Lattimore seems to prefer and uses more than any other camera."[23] Another informant believed Lattimore was too divorced from current American thought, and could not recall that he ever wrote one word of criticism of Russia or the Chinese Communists, but that his work was replete with criticisms of the American and Chinese Nationalist governments.[24] That an informant was "not able to specifically cite any statements made by Lattimore in criticism of the Communists," was something that the FBI believed significant.[25]

The FBI spent considerable time pursuing its many leads:

> By teletype dated April 11, 1950 to the Bureau, San Francisco and Omaha offices, the San Francisco and Omaha offices were requested to check their indices and to make discreet inquiries among reliable informants regarding Robert Bowman in an effort to ascertain if there is any truth in the allegation that Robert Bowman is, or may have been, a member of the CP, thereby lending some credence to the above allegation. . . . The San Francisco and Omaha offices were also requested to advise the Bureau and the Baltimore office of their findings so that a decision could be made as to whether or not Robert Bowman should be interviewed regarding any knowledge he might have regarding subject Lattimore.[26]

It was all quite preposterous.

Lattimore's Growing Notoriety

On this front, in creating doubts about Lattimore, the moral entrepreneurs could count themselves successful. Much of what was put about with regard to Lattimore was silly and by itself proved not to be damaging. However, the seriousness with which the charges were taken began to take a toll. All of the accusations could not be answered. The FBI seldom revealed what it had been told. Disproven rumors and innuendos were followed by more rumors and innuendos that also needed to be disproven. It was not possible for the authorities at the Johns Hopkins University to ignore reports, whispers, gossip, comment, and rumor.

Senator McCarthy devoted a chapter in his book, *McCarthyism: The Fight for America, Documented Answers to Questions Asked by Friend and Foe,*[27] to Lattimore. Written like a catechism, in question and answer form, McCarthy repeats and explains the evidence (see Appendix E) to support his charges of Lattimore's Communist party membership and Communist activities. The compilation, taken as a whole, makes Lattimore appear quite sinister. A book by John T. Flynn, *The Lattimore Story,* details how Lattimore's efforts on behalf of communism resulted in "the betrayal of China and Korea . . . the most immoral—perhaps the blackest—story in our history."[28]

In *Spies, Dupes, and Diplomats,* Ralph de Toledano's "effort to reexamine . . . the causes and mechanics of America's suicidal Far Eastern policy,"[29] Lattimore is given a prominent role as one of the individuals who helped "to push this Nation into Far Eastern armed conflict twice in a dozen years."[30]

> Stilwell, Carlson, and Davies—aided by writers like Edgar Snow, Guenther Stein, Owen Lattimore, T. A. Bisson—all helped sell the Chinese Communist cause to the American intellectuals and to the State Department. They were all friends of Agnes Smedley; she even conducted some of them personally to Yenan, the Red rebel capital. And through them, she influenced the group of foreign service officers who remained in China during World War II and helped engineer the destruction of the Nationalists.[31]

According to de Toledano, there was "no way to evaluate [the] evidence" of how deeply Lattimore was involved in Communist activities, but he was more than "merely a Johns Hopkins professor with a firm set of ideas, honestly held";[32] he was one of many who "misled and misinformed"[33] the country. Lattimore was being kept in the public eye.

Every turn in the Lattimore case was conspicuously covered by the press. The account of his testimony to the Tydings committee was a page-one story (with photograph) in *Time* magazine (see Appendix F). Anything Lattimore said or did, or was purported to say and do, became news—and the Johns Hopkins University became part of the story.

The Government's Travel Ban

For example, in the late spring of 1952 an informant in Seattle, Washington, told the Central Intelligence Agency that Lattimore had plans to visit (perhaps flee to) the Soviet Union. He purportedly had already purchased his ticket, and was scheduled to leave in about a month. This information was relayed to the FBI for investigation. It in turn told the State Department's Passport Bureau that Lattimore was making "arrangements for a possible visit to the U.S.S.R. and/or its satellites," that his intent was "illegal." It then asked the Customs Bureau of the Treasury Department to alert its agents not to allow Lattimore to leave the country. A government official acknowledged that the step had been taken as "a precaution against his [Lattimore] skipping the country."[34]

This stop order by the commissioner of customs was highly unusual. Since, according to the secretary of state, such an action was reserved for "fugitives from justice," "people who are mentally ill," and persons of "subversive affiliation or intent,"[35] the matter was widely discussed. The *Houston Post* began a report: "The State Department disclosed Friday night that it has alerted U.S. Customs guards to halt any attempt by Owen Lattimore to leave the country. . . . Lattimore, a Johns Hopkins University professor, is a former State Department consultant. He has figured as the target of repeated attacks by Senator Joseph McCarthy, R-Wis., who denounced him on the senate floor as a Soviet spy and as 'the chief architect' of President Truman's administration's Far East policy."[36]

At first, government officials had little to say on the matter. In the face of repeated inquiries by the press, the State Department would only confirm that Lattimore would under no circumstances be issued a passport to go behind the Iron Curtain.

> Speaking with obvious reluctance during an interview, Harry M. Durning, Customs Collector of the Port of New York, acknowledged that "as of now" the Johns Hopkins professor is to be denied passport privileges.
>
> If Lattimore were to attempt to leave, Mr. Durning said, he would be halted by customs officials at any port of embarkation by order of the State Department. His passport will not be renewed, according to Mr. Durning.[37]

The government made it clear that this was a special situation, and was not "merely routine."[38] Senator McCarthy, among others, believed that the State Department wanted Lattimore to leave the country as it was implicated in his conspiratorial activities.

The fact that Lattimore's passport had already expired and that he had no plans to go abroad only increased interest in developments. "The Johns Hopkins professor said that he went to England in January and that the passport he used for that trip is no longer valid. 'I just don't understand what this whole story is about,' he said."[39]

The university was more closely identified with these events than it would have liked. It was not possible to avoid the unwelcome attention. It became necessary to issue a formal statement that as far as the administration knew, Lattimore had no plans to leave the country. He had not consulted with the administration.

The university only knew of a tentative offer he had received to lecture at the University of New Delhi in the fall. It was added that the university would agree to grant Lattimore leave should he request it. It knew of no plans to do so. Only one trustee would go as far as to state that Lattimore "did contemplate making a trip abroad" and that "there was some talk about a leave"; the travel was to be to England or India.[40] However, generally trustees would not be drawn in; the other members of the board contacted by the press for information and opinion claimed that they knew nothing about the situation or referred the matter back to the administration.

The allegations that Lattimore was set to flee the country were shortly shown to be false, and the government rescinded its order and apologized for having cast suspicion on him. This did not immediately deflect attention from Johns Hopkins. It was prominently mentioned in the criticism of the State Department's apology to Lattimore in an editorial in the *Idaho Daily Statesman* that Senator Herman Welker had inserted in the *Congressional Record.*

> Nobody has yet proved that Owen Lattimore has ever been a member of the Communist party, but it has always seemed to us that this is strictly a quibble beside the point. The facts of the Lattimore record are that he long advocated, and, indeed, was in a position to get results, that the Communist forces of Asia should emerge as the dominant power on the mainland. There can be little or no question today that the virulent Lattimore views played an enormous role in switching this Nation's Far Eastern policy from support of Chiang Kai-shek to the abortive attempt to rig a "deal" with the Peiping Reds. The result was China's fall, and Korea.
>
> Lattimore is still a professor at the Johns Hopkins University, although his own weird academic background scarcely entitles him to the tile of "professor" which he currently holds.
>
> Probably this country would be better off if instead of restricting Lattimore from traveling behind the Iron Curtain a way could be found to send him behind it for good.[41]

More importantly, the incident prompted letters critical of the university.

> Dear Sirs: I see by the paper that the State Department of Washington, D.C. has forbade the customs officials to issue passports to Owen Lattimore. . . . From what I can learn, Mr. Lattimore is either a Communist or a dangerous radical, so

> dangerous that it is unsafe for him to be at large. But still he is free to teach at your school. . . .
>
> It appears to me there is something rotten in Denmark.[42]

New Targets

As time went on, the university became more and more subject to condemnation by the moral entrepreneurs. The fact that Lattimore had not been punished was their prime concern, and they placed the responsibility for this with the Johns Hopkins administration. Thus, the university became a secondary target. As they saw it, Johns Hopkins was willingly allowing itself to be used as a refuge. Given Lattimore's character, nothing more could be expected of him. It was the contention of the moral entrepreneurs, however, that there was no justification for what the university had become a party to; it was clearly culpable. Its administrators knew the difference between right and wrong. It still continued to protect Lattimore after all that had been disclosed about him, and the public needed to be reminded of this. It did not take long for individual trustees to become the subject of ridicule:

> The *Freeman's* dunce cap for the season rests on the brow of Carlyle Barton, [President] of the Johns Hopkins University Board of Trustees. As quoted in the *New York Times* of June 22, Mr. Barton declared that the two congressional inquiries into Senator Joe McCarthy's charges that Owen Lattimore was the "chief architect of our Far Eastern policy" and associated with Communists, "had proved nothing."[43]

In 1959, many years after charges were first brought against Lattimore, the lead article in *American Mercury,* "Johns Hopkins Flunks Anti-Communism Test,"[44] looks almost as closely at the failure of the university and its leadership as at Lattimore's political past. Although Lattimore's presence on the faculty is the catalyst for the story, the university gets considerable attention, considerably more than it welcomed. The reason Lattimore was kept on the faculty, the article contends, is because the university has "lost itself in the pursuit of expediency." The characterizations of Lattimore and the university are equally uncharitable.[45]

Lattimore is described as "a manifest misfit"[46] who had been a fur trader in Outer Mongolia before his appointment to the university. There is a recital of his work and views, and all of the mischief these have occasioned. His "devious political activities"[47] are also reviewed. This picture of Lattimore had become quite standard, and was to be expected. For almost a decade he had been castigated by a large segment of the press. The university had not always shared in this notoriety. It was unaccustomed to such stinging rebukes. The net of deprecation had been cast wider. The university had been made Lattimore's ally and co-conspirator. It was the university that had flunked the test.

Those in the university only marginally connected with Lattimore are reproached. The faculty is blamed for not recognizing or addressing the moral issues involved in the Lattimore case. There is the assertion that one faculty member who raised disturbing questions about Lattimore "has had a rough time" on campus, while another who supported Lattimore "has had a flourishing career at Hopkins since the controversy."[48] The trustees are accused of "pampering" Lattimore: "they have preferred to coddle a pro-Communist rather than subject themselves to the discomfort and billingsgate of a courageous stand." Although comprised of conservative professionals and businessmen, the board is guilty of "moral palsy."[49] Even Milton S. Eisenhower, who assumed the presidency of the university after Lattimore had been cleared by the courts and reinstated to the faculty, is faulted.

> The extent of the university's slide into mediocrity may be seen in the fact that the presidential chair which was once graced by Daniel Coit Gilman is now occupied by Milton Eisenhower.[50]

The sin of Johns Hopkins was not conscious pro-communism, but "the sin of half-heartedness." The leadership had shown a "dismal breakdown of character."[51] The indictment is uncompromising in its vituperation, and the zeal is unbounded. The push to inflict pain is obvious.

The broad and bitter attacks by moral entrepreneurs on those who were not as punitive toward Lattimore were effective. They mobilized many who otherwise might not have become active to press their agenda. Lattimore, his defenders, and the Johns Hopkins University were in a position of always reacting to events. The situation was defined by the moral entrepreneurs. Chapter 3 shows with alarming clarity how the moral entrepreneur's intense commitment put Johns Hopkins on the defensive, keeping it off balance during the entire episode.

3

The Outcry for Sanctions

One obvious way to punish or silence heretics, or deviants in general, is to threaten their livelihood. Economic sanctions can be used to bring about conformity and, in the extreme, bring economic ruin to those whose ideas unsettle a community. For someone like Lattimore whose occupation it was to express ideas in an academic setting, an obvious way to punish or silence him would be to work through the administrative authorities of the Johns Hopkins University. The board of trustees or the president and other officials might be induced to threaten or punish him. They could gag him or, if that failed, dismiss him. Disciplining Lattimore or making him back down would be exemplary.

Not unexpectedly, then, for approximately five years there was constant pressure on the administrative authorities of Johns Hopkins to apply strong negative sanctions on Lattimore, if not to secure conformity by forcing him to recant, then at least to punish him for the putative damage he had done to American interests. A surprisingly large number of people wanted Lattimore dismissed from the faculty of Johns Hopkins, and they expressed this wish to university authorities. The moral entrepreneurs prompted emotional letters from all sides. These spirited communications—along with the small number in support of Lattimore—are the primary subject of this chapter. Over 250 that were readily available are analyzed, although more than this number were written to university authorities. There are many and most are passionate. It is quite evident that they need little interpretation; the pressure on Johns Hopkins can be most fully understood by considering them at length.

Around the country, people knew about and were dismayed by Lattimore's heresies. Some wrote to the president, the board of trustees, and other administrative officers of Johns Hopkins to convey their sense of outrage and disbelief that, to their minds, such an ideological deviant could hold an academic appointment; others wrote to encourage the university to stand firmly behind Lattimore. Some wrote repeatedly. Although from merely reading the letters it is risky to draw conclusions about their authors, it is clear that the correspondents were from all social and educational classes. Some of the correspondence was long and detailed; about as many were short, with telegraphic phrases and few complete sentences. Fewer than a fifth made their case cogently and were to the point; as many were not. They did not know the facts and they rambled. Some letters began or ended with patriotic or religious themes. Some rely on metaphors and use images of cancer, contagion, and disease, but the overwhelming majority do not. A small number were written in pencil; others were typed. A handful were written on ruled paper; a few were on engraved personal stationary. The letters came from around the country, fairly equally from all segments of society. They were apparently prompted by the belief that the writers should take things in their own hands to influence those who could affect Lattimore's career. A significant proportion of those expressing support for Lattimore were from the academic community. No attempt was made to determine what proportion was crank mail or what proportion was credible. The meaning of these terms is largely in the eyes of the beholder; readers can make their own judgments.

Many who wrote were convinced that they had an obligation to make their views known. Only those letters that were opposed to Lattimore's continuing at Johns Hopkins were abusive and were the most strongly worded. Many writers expressed considerable anger, convinced that the university itself was engaged in treason. The sentiment of some was anti-elitist. A not insignificant number suggested that, like Lattimore, the university was engaged in a conspiracy. A greater number believed that it was their right and duty to express their opinions and that the university had an obligation to listen and act on their suggestions. Some were unclear as to whether or not the Johns Hopkins University was a private or public institution, yet this hardly mattered. The attack on Lattimore and Johns Hopkins was wide-ranging and persistent. Support was more sporadic. It came when the calls for Lattimore's dismissal were most fierce.

Few expressed the idea that the university is a public trust, that as such it had inviolable responsibilities. What many writers instead assumed was that a university—private or public—should willingly and promptly respond to public opinion. Students had to be protected. It was unwise and dangerous for them to be exposed to heresies. If university authorities did not understand this, the larger community certainly did. If one could complain to the telephone company or to the water authority and expect a response and perhaps an accommodation, why not to a university?

The picture one gets of many who wrote to express a conspiratorial view is not unlike Edward Shils' portrait of the "vociferous minority" who communicated with politicians during the Cold War.

> Prim little clerks, rough laborers, suspicious schoolteachers, prosperous and resentful janitors, well-dressed housewives in their early fifties, splenetic cigar-chewing businessmen and the nervous secretaries of building and loan associations can all be obsessed with the wickedness of bureaucrats and intellectuals and foreigners and Communists. It is these and people like them who make up the nativist lunatic fringe so much in the field of vision of certain congressmen.
>
> Obsessed with powerful prejudices, xenophobic, stridently patriotic, aggressively suspicious of the stealers of secrets and the subversive agents of the "Rosenfeld revolution," seeing Jews, bankers and Bolsheviks in a single ring operating behind every political event, this ragtag and bobtail of American political life make a noise very disproportionate to their voting power. The passionate letter writers and telegraphers are seldom organized; when they are, they are loosely and inefficiently organized. They are a small, cranky, and rambling body of spinsters, "lumpen" proletarians, fly-by-night promoters, unsuccessful businessmen, toughs with political notions, solitaries and strays, beset by personal misery and thinking only of salvation through politics. These are the pickets who used to be seen marching up and down in front of the White House.[1]

It would appear that this vociferous minority was a majority of those who corresponded with Johns Hopkins.

The letter writers often affirmed their patriotism and questioned Lattimore's. Not only did they exhort against the dangers of internal Communist subversion, but there were warnings about the New Deal, centralized government, and foreign influences. Consistent with Shils' description, they expressed xenophobic and isolationist sentiments. The letters reflected an unyielding attachment to traditional beliefs and institutions. They were suspicious of Lattimore, a cosmopolitan world traveler. Many expressed hostility about academics and academic life. They were intensely and angrily concerned about the drift of national and international events. Wherever they looked it seemed that the Left and the internationalists were in the ascendancy. Some correspondents knew quite a bit about Lattimore's activities and beliefs; others knew very little. A large number were grossly misinformed about what he had said and written. The majority got all or some of what they knew from local newspapers and the radio. Magazines, pamphlets with limited circulation, and television also disseminated the ideas that people repeated in their correspondence. Not very many had read Lattimore's books or articles. Not many more had listened to, read, or were familiar with his congressional testimony. They repeated the phrases they read in the press. (Many of the ideas expressed in the piquant full-page account in *Time* magazine of Lattimore's testimony before the McCarran committee reprinted in its entirety in Appendix G, which comes just short of ridiculing him, were found in letters mailed beginning the week of its publication.) The letters varied in topic and tone. Some were quite harsh. Some were incoherent; others reflected considerable thought. Many were reasonable; many were not. In some there were references to Shakespeare or other flourishes; most were very direct. Almost all reflected an indifference to academic freedom, a disdain for academic due process, a confusion between charge and proof, or a fusion of indictment and conviction.

The most common theme repeated was quite simple—Lattimore should be fired. He should be immediately fired. He was untrustworthy. Students were being put at risk. He had disgraced the Johns Hopkins University; he had become an embarrassment to the university. He was a detriment; the university's reputation was suffering. It was now under a cloud. He had forced the university to become enveloped in his predicament. From a member of the J.H.U. Alumni Association:

> In recent years I have been greatly puzzled to find an answer for myself or to give an answer to others who have discussed the matter with me, why Owen Lattimore has so long been retained on the faculty of your outstanding institution.
>
> I do not wish to discuss the merits of the matter itself, about which I am entirely uninformed, except through the press and radio; but I do know that any institution, no matter how prominent, cannot fail to lose some of its just prestige by such publicity concerning any member of its faculty or staff.[2]

This was a theme in numerous letters: the merits of the case were less important than what the public thought about the university. Someone else put it more succinctly: "Each time [Lattimore's] name is mentioned your institution is linked with him. . . . Can you afford to let this situation continue?"[3] As many writers saw it, if an individual is a detriment to an institution, the tie should be broken. It should be broken sooner not later. It is not only necessary, it is proper that the relationship be ended. A college or university could do nothing less. Not to do so was incomprehensible—and unreasonable. The university was blamed for the fact that charges were made against a faculty member and it did not call him to account. Its inaction was inexplicable, and unacceptable.

Even if he had not deliberately acted to further communism, some argued, what Lattimore had done and said showed that he was either incompetent or naive, and on either count he deserved to be fired.

> You've full faith in Lattimore, eh? He was the guy who was sent to advise Chiang Kai-shek and then came to Town Hall forum and went to bat for the Chinese commies. If he isn't a bolo [Bolshevist?] he must be the biggest nincompoop alive. Better explain.[4]

> Even if you believe he is not a disloyal citizen, his viewpoint is a dangerous one. If he is not guilty, then he is certainly a stupid man.[5]

Part of the pattern of reproaching the university administration was to belittle Lattimore, commonly rudely and in the strongest language.

Although most who wrote felt strongly that Lattimore should be fired, by no means all did. Some merely asked for information. They wanted an explanation of Lattimore's relationship to Johns Hopkins. They wanted to know what the administrative authorities of Johns Hopkins thought of his politics, why the university had not disciplined him, and if the university's laissez-faire attitude reflected tacit approval of radical political beliefs. Given the seriousness of the charges against Lattimore, the university's tolerance made no sense.

What was being repeated about Lattimore in the press and on the radio made him indeed sound like "a very dangerous man." The impression that he was almost single-handedly responsible for the enslavement of hundreds of millions of Chinese had been created. It is not an exaggeration to say that many were energized and re-energized by the press, most particularly by conservative syndicated columnists, wire service dispatches with critical facts omitted, and sensational headlines and reporting. What was reported in the press was often inflammatory. It was often certainly enough to arouse the public's curiosity and fear.

Even if only a small part of what was being said about Lattimore was true, that he would be allowed to pursue a respectable and responsible calling was beyond the ken of most. A respectable and responsible institution would not want to keep in its employ someone who was not respectable and responsible. An apologist for communism was anything but respectable and responsible.

The many postcards and letters received by Johns Hopkins made it apparent that people from all regions of the country and from all walks of life were convinced that punishment was long overdue. Rather than being punished, it appeared that Lattimore was being rewarded. The public unhesitatingly communicated its outrage to the administrative authorities of Johns Hopkins, with an unshakable conviction that the university had an obligation to act on its advice. The Johns Hopkins administration was expected to take decisive action. To do otherwise would be irresponsible and wrong. It seemed self-evident that the university had no choice. It was not considered relevant that Lattimore had a contractual arrangement with Johns Hopkins which he had not violated. Nor was it relevant that he had yet to be convicted of a felony or even a misdemeanor.

If the flood of mail sent to the university is any indication, public opinion was clearly not on Lattimore's side. It had never been. He had been on the defensive from the day that he had been publicly identified as a loyalty risk by Senator McCarthy. To personalize the loss of China made world affairs more understandable. To blame it on dark plots, on a Communist conspiracy, rather than on the limitations of American power and the failures of the Nationalist government suited the paranoid style of thinking of the moral entrepreneurs. Lattimore may not have been convicted by the courts, but he had clearly been convicted before the bar of public opinion, and by most of the media: "I wish to vigorously protest against Johns Hopkins carrying on its payroll any man of Owen Lattimore's stripe. There can be no compromise with communism; there is no middle ground when it comes to loyalty and patriotism to our country. In my opinion Lattimore is a dirty, lousy traitor to our country masking himself in the garb of a loyal citizen. This has been proven to the satisfaction of the general public."[6] This concern about Lattimore's appointment at Johns Hopkins sometimes ebbed, but it never faded, even after he had been cleared in the courts.

Forerunners of McCarthy

For some time prior to the inquiry into his loyalty, Lattimore's appointment at Johns Hopkins was a concern to a number of people, some of whom were quite influential. In early 1945, an alumnus, the former Tokyo correspondent for the International News Service, began a letter to the university provost, P. Stewart Macaulay:

> Dear Pete:
>
> The other day you may have noticed that Jesse Jones gave $300,000 to the University of Virginia.
>
> I think you should anticipate in advance that you cannot expect substantial support for the Walter Hines Page School so long as you have Owen Lattimore on your staff.
>
> You should make a very close study of Lattimore's past work and his various connections. . . .
>
> As . . . mentioned in our conversations when we had such a pleasant visit with you, Lattimore has regularly lived from the trough of public and private endowments, back to the days when he wore a monocle. . . .

After the gibe, the writer added the thought that although he and others would like to see the John Hopkins University become a leading center for Far East studies, he doubted that this would come about as long as Lattimore was on the faculty. He recommended that the university administration "clear yourselves of any connection with Lattimore"; "He is away now from your staff which might be a splendid opportunity to make the absence permanent."[7] Well before the publicity generated by Senator McCarthy and the Tydings committee hearings, the administration of Johns Hopkins was receiving advice that it should fire Lattimore.

In his response to this letter, Provost Macaulay solidly defended Lattimore. Having himself been a newspaper reporter for over a decade before joining Johns Hopkins as secretary to the university in 1936, Macaulay took pains not to offend a fellow journalist. He began on a light note, assuring the alumnus that he understood that Lattimore and he would not see eye to eye; that was why Macaulay had once suggested a meeting, so that there would be a "better understanding" or perhaps even "fireworks."

Macaulay went on to explain that he and university President Detlev W. Bronk were convinced that Lattimore was not a follower of the Communist party line.

> Owen admittedly has made some statements and written some things which would lead one to believe that he is too ardent a sympathizer, but I have talked with him many times about politics in general and Russia in particular and I cannot find in him any of the zeal of the real convert. He is almost as completely objective as any one you can find and if he appears to have leanings I believe the appearance is due to his anxiety to be scrupulously impartial.
>
> Unfortunately, on many occasions people who do not like Lattimore have picked up the vulnerable spots which can be found in any man's writing. . . .

Macaulay expressed the view that Lattimore would not be a financial encumbrance to the university. Whatever financial support his presence might discourage would be more than offset by funds he would attract. Even if this proved not to be the case, Macaulay argued, Lattimore had to be supported because his work was honest and original. The fact that others, even potential donors, might be offended by what Lattimore wrote or said is not something that should be taken into account in assessing his value. The important point was that he was "conscientious to a remarkable degree." That he was "a bit of an idealist" should not be used against him: "I don't expect to convert you or make you a Lattimore disciple, my best hope is that I have been able to suggest to you that a university cannot be based upon any one set of opinions, political or otherwise, and that it should be receptive to men who have diverse views and who are willing to express them honestly and fearlessly."[8] In spite of Lattimore's warranted shortcomings, the Johns Hopkins University administration appeared to be solidly supportive.

The alumnus was neither offended nor persuaded by this approbation and affirmation of the principles of academic freedom. The following spring he again wrote Macaulay:

> What is Owen Lattimore's position now with respect to Russia and Manchuria?
>
> Was he not one of the advisors who suggested to the late president that Russia get the Kuriles? How far was Lattimore involved in the Manchurian deal?[9]

In the minds of many, Lattimore was the gray eminence behind American foreign policy in Asia.

There was a climate of suspicion across the country about Soviet expansionism and those who were perceived not to be critical enough about it that clearly antedated Senator McCarthy's attacks on Lattimore. There was a common perception that Lattimore was, if not himself an important policymaker, close to those in the government who shaped foreign policy. He was thought to be quite influential; many believed they saw his hand in the twists and turns of the State Department's, and thus the government's, foreign policy. Over the years, he and numerous State Department officials denied this allegation. These denials were never believed. They were seen as merely more evidence of Lattimore's hold over others. The moral entrepreneurs were convinced that Lattimore was powerful and instrumental in shaping the government's foreign policy. He was too devious and sinister, they reasoned, for it to be otherwise.

Individuals in Baltimore, in Maryland, and around the country with no ties to Johns Hopkins wrote to share their apprehension:

> To whom it may concern at Johns Hopkins—
>
> I am looking at the Fourth Report Un-American Activities in California 1948 Communist Front Organizations and on page 199 it says, "among the Communists and Communist fellow travelers who have been writing textbooks for use in public schools are the following: Owen Lattimore!"
>
> Have you too become a Communist front? I wonder.[10]

Such charges were difficult to answer, and the Johns Hopkins administration generally did not respond to such letters. This did not sit well with many letter writers who felt snubbed and were offended by the apparent arrogance of the Johns Hopkins administration.

Indeed, the failure of anyone at the university even to acknowledge receipt of these communications may have led some to write more than once in the hope of eliciting a reply. In some cases it increased the frustration and righteous indignation. If the university chose not to take their advice, at least it could send a short answer, an explanation. The failure to do so was taken by a surprisingly large number as irrefutable evidence of unqualified support for Lattimore and for left-wing politics. Many more were sure that it was a sign that the administration was untrustworthy and remiss. No strong and conscientious official would not stand up against Lattimore—and communism—and proudly inform others about his position.

As a rule, the administration did not respond to postcards or the most virulent letters. Those who called the administration or faculty Communists were least likely to receive attention. Officials were most likely to acknowledge letters from someone they knew as well as from those who expressed sympathy about the university's dilemma. They were aware that by not replying they would in many cases provoke greater condemnation, but more often than not they gave every appearance of ignoring criticism. As a middle course, sometimes a short, general, noncommittal response was sent, the feeling being that any answer, no matter how lacking in substance, was better than none.

> Dear Det:
>
> If we fail to answer this letter we run the risk of having a story built around the failure. Yet I do not see how we could attempt to answer the very specific questions. My suggestion—and it may not be a good one—is a two-sentence reply: "The university is not prepared at this time to answer the questions raised in your letter. If and when any statement is made, I shall be glad to see that a copy is sent to you."[11]

After noting that the "title fight" between Lattimore and McCarthy was doing Johns Hopkins "no good" and that Lattimore's unapologetic handling of the situation was also not helping matters, an attorney wrote asking what the term 'Far East expert' meant and what qualifications were necessary to be designated as one.[12] Receiving no reply after waiting a month, he again pressed for answers.

> Your man Lattimore continues to create considerable comment in the current news, and generally with the background of the university thrown in.
>
> In August I wrote you inquiring just what his qualifications for Far Eastern expert were, but received no reply. His continued public appearances, some of which at least are not relished by a large number of people, justify my inquiry. While on these various tours, does he receive any salary from the university? . . .

> It is a fair question to ask, just what is this man's job with the university, and is he being paid while on these various press conference expeditions to various parts of the country?[13]

Some who wrote more than once refocused their criticism from Lattimore to the university's failure to respond.

A vice president of the Thomas A. Edison Company wrote seven times in 1951 and 1952 asking when the university planned to terminate Lattimore. In early August 1951 he first inquired:

> How long are you going to keep that stinker, yes I mean stinker, Owen Lattimore as professor at the Johns Hopkins University where he can distort our way of life and foul the minds of the youth of the Nation?
>
> By keeping this stinker in that position you are rendering a great disservice to our way of life. Why don't you remove that stinker without delay and thus in a measure purify your college?[14]

A week later, referring this time to Lattimore as a "slicker," he warned that if the university did not fire him it would "become known as a Communist hangout, and I think rightly so."[15]

At the end of the month, making more of an effort to engage President Bronk and suggesting that there were personal risks, he again asked:

> Attention of the President
> Gentlemen:
>
> When are you going to clean this Communist out of your university? To be more specific, when are you going to get rid of that guy, Lattimore, who says everybody is a liar but himself? I think he is the liar and I think you are evidencing communistic sympathies by carrying him on your rolls and permitting him to disseminate his poisonous doctrine in America.[16]

Before the end of the year he again wondered: "why don't you get rid of that man Lattimore?"[17]

The following March he was much more indignant.

> Get rid of Lattimore and all other pinkish liberals who would sink our way of life. If you keep him, it will be prima

> facie evidence that you are a subscriber to Lattimore's philosophy which is anything apparently that aids and abets the Communists.[18]

The sixth letter was a series of angry questions.

> When are you going to get rid of Lattimore? Do you need any more information than has already been made crystal clear that he doesn't fit in any educational institution, especially Johns Hopkins? Why have this Communist sympathizer who sold Chiang Kai-shek down the river hang around Johns Hopkins and dirty its name if you are not in favor of the Communists too?[19]

By his final letter, there was no question in his mind what political views guided administrative decisions at the university.

> Why do you keep Owen Lattimore—the questionable character, to put it mildly—on your payroll? Is it because your institution is red or pink? What other reason could you have for keeping him if you don't sympathize with the thing that he stands for, which is communism?[20]

The university gave the appearance of being quite passive.

There was clearly a reservoir of suspicion about Lattimore, particularly by those who saw everything left of center as error, by those who conflated liberalism and communism. That the university would not fire Lattimore was incomprehensible to many. At best it was seen as weakness, stupidity, or naïveté. It was often seen as arrogance or complicity and yet more evidence of Lattimore's great power. By not ending Lattimore's connection with it, the university put itself under the same cloud. The newspapers almost never mentioned Lattimore without also mentioning Johns Hopkins. By the time he completed his testimony before the Tydings committee, postcards and letters began arriving at Johns Hopkins with great regularity. There was a groundswell of indignation and disbelief that nothing appeared to have been done to put an end to his pronouncements and career.

At this point, as indicated by internal memoranda, the administration received a larger number of telephone calls, relative to postcards and letters, than at any other time.

> Mr. Louis J. Briel, Jr. of 405 Cedarcroft Road telephoned today and asked me to tell Dr. Bronk that "rumors are going

> around that there are a number of faculty members at JHU who are pink if not red." He suggests that Dr. Bronk not endorse Mr. Lattimore and that he ask him to leave the university immediately.[21]

Over a third of the correspondents had specific suggestions about what the university administration should do about Lattimore's appointment. The view most often expressed was that Lattimore's presence on campus was harmful—that his ideas were harmful to America, that he had a destructive influence on students, that he could not be trusted, that, above all, he should be promptly dismissed. In the first place, there was no way of telling what the adverse effects of Lattimore's teaching on students might be:

> One might not like to have teachers be subject to the scrutiny of a FBI but if we are going to breed so many Communists in our colleges perhaps it will be a good idea to screen some of the teachers. Certainly I think anyone who studied under Mr. Lattimore should be carefully screened by the FBI before given a job of any kind.[22]

Lattimore had tainted not only the university, but most particularly his students.

That Lattimore might have a corrupting influence on young minds was alleged with greater regularity by those with no relationship to Johns Hopkins than by those with one—alumni, parents of students, or relatives, friends, or even acquaintances of someone with a connection. Here the belief was that if Lattimore's teaching was of demonstrably questionable quality, he could permanently harm students:

> May I ask, if Owen Lattimore's memory is as "faulty" as he and his wife claim, how can he be entrusted with the education of youth? Is it possible (I think otherwise) that he is already too senile to occupy his professorship? Otherwise how can you feel fair, under your heavy obligation to youth, that your students are not being handicapped by his acknowledged omissions of memory? Surely your educational standards are higher than that!![23]

> The time has come to rid the university of Dr. Lattimer [*sic*]. . . .

> If I had a son or daughter of school age they would never attend while Lattimer and a few more Communists were at the university.
>
> Lattimer is a Communist and as a Baltimorean I ask you to demand and receive his resignation at the earliest date possible.
>
> With regards to you, I beg to remain,
>
> Yours very truly[24]

> Will you please discharge Owen Latimore [*sic*] from your faculty. We cannot afford in this country to [have] men of his caliber and political beliefs teaching university students. The man is a liar and a Communist and there should be no doubt in your mind after all the investigations about him that he does not belong here. Why does he not emigarate [*sic*] to China or Russia where his frinds [*sic*] are? When we get rid of the crooks in gowerment [*sic*] all the way from the White House to very many of the departments we shall insist that public institutions as yours also get rid of their pet commies. So get him out now.[25]

In 1950 when the bulk of the correspondence began, a postcard was still one cent, and one could at small cost demand redress or express an opinion.

The greatest number of postcards and letters began arriving in 1952 after Lattimore gave testimony to the McCarran committee and the committee publicly castigated him and recommended that he be indicted for perjury. This wave lasted for nearly eighteen months. Not surprisingly, the largest proportion of postcards and letters received in this period had a Baltimore postmark, but this number was not a majority. The correspondents lived in all parts of the country, an indication that people from all regions knew about the Lattimore case and had strong and set opinions about it. Males and females wrote in almost equal numbers. Over three-fourths of the correspondence was addressed to an administrative officer of the university, usually the president. About half of the time, the writer did not know the proper name, title, or address of the person to whom he or she was directing the correspondence. Fewer than one-sixth of the writers indicated that they or some family member had some formal connection with the university.

As is evident from a large number of these postcards and letters, there was an immense and fervent loathing for Lattimore across America. People had feelings about him that went well beyond calling him variously a "liar," "commie," "red," "traitor," "spy," or "pinko," that went well beyond offering derogatory nicknames for him. The hostility was from people from all walks of life—from prominent businessmen and professionals such as physicians, dentists, architects, attorneys, and the clergy to many with apparently limited education and, by their own admission, with little understanding of what went on in institutions of higher learning. Judging from misspelling and grammatical mistakes, it would appear that about one-fifth of the writers were not fully literate.

In close to half of the cases it is clear that it is not merely Lattimore and what he reputedly did that bothered a writer, that fed the excitement and rage and occasioned the shrillness. The concerns were greater. It was the opposition to all things on the Left, most particularly all things on the far Left. It was the fear of the country being overthrown and ruled by communism, of losing freedom and possessions. It was an uneasiness with ideas new and different, and which had not been given legitimacy by large numbers of political and religious leaders. It was the rejection by Communists not only of Western religion but of all religions. Any threat to religion was seen as a threat to freedom, order, and morality—and to the family. (In the minds of many, communism and atheism were often coupled. One correspondent referred to "the unspeakable ideologies of atheistic communism in China," another to "the godlessness of the Communists," and a third to "their rejection of real TRUTH.") It was some of the threads of populism—anti-intellectualism, ambivalence about elites and their institutions, the assumption that if a majority holds an idea it must be valid—that have captured the American mind. The Lattimore case was particularly volatile because it brought together features of American society that had been festering years before the Cold War. Why else refer to Lattimore as a "skunk"? Why else wish him not simply deported, but dead? Why else would Sam Hiram Houston from Texas send the following?

> From out of the fog of deceit, trickery, half-truths, evasions, and deliberate falsehoods . . . the indisputable, undeniable facts emerging, place the indelible stamp upon one . . . Owen Lattimore . . . as an UNMITIGATED LIAR . . . a soft shelled "COMMIE" or a "PINK DUPE" . . . ONE that along with many others . . . caught in bad, or highly questionable company . . . pursues the regular Communists line of lying,

> shouting . . . forgetting . . . in an effort to free himself from his own entanglements.
>
> His line-up with *ONE WORLDERS* . . . *APOLOGETICS* . . . *HALF-BAKED* . . . *FREEDO-AMERICANS* of the "STRIPED PANTS" VARIETIES . . . that infest many of our *HIGHER INSTITUTIONS* OF LEARNING . . . leave little doubt as for *the underlieing* [*sic*] *cause* for the flood of socialism, communism, atheism and the athletic scandals now engulfing so many of our institutions.
>
> He . . . LATTIMORE . . . will, in due time, get what he has asked for . . . a one way ticket to
>
> POLITICAL and SOCIAL OBLIVION.
>
> IN AMERICA AND FOR AMERICA
>
> [P.S.] Charges by Sen. McCarthy proved and multiplied about 110% by Sen. Pat McCarren—Yes?[26]

Many others also linked quite disparate issues in an unintentionally comic fashion.

Lattimore was a "disgrace to true Americanism." In the words of "Semper Paratus" from New York: "He is an ugly duckling with pink feathers which are turning red. Disgustingly yours."[27]

Other Targets

As time passed, administrative authorities at Johns Hopkins who were reluctant to take action against Lattimore and who had little to say publicly about him also became the targets of a great deal of scorn: "Don't you think it high time to clean the traitors out of Johns Hopkins? Also it is high time for you to resign and make way for a decent and patriotic American in your Red-infested university."[28] It was common in these correspondences to accuse the president and the entire administration of Johns Hopkins of being on the political Left. It was accepted as a fact by many that a significant number within the institution shared Lattimore's views—and none were above suspicion.

> Dear Sir: Re: Lattimore.
>
> Your letter to the above would tend to indicate by continuing his salary you are in full accord with him and will fight shoulder to shoulder on the side of any un-Americans.[29]

In the eyes of the majority of moral entrepreneurs, by the time the Tydings committee hearings were completed the administration of Johns Hopkins was as suspect as Lattimore.

It was a widely held belief in the 1950s that a significant number of colleges and universities had been "infiltrated with Communists and socialists," and that those with tainted political values could be found even at the highest levels of academic administration. The failure of the Johns Hopkins administration to show the public that it disagreed with Lattimore by punishing him fed this perception. In two different letters, a prominent citizen accused the university of following a course that was politically dangerous.

> It is an established fact that our public schools and colleges, once described as "the fortresses of our freedoms," have failed us and they have become asylums for the protection of seditious forces. And in many cases they have become the friendly defender and encourager of that which comes pretty close to treason.
>
> This is conspicuously true of Harvard and Columbia. And what is Johns Hopkins going to do with this Lattimore fellow? It is a disgrace to keep him on your payroll and the trustees and administrators of Johns Hopkins themselves become contributors to this treachery against our country if they do not kick him out.[30]
>
> Dear Sir,
>
> Now—how much longer is Johns Hopkins going to keep that fellow Lattimore on its faculty and payroll? Have Americans no longer a right to expect militant patriotism in [their] colleges? Has the courage of our culture collapsed? You have condoned sedition until you are now forced to face it.[31]

Many less prominent individuals expressed the same sentiments.

For years it had been taken as an article of faith that too many faculty were too far to the Left. ("Would like to say to my mind one half of the Profs in our colleges in our country today are either atheists or Communists."[32]) This is a common view even today. To some, Lattimore was seen as just one Communist professor among many. Some correspondents even specified how many, the number or proportion—ten, twelve, fourteen, one-quarter, one-third, one-half—of other Communist faculty members there were at Johns Hopkins. That administrative officers would also be seen as sharing and advancing these dangerous views was what was new.

From when the suggestions of how the university should deal with Lattimore began to trickle in during the early spring of 1950 until 1960, when only occasional comments were received, over 80 percent of the correspondence was negative. Of the postcards and letters not supportive of Lattimore close to 45 percent were quite hostile. This was often readily apparent from how a postcard or envelope was addressed:

> Mr. Detlev Bronk
> Pro-Communist President of the Johns Hopkins University,
> Russian Espionage Headquarters for the United States
> Johns Hopkins University
> Baltimore, Maryland[33]

Not surprisingly, the texts of such postcards or letters generally conformed to the address and salutation.

> President Bronk,
> Defender of Traitors
>
> You will please note that a former Russian agent by the name of Bogolepov testified today that at an espionage meeting in Moscow in 1936 your dear friend the Russian spy Owen Lattimore was appointed by Maxim Litvinov as the agent to soften up American opinion.
>
> IT IS HIGH TIME THAT YOU BE EXPELLED FROM JOHNS HOPKINS AND OWEN LATTIMORE BE SENT TO THE ELECTRIC CHAIR.[34]

> DETLEV W. BRONK
> PRESIDENT OF THE JOHNS HOPKINS UNIVERSITY
> DEFENDER OF THE COMMUNIST TRAITOR OWEN LATTIMORE,
> WHO IS BLOODY JOE STALIN'S TOP SPY IN THE U.S.

> TRAITOROUS UNIVERSITY PRESIDENT
> DETLEV W. BRONK
> DEFENDER OF COMMUNIST TREASON AND TRAITORS
> AT THE JOHNS HOPKINS UNIVERSITY
>
> IT IS HIGH TIME THAT YOU KNOW THAT HIS EMINENCE CARDINAL SPELLMAN IS BEHIND SENATOR McCARTHY.
>
> YOU ARE PLAYING A DANGEROUS GAME IN PROTECTING THE TRAITORS AMBASSADOR PHILIP JESSUP AND THE COMMUNIST SKUNK OWEN LATTIMORE.

> PATRIOTIC AMERICANS ARE GOING TO PUT AN END TO YOUR TRAITOROUS ACTIVITIES. YOU AND YOUR ILK SHOULD BE DEPORTED TO RUSSIA. LATTIMORE AND JESSUP SHOULD BE HANGED.
>
> The Anti-Communist Sodality of the Third Order of St. Francis[35]

Of course, all writers whose postcard or letter indicated considerable animosity toward Lattimore were not necessarily as rude. A single-sentence note describing Lattimore as "an insignificant little tramp who should be deported or exported as trash," closed: "Yours truly."[36]

All correspondents were also not overtly angry. Some were ironic.

> Dear Sirs:
>
> Several months ago I read where Russian doctors had found that horseradish cured cancer.
>
> Since you harbor Owen Lattimore, I am sure that you have constant contact with Russia and might know more about this horseradish cure, or you may have been ordered by the fatherland to conduct experiments here.
>
> Since I have heard no more about the horseradish cure it most likely is just so much horseradish as the saying goes, but if it holds any promise will you please let me know.
>
> Yours respectfully[37]

> Professor Owen Lattimore of Johns Hopkins University
> A nice boy if you like them rare.[38]

Seldom was a negative letter conciliatory.

A significant number of these more critical notes were unsigned. Some writers were apparently apprehensive about retaliation by the university.

> My, you must be proud of this guy the way you hang on to him. Am not signing my name because I am afraid of reprisals. You and your gang are a great danger to the good old USA. I expect that as soon as you realize the danger you will do a "Henry Wallace."[39]

> Our family has heard some very disreputable things about your college. We just could not believe them of the high rated Johns Hopkins.

> This affiliation, we regret to state, has tipped the scales. It is now clear this man has cast his lot with the Jews and communism and against his own country.
>
> For two generations we have patronized your college and your hospital. This thing, therefore, does not make us feel very good.
>
> From several alumni and patients, and we will add, now assisting the FBI all we can. It is for this reason we are (all of us) anonymous.[40]

At worst, most of these correspondents were nothing more than unpleasant ("with Prof. Lattimore's indictment for *perjury,* you should be indicted for negligence and softheadedness"),[41] but a handful of correspondents may still have thought that the university could or would report them to a governmental agency or take some legal action.

Essentially the angriest postcards and letters never went beyond name-calling and abusive language.

> You should be ashamed to sit and do nothing after all this that Owen Lattimore is saying before the senate committee. To be stupid and ignorant is one thing but to go on and on, never awakening, you bring yourself, all higher education, the whole civilization that you represent into disrepute. Won't you just move so we can know whether you are dead or not?
>
> Many so called universities and their staffs have arrived at their dead end, I mean the bulldozer stage, where everything has to be buried and start all over again. I think you, your Johns Hopkins University are there.
>
> I am not afraid of you or communism, I know that a fight cannot be dodged very much longer, you will know when you are through this—I at least hope so anyway.
>
> Won't you just come out of it and elect to be an American from here?[42]

Actually, most threats were quite benign and unfocused. The majority that were specific indicated that they would use the legal system against Johns Hopkins.

> Sir:
>
> Just a line to inform you people that if you do not get that Communist Owen Lattimore out of your university I shall take action with the Maryland Ober Act to have him removed.

> We do not want reds in this country in such where American people go. So you have 14 days to act or I shall by force remove him for you. It has been proving [*sic*] he is red Communist follower and look very low for your university to have such trash as him there.[43]

Others suggested that they might harm the university publicly, or that others would do so.

> Dear Sir—
>
> That you could retain on your faculty, Owen Lattimore, in the face of public charges by congressional committees that he has committed public acts of perjury, is beyond my comprehension. Under the circumstances, I could not recommend your institution as a reputable place of learning to any self-respecting red-blooded American.[44]

> ALWAYS IT WAS WONDERED WHY JOHNS HOPKINS CARRIED HIM ON A FAT PAYROLL, WHY AMERICAN MONIES & PRESTIGE SHOULD UPHOLD THIS UN-AMERICAN ASSASSIN OF OUR NATIONAL CHARACTER—and play a game with worst enemies.
>
> THAT'S A QUESTION REPORTERS WILL SOON BE PUTTING TO YOUR PREXY—and you'd better have a mighty GOOD ANSWER to avoid innuendos against the ancient & honorable institution we love.[45]

Some letters were less general, although several stated that they would not allow their children to attend Johns Hopkins.

> I wouldn't send a boy there so long as you have the flabby policy of keeping a man against whom there is preponderant evidence that something is wrong with him. I heard him speak and I wouldn't trust him across the street. You would do well to get rid of him.[46]
>
> My son will be entered in the University of Buffalo instead of Johns Hopkins! Not much you say! I shall influence others.
>
> "All American"[47]

> I have a small son. He may want to go to college when he grows up. I do not know which college he may wish to attend

> but I know of several he is not going to attend. Not on my money anyway.[48]

Still others thought that not only undergraduate education but all aspects of Johns Hopkins should be boycotted.

> Dear Sir:
>
> American boys are dying in Korea, you sir with unbelievable callousness allow an arrogant red rat to teach American youth.
>
> I am suffering from high blood pressure, my doctor advised me to go to a doctor at Johns Hopkins. Believe me, I would rather die than go to an institution that tolerates and encourages treason.
>
> How the boys can stand this rat in their classes is a sad commentary on our American youth.
>
> Yours very truly,
> Phila, Pa.[49]

Some obviously believed that the university only had one traitor on its faculty.

Not surprisingly, the threat that the Johns Hopkins administration seemed to take most seriously was the promise of withholding contributions from the university. Almost all such communications that threatened not to support the university financially were in the form of a letter, and most came from alumni. This subject is considered separately and in some detail in the next chapter.

It is worth noting that not all writers of critical mail were churlish. Some letters were lengthy and well-reasoned. (Two examples, one from New York and the other from Texas, are reproduced in full in Appendix H.) A great many more were short and to the point. A newspaper executive from Oklahoma:

> Our college presidents are intellectual cowards. They give sanctuary to treachery, even treason, and the freedom of speech that denies freedom. How long is Johns Hopkins going to keep Lattimore?[50]

A physician from Los Angeles:

To the President
Johns Hopkins

It seems to a lot of Americans that it *is time Lattimore* left *the sanctuary of your university.*[51]

An alumnus:

Dear Doctor Bronk—

Clean the UNIVERSITY of the COMMIES. Yes Alger Hiss rose to high esteem and office, and betrayed his UNIVERSITY and COUNTRY. . . . In view of the BUDENZ and McCarthy testimony—LATTIMORE is also in the group. His recommendation as to CHINA, you note paralleled the COMMUNIST recommendation, word for word—was it a coincidence? Where there is smoke, there is fire. . . . Doctor do not wait for LATTIMORE to receive the fate of HISS, before you take notice. With best wishes for you and the UNIVERSITY.

AN OLD TIMER, HOPKINS GRAD[52]

The public from around the country:

Dear Sir: Many folks out here in the midwest wonder why you keep a traitor like Owen Lattimore on the payroll of your school.

Query[53]

Lattimore stinks to *Hi Heaven*. J-H begins to smell of him. He is worst blot on J-H record—[54]

How much longer will you keep a stinker like Owen Lattimore on your payroll?

We can smell him this far away. Please show him this note.[55]

The letters came in like chain shot. As the months went by, more and more demanded Lattimore's immediate dismissal.

Correspondents used techniques besides insults and threats in their efforts to get the attention of university authorities. They often began a letter with a personal statement about themselves, presumedly to show a human side. Sometimes they were brief; other times they were full of details. A physician from Albuquerque described himself as "a young and unquestionably patriotic American."[56] Accounts were generally less modest and more informative.

> I am a member of the Masonic orders, have my name on the rolls of the Christian Church, have cards in the Spanish War Veterans, the V.F.W., the American Legion; have honorary citizenship card in Boys Town, and probably might be called a nine-run citizen. Am also a member of the local Rotary Club.
>
> I don't claim to be a reformer, or an outstanding moralist, but I do make claim to loyalty to my country.[57]

Copies of letters written to other academic administrators, public officials, philanthropic organizations, and members of the press were used to make an impression. Someone sent a copy of a letter in which he reminded the broadcaster Edward R. Murrow that it was a mistake to trust Lattimore, since it was in his nature to lie, as it was any Communist.

> How perfectly he exemplified the technique of the Communists at the top. . . . In every country which has bowed to communism there have been undercover men who always denied their affiliation until the red flag was run up in sign of victory, then they came forth to sit in the high places as a reward for services performed. . . .
>
> You must know, of course, that the discrediting of Budenz, like the liquidation of Trotsky, is an essential part of the Communist program. I think, however, that Lattimore overdid it today—the performance, with all the stops pulled out, was too pat. . . . [58]

A second writer pressed the attorney general to prosecute Lattimore, with more vigor and speed.

> I have just learned that the trial of "Professor" Owen Lattimore is to be postponed until next October. WHY? Petty thieves and gamblers can be thrown instantly into jail and poor men who are unable to pay the exorbitant taxes imposed on them are subject to fines and imprisonment. . . . Certainly, the FBI has enough on Owen Lattimore to hang him, and if you are interested in the survival of our Nation, it is your sacred duty to bring speedy action against him. . . .
>
> I beg you to place your loyalty to your country above all political considerations, and see to it that those who would impose the Soviet form of slavery on this helpless Nation are immediately made impotent. You can do no less.[59]

Another forwarded a copy of her analysis of Lattimore's writing and character which she had sent to Senator McCarran.

> He always starts out by telling us HOW to fight our mortal enemy in this not-so-Cold War and ends up by giving a plan that is right down Stalin's alley. He should be asked why he resorted to the lie in speaking of "Communist ascendancy in Asia" that it stood for "peaceful constructive activities in FREE COUNTRIES, and peaceful cooperation among FREE PEOPLE." The capital letters are mine. No one except Communists ever had the impertinence to call Communist countries and Communist peoples "free. . . ." I personally consider him diabolically clever, subtle, foxy. One of [the] Grave Diggers of America. I consider the damage he has done to my country simply incalculable. . . .
>
> I, for one, will take the word of the ex-Communist rather than the word of Lattimore. His words just do not ring true.[60]

All were certain of Lattimore's guilt, and all were unforgiving.

Others used their relationship with important and influential personages to the Johns Hopkins University in their efforts to influence the administration. Someone from Connecticut began and ended her letter invoking the name of and her relationship to the family of the much revered first president of the university, Daniel Coit Gilman, who had passed away over forty years earlier.

> A Gilman would never have permitted a Lattimore to lecture and hand out insidious propaganda within the halls of Johns Hopkins, yet you permit him to rant and shout at all times. . . . The man, in the words of a great dramatist, "protests too much." All of Gilman's associates had to be above suspicion.
>
> Today the college that harbored a Gilman now shelters a Lattimore, the companion of Jaffe, Service, etc. (His recent attendance at the Jaffe home to witness the marriage of Jaffe's Communist niece and her Chinese lover, another Communist, is rather significant.) . . .
>
> The Gilman family lived in Norwich. The three Gilman sisters were loved and admired by all. I knew them well and received many favors from them. In their home one found gracious living, true culture, and an eagerness to help those who yearned for higher education. Race, color, and creed did not influence this Christian household. Loyalty was their creed.[61]

Someone from North Carolina attempted to trade on his relationship with the Page family.

> How your good university can possibly retain Owen Lattimore as a member of your faculty under the Walter Hines Page Memorial is beyond my understanding. It was my good fortune to have known Walter Hines Page and all his family intimately. We were neighbors for years. Rest assured, I will do all in my power to prevail upon his heirs to force the removal of this un-American little rat Lattimore from your institution.
>
> Yours very truly
>
> P.S. I'm leaving here today to go North and meet with one of Walter Hines Page's own sons in this connection.[62]

A number of the critics of Lattimore and Johns Hopkins expressed the view that some personal characteristics of Lattimore, in addition to what were widely regarded as his political beliefs, made his continuation on the faculty problematic. For example, Lattimore had spent nearly all of his childhood and young adulthood in Asia and Europe: When he was about a year old, his family moved to China where his father taught in a program of general Western education. At the age of twelve he was sent to complete his schooling in Switzerland (one year) and England (five years). He returned to China when he was nineteen and worked for one year for an English newspaper and for six years for a British import-export firm. During this period he studied and traveled throughout Mongolia and Sinkiang. Lattimore returned to America in 1928 and spent one academic year in the Division of Anthropology at Harvard University. The early 1930s were spent in Peking and traveling in Mongolia. After he assumed the editorship of *Pacific Affairs* he set up residence in Peking and returned to America only shortly before he took the post at Johns Hopkins. Because of these facts that could have been used to prove experience and authority, he was viewed by some as too foreign, as someone less than fully American. He was a little too worldly.

Moreover, the fact that Lattimore did not have a bachelor's degree, let alone an advanced degree, bothered other correspondents. Some were convinced that this had some sinister meaning and reminded the university administration of this fact. Even Senator McCarran wrote in his capacity as chairman of the Internal Security Subcommittee of the Senate Committee on the Judiciary for an explanation:

My Dear Mr. President:

I have received the following letter and am at somewhat of a loss just what to tell this gentleman. I shall be very grateful if you will advise me.

"It is common knowledge in North Baltimore that Mr. Lattimore has no degree, yet he is a member of the faculty of the famed Johns Hopkins University. The shop was closed in a certain Maryland high school my boy attended because they could not get an instructor *with a college degree* to handle the class. Am I nuts, or is something rotten in Denmark?"

Sincerely[63]

Provost Macaulay responded for the university:

Dear Senator McCarran:

This is a reply to your letter of March 20 in which you quote a paragraph from a correspondent who apparently is a resident of Baltimore.

The fact that Mr. Lattimore has no degree is common knowledge. He is so listed in the university catalogues and his biography in *Who's Who in America* indicates that he has no degree.

Sincerely yours[64]

The university administration could respond, but it could not mollify Lattimore's or its critics.

Many others were also convinced that Lattimore's lack of formal degrees not only at the minimum disqualified him from holding a faculty appointment, but it might even be hard evidence that he was a charlatan, an impostor. Someone from a Knights of Columbus chapter wrote:

Gentlemen:

I have been waiting for some time now for a dismissal of "Professor" Owen Lattimore from the Johns Hopkins University.

I am beginning to wonder if the administration at the university are [*sic*] awake or what has to happen to convince them [*sic*] that something is wrong with Lattimore.

> Moreover, one wonders how Johns Hopkins has such a reputation for scholarship and yet has on its staff Owen Lattimore, who bears the title of professor and is head of the School of International Studies [*sic*], yet Mr. Lattimore enjoyed little formal education, never attending college nor graduating from high school and holds no academic degrees. One wonders how a man of such calibre was appointed, who suggested or ordered it and by what authority?
>
> Evidently there must be others at the university who either endorse or follow Mr. Lattimore's policies otherwise something should have been done previously. . . . [65]

Others expressed their opinion and concern.

> The dean of the university:
>
> Well I suspect that old Johns Hopkins must be writhing in his grave to think the school his name is on should hire and retain as a professor such a sixth grade size (NO degree of any kind); such a wild Communist tainted, double talking smoothie as Owen Lattimore.
>
> Your tacit approval of his line of thought and undignified contemptuous line of thought must make your faces red some time.
>
> I know his continued sponsorship by you (evidenced by no disavowal of his methods or point of view) has materially lowered the people's ideas about you, at least out West.
>
> [P.S.] Why don't you can him cold—and clean your reputation—or don't you care?[66]

> President Johns Hopkins:
>
> Kindly see that Owen Lattimore cannot teach at the Johns Hopkins University, as he is no high school graduate, and has no degrees of any kind. He is not worthy of teaching our young people of today. It would be a disgrace and being a mother I would not want my children taught by him, and there are thousands who feel the same way. He should not be able to teach anywhere here in our United States, that we love so *very very* much.
>
> A Chicago Mother[67]

Any argument that might persuade the administration to fire Lattimore was used.

Many were also as offended as Senator McCarran and his colleagues by Lattimore's pugnacious behavior before the senate committee, and wrote the university to express their displeasure. Lattimore was faulted for being nonprofessional, for being an obstructionist in order to hide his misdeeds.

> Dear Sir:
>
> As a native son of the Free State of Maryland it is becoming increasingly hard for me to bear to read in the daily press of Owen Lattimore's contemptible, arrogant prevarications. That this cowardly betrayer of America and China—who so nonchalantly and insolently laughs off the enormity of his moral crime—continues to hold a post at one of America's most respected institutions of learning is beyond all understanding and can only indicate that Marylanders no longer have the guts and patriotism they once had.
>
> Academic freedom is fine and dandy but it does not include deliberate falsehood, subversion, and downright traitorousness. . . .
>
> Yours for "America First and My Country, Right or Wrong"[68]

Another letter was received on the stationery of the Philadelphia Veterans' Advisory Committee.

> In view of the conduct of Owen Lattimore at his recent hearing in Washington your institution stands out as nothing more than a festering sore in the minds of many Americans. . . . We ask that he be dismissed immediately and a general housecleaning be made to scare out all Communists in the university—to continue his employment brings only a red smear at this institution.[69]

The letters from those who wrote on behalf of organizations were no different from those who only represented themselves.

The Power of the Media

Clearly the great attention by the media to the Lattimore case precipitated a large number of these letters. As many letters seemed to be affected by news stories as by editorials, radio broadcasts, letters to the editor, and opinion pieces. Because most references to

Lattimore in the press mentioned his appointment at Johns Hopkins, the university seemed an appropriate place to write to ask questions, express concerns, or make demands. The postcard and letter writers seemed to assume that because the charges were made and repeated by prominent politicians, journalists, or other public figures then they must be totally or in large part true. More than one correspondent reminded the university administration: "It is surprising that you permit the man Lattimore to remain as a teacher at the institution since a number of charges have been made against him at various times and at present he is under indictment. Where there is so much smoke there must be some fire."[70] Press reports even induced trustees to write university administrators.

> Most of the statements before the McCarran committee as reported in the newspapers have been pretty vague and indirect. However, the *Washington Evening Star* of yesterday carried a report of some testimony of a Russian Colonel which I had not seen before and which I think is a little nearer the issue. I am enclosing the clipping from the *Star* in case you haven't seen it.[71]

Many writers enclosed pictures, news items, headlines, editorials, magazine articles, or political cartoons to remind the Johns Hopkins administration that Lattimore was an object of distrust.

> Referring to the enclosed article [headlined: "Probers Name Lattimore as Soviet Agent"], just one of many similar ones, it seems that it is high time that your university purge itself of this obnoxious character, at the earliest possible moment. . . . Whether all of the accusations against Lattimore are true or not, there is enough against him to make him totally unfit for the position which you are permitting him to hold. This is the opinion of many of our best citizens.[72]

> I am enclosing a clipping from Roanoke, VA. paper, [*The Roanoke Times,* August 1, 1951] in which Lattimore is once more mentioned as Red in the employ of Russia.
>
> If we only had men like either Teddy Roosevelt or Grover Cleveland, this would not be going on in this country.
>
> A word to the wise is sufficient.[73]

> I wish that you would read over the abstract of "Eleven Years in Soviet Prison Camps" by Elinor Lipper which appears

> in the June *Reader's Digest.* Below is a clipping concerning Freda Utley's *The China Story* [which is quite critical of Lattimore].[74]

> I do not have the pleasure of knowing you but we see plenty of information in the papers from time to time regarding the Johns Hopkins University and Mr. Owen Lattimore, who seems to be an individual of some importance in the United States. I call your attention to *The Freeman* of June 30, 1952. Commencing on page 643 it carries an article entitled "How the IPR Helped Stalin Seize China," which may be of some interest to you.[75]

Besides materials which appeared in the press, pages and even entire copies of the *Congressional Record* were mailed to the university.

Newspaper clippings arrived full of marginalia. An article with the headline "Probers Link Lattimore Aid to Red Party," the subheadline "Demand Investigation of Prof's Defender," and a long report of how Lattimore attempted to conceal from the McCarran committee the true facts of his relationship with an associate who took the Fifth Amendment when asked about whether he had been a member of the Communist party, arrived with the questions "what kind of a school are you running out there, mister?" and "can't you get along without these guys?" scribbled on the top.[76]

Most materials clipped from newspapers and magazines with the added commentary were quite unfavorable to Lattimore. One headline that read "Aid to Spy Laid to Lattimore" had the advice "give this to Lattimore and ask him to resign" written in thick, dark ink.[77] A long provocative piece from the *Chicago Tribune* Press Service with the headline "Bare Lattimore Wiles to Win China for Reds" and a smaller headline "Propaganda Snare for Banker Lamont Fails" describing how Lattimore was the ghost writer of a letter which sought to influence the American government on behalf of the Chinese Communist armies in 1945 had "such a *skunk* should be deported to a lone island" on the first page and "no doubt—you have no son murdered by the dear China Communists" on the second.[78]

The university received retouched editorial cartoons and newspaper photographs of both Lattimore and university President Detlev W. Bronk. Some newspaper pieces were sent without comment, merely with sentences or paragraphs underlined. Others arrived with the briefest note of a few words. Some correspondents sent detailed accounts from periodicals.

A lengthy article with the headline "Lattimore Aide of Red Police, Senators Hear" was accompanied with the short letter: "Dear Sir: The enclosed clipping regarding a member of your faculty may interest you."[79] A hostile column in the *New Leader* titled "The Political Views of Hopalong Lattimore," ridiculing Lattimore's denial that he was a Communist, Communist sympathizer or fellow traveler, had the following typewritten along the top and bottom:

> This article is "McCarthysim" as defined by the Communist Brain Trust and our befuddled liberals. To them, Senator McCarthy became Public Enemy No. 1 and Lattimore an abused saint, instead of one of the leading architects of our pro-Moscow policy in Asia. The McCarthy-Lattimore controversy clearly proves that the ideological war is more important than the shooting war.[80]

Headlines with letters over one inch high announcing "Indict Lattimore as Liar"[81] arrived without the accompanying story or any comments.

About half of these press clippings were not news accounts but opinion pieces, almost all unflattering to Lattimore. A piece by Fulton Lewis, Jr., describing how Lattimore had, by someone's testimony before the McCarran committee, been made to look like a "clown," and as a result had been forced into silence, had "is this bird still on the payroll or getting Russian rubles?" scrawled across the top.[82]

Senator McCarthy's charge that there was a Lattimore-Acheson plan for Asia that would subjugate the entire region to communism was often enough repeated in the press to become imprinted on the American consciousness, and precipitated letters.

> Why should a university of your standing employ a man who does not have even a bachelor's degree from any college. Either Lattimore is a fool or a traitor—in either case he should not be employed by a reputable university.
>
> . . . When one thinks of all the traitorous teachers in our schools and colleges, we do not wonder that we are a morally bankrupt Nation and are afflicted with a shallow, vindictive little man like harry truman [*sic*] as president, a Secretary of State who is either hopelessly confused or is pro-red, and military leaders (?) who are but stooges of Generalissimo Acheson.

> If we don't wake up and return to the principles and ideals upon which our Nation was founded, we deserve to be annihilated. No country was ever more blessed by God than America, and no country has been less deserving of such blessings. We need AMERICAN teachers and not socialists, reds or fellow-travelers.[83]

A long newspaper article which quoted FBI Director J. Edgar Hoover's warning that "a hard core of 43,217 Communist party members in the United States may be expected to strike 'with sabotage and revolt against this country if and when the time comes' " and repeating Louis F. Budenz's charge that Lattimore was a member of the Communist party arrived with a brief note "Dear Sir: You may find the enclosed clipping interesting."[84]

When a Minnesota newspaper ran a report that the university did not plan to take action against Lattimore even after a McCarran committee witness "called him 'the principal agent for the advocacy of Stalinist ideas' among American experts on the Far East," a physician pasted the article on a postcard and sent it to President Bronk with the message:

> DISCHARGE THE RUSSIAN SPY OWEN LATTIMORE. Johns Hopkins will soon have the same reputation as Harvard as a seminary of treason and a hotbed of pro-Russian subversion.

He addressed the card:

> Detlev Bronk
> President of the Johns Hopkins University
> Defender of the TRAITOR and RUSSIAN
> ESPIONAGE AGENT Owen Lattimore
> Johns Hopkins University
> PERSONAL ATTENTION OF MR. BRONK[85]

The similarily of the address on this card to others received from different parts of the country is apparent. It was not possible to ascertain whether this similarity is simply due to chance or to a concerted letter-writing campaign.

The Effects of the Korean War

The military action in Korea between 1951 and 1953 greatly intensified the American people's anger and apprehension about the spread of communism around the world, and became a dominant theme of a number of the postcards and letters addressed to the Johns Hopkins administration regarding Lattimore. It was believed by many that had China not turned to communism, there would not have been a war in Korea. A corollary of this article of faith was that those who did not prevent the defeat of the Nationalist army to Mao Tse-tung's forces were responsible for the Korean conflict: "The Democratic administration led by Truman and Acheson didn't know too much about the Asiatic situation and took the advice of a so-called expert by the name of Lattimore. I feel that he has done this country an incalculable harm. He has hobnobbed with the Russians, let them dictate the Asiatic policy of our country and this policy led to the loss of China to the Russians and eventually the Korean War."[86] Lattimore was not just an unreliable advisor, he was fully responsible for the many American setbacks in Korea.

Many remained convinced, notwithstanding his repeated denials, that Lattimore dictated American foreign policy or dominated those who did. They were also convinced that a mistaken American foreign policy led directly to the fall of Chiang Kai-shek. The Democratic administration had been weak and stupid, maybe not even committed enough to American interests. As a consequence, the country had to pay a steep price for this incompetence—or perhaps even treachery. It seemed highly unlikely that Lattimore was not culpable.

It appeared that each letter which worried about America's fortune in Korea was more irate than the last. As American casualties increased, so did the fury:

> We who have our sons fighting in Korea because of the stupidities of such men as Lattimore, are waiting for some action from Johns Hopkins.[87]

> I am writing to you relative to your continuing to have a man as Owen Lattimore teaching in your university. Really how red-blooded Americans knowing what part he must have had in the betrayal of China to the Communists and with this growing into the Korean War where thousands of our young men have died for naught, believing there must be something wrong with those in charge of the once great university. It is too heart sickening for words.[88]

> Would you Mr. President look Mr. Lattimore up and ask him if he will relinquish his job so I too can travel to China and

> see the democratic forces who are killing our boys. Does the good semi-professor explain to his classes that he is responsible for this carnage and that you the president should be commended for your pugnacity in keeping this bum on the payroll. Have you Red spots too? Isn't there a spark of manhood in your whole carcass to notice that the once great university is now being humbled and humiliated by this two-faced, double crossing pinko-stinko who has been whimpering ever since he was exposed, and if Benedict Arnold were alive they could be Palsy-Walsies of the same type.[89]

The heightened concern about Lattimore and his ideas engendered by the escalating war in Korea is most evident in a series of a half dozen letters written over a short period of time by a man from California whose life had been profoundly affected by the conflict. Many are quite long, and all are redundant. All are also written with considerable feeling. Excerpts can be found in Appendix I. There is no way of knowing how many correspondents had personal reasons—for example, a relationship with someone who was in the military or even someone who had been wounded or killed in Korea—for their interest in the Lattimore case, but for many their interest was intensified by developments in Korea.

Countervailing Pressures

In a letter Provost Macaulay wrote in July 1952, he remarked that members of the board of trustees were "deluged—with communications from both sides."[90] This is true as far as it goes, but it does not convey the total picture, most particularly as to the balance of postcards, letters, telephone calls, and the like from "both sides."

As indicated earlier, for every ten postcards or letters critical of Lattimore and calling for sanctions or reproaching the Johns Hopkins administration for its failure to move against him, there were only about two that were supportive of Lattimore or the university.

Although the ratio of unfavorable to favorable communications was quite lopsided, the fact that there were "communications from both sides" shows that not everyone in America believed that Lattimore and his ideas were that dangerous, that his behavior before the McCarran committee was inappropriate, and that the Johns Hopkins University should call him to account. Some felt that the entire matter should be ignored. A very small and vocal number were of the opinion that what Lattimore had done was deserving of praise, not punishment. There were countervailing pressures on Johns Hopkins to retain and in no way disturb Lattimore's tenure.

The content of a number of these letters had little to say about Lattimore or what he was said to have done. They were rueful about the Cold War, political repression, the intemperate tactics of Senator McCarthy, the circus-like atmosphere of the congressional hearings, and the climate of hysteria regarding the Soviet Union and communism sweeping the country.

Some of the letter writers expressed admiration for the president and board of trustees for standing firm, for not "taking the easy road" by simply dismissing Lattimore. These letters encouraged them to continue to hold fast in the face of the considerable pressure from politicians and opinion makers to apply sanctions. A few even suggested that the university repudiate the charges against Lattimore and were critical of the university for not offering a more vigorous defense of him. Those that congratulated the administration for acting in an impartial manner were, however, more common.

Many of these advocates seemed impelled to point out that they were not personally acquainted with Lattimore, that they were writing to defend a principle, not an individual.

> I have no connection with Professor Lattimore, but as a lover of justice and fair play, I am shocked and greatly disturbed over the ordeal through which he has been passing. . . . I am sending this simply to give you some idea of your correspondent's background. As a Mayflower descendant and a former member of the S.A.R., I have no Communist affiliations.[91]

Although a distinct minority, a significantly larger percentage of letters endorsing Lattimore or the university's stand received the formal attention (in the form of a response) from the academic authorities of Johns Hopkins than those that were critical. The response was often merely an acknowledgment and an expression of gratitude for understanding and support.

> Under ordinary circumstances it is at best in questionable taste to praise a university for pursuing a course that is strictly correct. But when the pressure toward hasty and possibly ill-advised action is tremendous, rectitude becomes admirable indeed.

In the Lattimore case the Johns Hopkins has justified the pride of its friends, who will have no occasion to apologize for it, regardless of the outcome of the trial.[92]

My dear Mr. Johnson:

Thank you so much for your good letter of December 21, in which you kindly express your approval of the action of the Johns Hopkins University in the case of Owen Lattimore. Because of my high regard for you and your noble ideals, I especially value your expressions of approval and confidence.

With warm appreciation and best wishes. . . . [93]

From reading the *Baltimore Sun* it is our opinion that the university has demonstrated an objective impartial attitude with respect to Professor Owen Lattimore.

It is our opinion that private citizens should be articulate in matters as important as this. For that reason may we take this method of extending our personal tribute to you and the board of trustees for your fairness and impartiality.
cc: Editor, *The Baltimore Sun*[94]

Thank you very much for your very kind and cordial letter of December 20. I have shown it to Mr. Barton, President of the board of trustees, and he joins with me in expressing appreciation for your confidence.[95]

Of course, unlike the negative letters, it was possible to answer these letters. Almost all were signed (some exceptions: "A Friend of Liberty," "A Former Student"), had return addresses, and were reasonably well argued. A significant number were from academics who had friends or acquaintances at Johns Hopkins; a number were from professionals—physicians, dentists, attorneys, schoolteachers. Some appeared to be from alumni. There were none with a letterhead from a business or industry. Some were from prominent citizens—politicians and others in public life—but most were not. Those that were invariably received a reply.

TO ONE AND ALL:

I wish to seriously and deeply commend you for not persecuting and sacrificing Owen Lattimore . . . .

Your institution is entitled to the very highest respect of all those believing in freedom of speech. It will be noted that I do not even know the name of the president of your university, nor even of a single professor (unless probably they were called to my attention) and this is sent as a full out respectful letter.

Sincerey yours,
Maury Maverick[96]

I want to tell you how much we appreciate your letter of commendation. You must realize the great difficulties that we have faced in connection with the Owen Lattimore situation. We believe that we have acted in the spirit that should be followed by an institution of this type, and it is a pleasure to be commended for our action. I shall take the occasion of calling your letter to the attention of our trustees.[97]

Knowing the propensities of Americans, I suppose that you will be receiving a good deal of comment and perhaps criticism regarding the action you took on Mr. Lattimore following his indictment.

I want you to know that I think the move you made was wise, objective and unemotional.[98]

It was extraordinarily kind and thoughtful of you to have written me as you did concerning the action of the Johns Hopkins in the case of Mr. Owen Lattimore. I can't tell you how much I appreciate your kindness. As you say, there are some who feel that we were unfair to him by disassociating him from the university following his indictment and others who feel that we should have dismissed him before he was tried by due process of law. However, we have felt that this would best show our regard for established American institutions and especially for the judicial process.

Dr. Victor Johnson
Mayo Foundation
University of Minnesota Graduate School[99]

The plaintive tone of these replies suggests that the administration was feeling considerable pressure.

A few who wrote defending Lattimore sent money to be used to cover his legal expenses.

> I believe in the loyalty of Owen Lattimore, and I am writing to him today expressing my confidence and enclosing a small check toward a fund which I hope will be raised to enable him to seek justice in a higher court. I hope that his friends in your great university, and others who believe in the traditional justice of our country, will rally to his support.[100]

Others put forth the idea that the university raise funds "to enable [Lattimore] to have the best possible legal aid"[101] or asked for information as to how they might contribute. The administration did not encourage these initiatives.

> If my views are correct, both because he deserves a fair trial and because it will ease my conscience, I would like to contribute to Dr. Lattimore's defense.
>
> If you are free to do so, please let me know how your faculty feels in this matter, and if a contribution is in order, how it would be best for me to make it.[102]

> In reply to your recent letter of January 26, I find it difficult to state how the faculty of the Johns Hopkins University feels with regard to the many facets of the situation regarding Mr. Owen Lattimore inasmuch as there is a wide diversity of views regarding the many aspects of the problem. Accordingly, you will see that it would be impossible for us to interpret the opinions of the faculty.
>
> Yours sincerely[103]

It was enough that the university not punish Lattimore. In keeping with its initial posture, administrators clearly did not want to become, or even appear to be, active in his defense.

4

The Response from Johns Hopkins

The defense of Lattimore on the Johns Hopkins University campus ranged from the spirited and determined to the proper and obligatory. Led by faculty, it was extensive, steadfast, and never overwrought or reckless. It engendered the minimum amount of public criticism, no more than any defense of Lattimore would.

Spring 1950

The lead story in a Baltimore evening newspaper on March 13, 1950, was preceded by a headline more than one inch high and described in detail Senator McCarthy's assertions before the Tydings committee that Lattimore had over the years collaborated with known Communists and Communist organizations. A separate article told of Lattimore's wife's (Eleanor Lattimore's) denial, on behalf of her husband, of Senator McCarthy's dramatic denunciation and of the initial reaction by the Johns Hopkins University administration to the accusations. As would prove to be characteristic, President Detlev W. Bronk's response was terse. (One of the few points Lattimore's supporters and critics agree on was that it was too terse.) He was quoted in the press as saying the allegations were "news to me." He added the assurance that Lattimore would "be quick to deal with the charges on his return to this country."[1]

Three days later President Bronk issued a one-paragraph formal statement that fairly well reflected the thinking of the majority of the senior faculty at the university and set the tone for what would be said publicly in the immediate months to come.

> I have known Dr. Lattimore during the year that I have been at the Hopkins. I have never heard him say anything that would indicate he was opposed to the ideals of American democracy or was disloyal to our government. Accordingly, I will abide by the traditional American principle of believing Dr. Lattimore to be innocent of disloyalty to the American government until he is proven guilty by his own statements or by due process of legal governmental action. I am sure all members of the university will agree with this attitude.[2]

Although supportive, this was not a ringing endorsement, and some Lattimore partisans were convinced that a firmer initial position by Bronk, who was a distinguished biophysicist having been among other things president of both the American Association for the Advancement of Science and the National Academy of Sciences, would have mitigated subsequent attacks on him and the university.[3] The advocacy for Lattimore from faculty was in general firm and less restrained.

Just a few days after Senator McCarthy gave his testimony, Sidney Painter, the chairman of the Johns Hopkins History Department, stated to the press that he knew Lattimore better than Senator McCarthy did and that he had never seen any indication of Communist leanings. He noted that Lattimore's connection with the State Department was slight, consisting mostly of giving advice to friends. He added that it made little sense to suggest that Lattimore was "in" the State Department. The facts did not support such a conclusion. He went on to point out that Lattimore's belief that the Communists had been successful with their policies toward the backward population of central Asia did not mean that he was expressing approval of these policies. The statement was merely descriptive; it was not a value judgment. Lattimore was convinced, he added, that the effectiveness of the Communist program must and could be matched by an equally effective program by a non-Communist alliance.[4]

Specialists in Far Eastern studies from around the country sent endorsements of Lattimore to Senator Tydings, to the Johns Hopkins administration, and to Arnold, Fortas & Porter. Their purpose was both to show support for Lattimore and to give an account of his opinions or beliefs.

> Dear Senator Tydings,
>
> Senator McCarthy's allegation that Owen Lattimore is a "top Soviet agent" seems to me completely incredible, on the

basis of my long acquaintance with Mr. Lattimore and with his writings. . . . I have never heard him express views or make statements which were disloyal in character, and I firmly believe him to be a thoroughly loyal and law-abiding American citizen who is devoted to the free, democratic way of life [in] this country. . . . I have not agreed with everything that Mr. Lattimore has said in [this] very extensive body of writing, but I am absolutely convinced in my own mind that its general tenor has been loyal and not disloyal to the United States and that it has not been "pro-Soviet" nor pro-Communist.

On the contrary, I regard Owen Lattimore as one of the most creative and independent-minded of American scholars on Asia. I further believe that his unusual capacity for thinking in terms of the broad and abstract principles of historical change and international relations has undoubtedly led him to make statements in some of his books which can be extracted from their context and pointed to by some persons with suspicion, providing the context of such statements is disregarded. . . . [I]n no case have these statements seemed to me to involve disloyal, anti-American or pro-Communist leanings.

Considering our urgent national need, in the dire struggle against Russia in Asia, for expert knowledge of Asia such as Mr. Lattimore demonstrably possesses, it seems to me the national interest demands that the accusation of disloyalty against him be thoroughly investigated and publicly disproved. . . .

John K. Fairbank
Professor of History
Harvard University[5]

Policymakers on and off campus were also showered with information from Lattimore's colleagues and former and current graduate students.

. . . Lattimore has *not* followed the Communist line. He is an independent thinker with whom I have sometimes agreed, sometimes disagreed. But I never had any reason to think him a Communist or to doubt his good faith and loyalty.[6]

Upon my return from wartime naval service in the South Pacific and occupied Japan, I studied for three years (1946–1949) at the Johns Hopkins University, and took several Far East seminars under Mr. Lattimore's direction. I became well

> acquainted with his political and economic ideas by reading his books and through informal conversations with him. . . .
>
> At no time during my stay at the Johns Hopkins University did Lattimore impress me as a member of the Communist party or as a "Russian espionage agent."
>
> Since leaving Hopkins I have been giving courses in international politics and in governments of the Far East at Boston University. I use Lattimore's recent book, *The Situation in Asia,* as one of several references in the Far Eastern course. There have been no classroom allegations whatever that the book was "Communist" or "pro-Russian."
>
> Instead passages from the book show Lattimore's desire to see Oriental nations become independent and free of Russian domination.[7]

Students also defended Lattimore. They were skeptical of Senator McCarthy's evidence and tactics. After deciding not to burn Senator McCarthy in effigy, having "rejected it as childish," the leaders of six undergraduate organizations drew up a statement for Senator Tydings.

> As heads of student government, publications and honorary groups at the Johns Hopkins University's undergraduate schools, we affirm our abiding faith in the accepted American traditions and laws. We believe that Owen Lattimore is innocent until Senator McCarthy's charges are proven indisputably correct.
>
> We urge the Senator to repeat his charges in public without the protection of his congressional immunity.
>
> Moreover, we hope that Mr. Lattimore will be given ample and complete opportunity to tell his side of the story.
>
> Realizing the seriousness of these charges, we ask the public to refrain from passing judgment until all sides have been heard and sufficient information has been made public to permit an objective decision.[8]

If certain individuals in the Johns Hopkins administration believed Lattimore had Communist ties, they did not say so in public. The FBI had interviewed the former university president, Isaiah Bowman, who knew Lattimore quite well. Bowman told them that from the many conversations he had had with Lattimore going back to 1938, he was convinced that he was not a Communist. He was aware that Lattimore had been so labeled "on occasion," and he could well understand why. He is reported to have described Lattimore as someone who "likes to play in the shadows," who has no sense about the company he keeps. He is also said to have told the FBI that Lattimore had spoken to some groups having a "questionable nature of a Communist tinge," and that Lattimore did not object to being seen under compromising circumstances. He described Lattimore as the type who would have no hesitancy in openly contacting a known Communist. These observations, incidentally, were described by the Justice Department as "one of the most honest and fair appraisals of Lattimore."[9]

On March 20, Eleanor Lattimore sent a letter and a five-page statement to President Bronk through Provost Macaulay refuting Senator McCarthy's principal charges against her husband.[10] In forwarding this material to President Bronk, Macaulay wrote a letter in support of Eleanor Lattimore's suggestion that the university administration make it clear to Senator Tydings that it was only Lattimore's presence in Afghanistan that prevented him from responding to Senator McCarthy and asking for an early opportunity for him to do so before the senate committee on his return to the country.[11] President Bronk promptly wrote such a letter.

> Dear Senator Tydings:
>
> Senator McCarthy's recent charges against Owen Lattimore are a matter of serious concern to me and to the university in which Mr. Lattimore holds a responsible position. It is particularly unfortunate that these charges were made at a time when Mr. Lattimore was in Afghanistan on a mission for the United Nations and therefore not in a position to defend himself.
>
> I am sure you will agree with me that both the national interest and simple justice require that Mr. Lattimore be given the earliest possible opportunity to appear before your committee, and this letter is a formal request to you that he be permitted to do so immediately upon his return. . . .
>
> Mrs. Lattimore has assured me that he will be available to your committee at any time after his return and has asked me to send along for your personal information and not for publication the attached statement which she has prepared and which represents her factual knowledge of the circumstances surrounding the charges made by Senator McCarthy.[12]

Three days later, Senator Tydings gave a positive response by telegram: "Thanks for your letter of March 24. Whenever it suits

Doctor Lattimore to come before our committee we shall be glad to hear him." Senator Tydings also released President Bronk's letter to the press. That same day attorneys made public a letter from him refuting Senator McCarthy's attack and demanding a retraction. This too was reported in toto and with banner headlines in the Baltimore newspapers.[13] A second formal statement by President Bronk also received full coverage. Again, President Bronk made the point that it was too early, and therefore it would be wrong, for him or others to pass judgment on the matter.

> In fifteen months' acquaintance with Professor Lattimore, I have had no evidence of disloyalty. In my view it is up to Senator McCarthy to present actual, definite, proven evidence. If he does, then it will be up to Professor Lattimore to reply in kind.
>
> Meantime, I hope other persons will go slow in taking sides.[14]

President Bronk was quick to add that neither Senator McCarthy nor his sources had investigated Lattimore through the president's office at Johns Hopkins.

Just prior to Lattimore's return to the United States, faculty and students from Johns Hopkins accelerated their concerted letter-writing campaign to newspapers and to Senator Tydings repeating the demand that McCarthy come out from behind senatorial immunity to repeat his charge that Lattimore had acted as a Communist agent. Like President Bronk, the writers asked that no premature judgment be made about Lattimore, that both sides had to be heard. They also expressed the view that Lattimore should be considered innocent of any wrongdoing until proven guilty.

A Faculty Dinner and Reception

Two weeks after his counterattack on Louis Budenz before the Tydings committee, where he denounced him as someone with "sordid motives" whose real intention was to further his career and turn a profit, Lattimore was honored by a dinner and reception by his university colleagues. According to the faculty organizers, the purpose of the event was to show Lattimore and the public that the faculty solidly supported him and that he was not the only target of the attacks; the attacks were also seen as an assault on free speech and academic freedom. The event would demonstrate to the wider community that the faculty of the Johns Hopkins University had complete confidence in Lattimore, that it had faith in his integrity as a scholar and loyalty as a citizen. The administration and board of trustees did not sanction the tribute and kept at a discreet distance.

Although seating and accommodations for the dinner were limited, all faculty and their wives were invited to a reception to be held later in the evening at which time Lattimore was invited "to speak his mind to us."[15] The sponsors reported that individuals from every department of the university, representing a wide array of political opinions and beliefs, had agreed to participate.

Not everyone connected with the university agreed that a testimonial for Lattimore was truly appropriate. For example, a physician with a long-standing medical school affiliation sent a letter stating that he was "opposed to faculty homage being paid at this time." Since the charges against Lattimore had not been disproven and he was still, in the minds of many, the object of suspicion, those within the university should refrain from a public commitment which at a later time might prove embarrassing.

> I think, to give faculty patronage to this reception is to jeopardize the name and principles of the Johns Hopkins. It is not scientific, nor *truthful,* to come up with the answer before the facts are known. It is school-boy behavior, but *not* academic freedom.
>
> Such action at this time by learned men is impertinent and in exceedingly bad taste.[16]

In general, however, faculty favored the communal act of cordiality.

The dinner and reception received wide coverage in the press, and others besides those with some connection to Johns Hopkins who read about it wrote or called, mostly to object to its taking place on campus. With a touch of irony, someone who identified himself simply as "not an alumnus" wrote from Michigan indicating his disagreement with the decision to honor Lattimore.

> Dear Sir:
>
> Please accept my apologies in having been unable to attend the testimonial dinner for Mr. Owen J. [*sic*] Lattimore.
>
> However, if you will be so kind as to notify me of the time and place of the blowout for Alger Hiss, I shall be most happy to attend.
>
> Yours very truly

P.S. At the above dinner was the red herring served as appetizer or entree?[17]

This jab was an early, but far from the last, instance where the university administration was called to account for something with which it was only marginally connected.

Clearly, a number of people, not just Senator McCarthy, were beginning to see parallels in the Alger Hiss and Lattimore cases, the most obvious being that both involved "deviousness and betrayal" at the higher levels of government which could only lead to misadventure for America. It was rumored, and readily denied, that had Hiss, a Hopkins alumnus, not been convicted, he would have been selected as the next university president.

Dear Doctor [Bronk]:

Writing as an OLD TIMER (HOPKINS), don't you think, and possibly regret, that it is just as plausible to now hold a testimonial dinner for ALGER HISS on the HOPKINS campus. Am sure ALGER HISS would command as large if not larger AUDIENCE of AMERICANS than did LATTIMORE. I with other HOPKINS men suspect the LATTIMORE audience was handpicked and the same audience would attend a testimonial to ALGER HISS, WADLEIGH, EARL BROWDER, JUDITH COPLON.

Doctor, would it not have been in good taste, to have postponed that dinner until LATTIMORE had been cleared by an IMPARTIAL committee, not by a committee bent on hiding any evidence which would tend to uncover any mistakes or worse in the administration, which has brought this country to its present state, and which may lead us into another WORLD WAR?

I am just expressing the feelings of the other HOPKINS men of the "OLD SCHOOL."[18]

Others believed that great implications could be drawn from the fact that there would even be a dinner and reception on university property. One left a message for the president.

Mr. David Lopheimer, 931 N. Calvert Street, telephoned today. He is a teacher and does not think that the affair (Lattimore reception) to be held on campus should be held. He says that it

> is most disgraceful of JHU and Dr. Bronk to allow it to take place. He also hears that Dr. Bronk is "pink." He asked that this information be passed on to Dr. Bronk.[19]

At the reception, Lattimore was enthusiastically and warmly greeted by an overflow crowd of approximately 600 guests. In his extended remarks, he warned that there existed in the country a situation in which the freedoms of inquiry and expression were in danger. He argued that this condition was threatening not only academic freedom but basic political freedoms. Freedom of thought was endangered by "assassination by guesswork." He also did not miss the opportunity to rake Senator McCarthy once more, referring to him as "disreputable" and to his efforts as "a hit-and-run campaign of libelous charges under senatorial immunity." His description of Senator McCarthy as a "ruthless, machine-gun-toting politician whose financial dealings, political practices and integrity as a judge have all been questioned in his own state" was well received.[20]

It was hardly surprising the audience would be appreciative of Lattimore's observations about, in general, what was happening to him and, in particular, Senator McCarthy. For a growing number of the Johns Hopkins faculty, the offensive against Lattimore represented an offensive against the rights of academics to pursue any line of inquiry and to speak out on any subject, however controversial. In the minds of many, Lattimore's fight had come to symbolize the fight for academic freedom.

Faculty were supportive of Lattimore in other ways. There were telephone calls and letters to Lattimore. Many also wrote to members of the university administration. Edwards A. Park, a distinguished physician, who for many years headed the Department of Pediatrics at the university, over the phone and in writing raised the possibility with President Bronk of the university's issuing an endorsement of Lattimore. The president begged off, responding that there was not unanimous support for Lattimore among faculty, and he did not want to appear partial. The administration had apparently convinced itself and a substantial number of faculty that it was only being judicious and was not showing a lack of courage in not defending Lattimore; the dubious contention that consensus was necessary before it could take a stand was not challenged by many.

Park, believing that it was imperative for someone in the university to defend Lattimore, was not daunted by Bronk's demurral: "I now write to ask if it would not be possible to obtain an endorsement from a large group of the university faculty. If, for example, 20 or 30 distinguished members of the faculty signed an expression of complete confidence the effect might be a powerful one."[21] Other faculty were just as eager to come to Lattimore's defense.

The Johns Hopkins chapter of the American Association of University Professors (AAUP), the organization most dedicated to and effective in defending faculty rights, unanimously passed a resolution asking Senator Tydings to "make a definite pronouncement . . . on the truth or falsity" of the charges against Lattimore. As Lattimore's colleagues saw it, not to vindicate him would result in hampering his "free expression"—and the free expression of others.[22]

Within a month after the Tydings committee published its report exonerating Lattimore, a member of the university board of trustees wrote letters to the president of the board, the university president, and the chairman of the finance committee of the E. I. duPont Company which, among other things, raised the issue of Lattimore as a public figure. In the third letter, the one to the industrialist, of which he sent copies to the other two parties, he stated that he was persuaded by Lattimore's defense against Senator McCarthy's charges and that he could not believe that Senator Tydings' investigation into the State Department, which may have been lax at times, was a wholesale whitewash. He saw it as merely the consequence of individuals holding true to political party loyalties.[23] In his letter to President Bronk, which he copied to Board President Barton, he was most concerned that the university avoid becoming entangled in political controversy.

> Certainly in the interests of Johns Hopkins it is tremendously important to avoid any presumption that could be formed in the public mind of involvement in any way in the tragic aspects of the McCarthy investigation and treatment by the senate committee, of which Senator Tydings is chairman.[24]

In a second letter to Bronk, also copied for Barton, the trustee noted that he had received a complaint about Lattimore's public stand that the People's Republic of China should be admitted to the United Nations, and reminded the president that the university needed to take steps to obviate "the dangers of adverse public reaction which could affect seriously the intended program of development on the part of the Johns Hopkins University and Hospital."

At the same time, he was careful to point out that he was not suggesting that anything be done in the way of reprimanding Lattimore. He was not even sure himself whether or not the People's Republic of China should be recognized and seated in the United Nations. He made it clear that he understood that Lattimore's appointment at Johns Hopkins did not extinguish his right to express his opinion. He repeated his belief that Lattimore had been convincing in denying Senator McCarthy's accusations. He thought that it was most important, however, that the university make it clear that Lattimore's views were not its views: "the utmost should be done in the interests of Johns Hopkins to remove any stigma attaching to the institution itself." He closed by asking the president for a "treatise," the substance of which he could use when he encountered "reflected concern over presumed (false or not) communistic tinges pertaining to Johns Hopkins."[25]

In his response, President Bronk agreed that it would be improper to attempt to curtail Lattimore's freedom of speech and that "we"—the university administration—must do everything to dispel any impression that Lattimore's opinions represent an official university position. He, too, believed that the university must distance itself from Lattimore. He regretted that Lattimore chose to quarrel with Senator McCarthy instead of simply stating his position and letting the matter rest. (He did not express regret that Senator McCarthy initiated the quarrel.) He cautioned that denials by university authorities which would not represent the opinions of all faculty would stir up more controversy. He thought that publicly emphasizing other activities of the university, particularly those contributing to the national security and welfare, would enhance its image. He also reiterated his public response to questions about Lattimore.

> I have known Mr. Lattimore for somewhat over a year. I have not seen any evidence of disloyalty to the United States, but I have never had any occasion to investigate it. Nor would I have had any facilities for doing so. If I were to make available to Mr. Lattimore any information affecting the national security, I would insist upon adequate clearance by the appropriate agency based upon an investigation by the Federal Bureau of Investigation. I would require the same for my own father. . . .

He concluded with the hope that the public controversy would soon subside.[26] It did, and for nearly two years the public clamor that the university fire Lattimore diminished significantly.

Not everyone was persuaded by the conclusions of the Tydings committee that there was less than met the eye. Some were sure that there was a great conspiracy, that Democrats and liberals were promoting it, and that they needed to redouble their efforts to protect America from its enemies, foreign and domestic.

A Baltimore attorney, George Blome, wrote a circular letter to the Johns Hopkins University board of trustees to express his concern "over the teaching of socialism and communism in our colleges," and to warn it about the "gravity" of the situation. He reminded the board that no school, college, or university in the United States taught Americanism or free enterprise. He also pointed out that Karl Marx had been employed by the socialists in England to draft a blueprint by which they might destroy the free enterprise system, and for a century they had "insidiously carried out his directives." There was no doubt in Blome's mind that Marx's disciples had "sold their plan" to President Roosevelt, who under the guise of the New Deal had followed the "blueprint to the word." In fact, thirty-eight of the "Marxian disciples" had moved into the White House as the Brain Trust, "and their work of destruction was begun."

According to Blome, schools were a primary target of Marx. One of his directives was to infiltrate them "and channel the thoughts of the impressionable, unwary youngsters." He told the trustees of a twenty-two-year-old graduate of Johns Hopkins who had been taught that most Americans are crushed and exploited by the capitalist. He also told them of a fifty-five-year-old woman of means who had become a socialist firebrand after taking some social science courses at the university.

One particular reason Blome had written was to inform the trustees that he had learned from a respected businessman of a report by an FBI agent "that one of the most powerful Communist cells in America is located at Johns Hopkins." He concluded by cautioning the trustees that "freedom of speech is not freedom to teach treason": "If . . . you are true Americans . . . then for the love of God and our once great country, place your house, your university in order."[27]

Concerned by the story that the FBI believed there was an organized Communist group operating on campus, President Bronk and other senior administrative officers met with the university counsel. It was decided to "confer with the FBI promptly" and to meet with Blome to substantiate the charges. If evidence of Communist activity were uncovered, the president wanted to "take vigorous and effective action." He did not want to "be accused of indifference" by the public or by the board.[28] Board member Francis White was "in hearty agreement" with President Bronk's plan of action.[29]

Blome would not or could not identify for the FBI the businessman who had related the information about the Communist cell at Johns Hopkins, and he was asked by the FBI to write the board of trustees to explain his "misstatement." In his letter he quoted congressional testimony to the effect that there were individuals at Johns Hopkins that were working to organize youth groups. He reminded the trustees that "we are engaged in a life and death struggle for survival. Our lives, the lives of our loved ones, our property our freedom are the stakes." He explained why he preferred to meet with members of the board rather than with university administrators:

> Mr. Charles Quandt, an attorney for the Hopkins, has asked me to meet with Provost Macaulay and Dean Shaffer at my office. It is my opinion that such a meeting would have accomplished nothing save a waste of time. These gentlemen are members of the administrative staff of the university. If they do not today know what is being taught by their instructors, I am sure I shall be powerless to aid them. If they do know, then they apparently listen favorably to the propaganda of the National Education Association and its insistence that the instructor be free to teach anything he wishes. If, however, you think I can be of any assistance to you and you should wish me to meet your board or any members of it, I shall gladly do so. I shall be everlastingly grateful if I can do anything to aid the Hopkins for which we each have a deep affection and, let us pray, we all will continue to have a lasting pride.
>
> Please understand that this letter is not written in a spirit of criticism. The fallacious propaganda of those who give their allegiance to the Politburo has placed you and the trustees of far too many of our universities in a most embarrassing and difficult position. You are faced with a dilemma which, I sincerely believe, can no longer be ignored. This intolerable situation cannot continue and it must be faced eventually. This you know as well as I. Either you will eject them; or the day will arrive, as it has elsewhere, when they will eject you. And time is running out. Rest assured that when you do cast out these people, you will hear their usual screamings, rantings and accusations; but you will have gained the approval and heartfelt thanks of every loyal, intelligent American.[30]

After receipt of Blome's second letter, Board President Barton invited him to meet to discuss the entire matter; Barton most particularly wanted more details about faculty misusing the classroom to propagandize. He apparently believed that Blome had evidence to support his claims. Blome agreed to the meeting, but then inexplicably canceled. Barton could get little concrete information from him: "I had also asked Mr. Blome to be more specific in his references to former students, but he gave me no names and discussed at length the views of a student who had graduated in 1936 and who stated that he had learned about socialism at Hopkins at the time." Blome indicated that at a later time he would meet with one or more of the trustees, but according to Barton "was absolutely unwilling to talk in the presence of any member of the university staff."[31]

In spite of the fact that Blome could not substantiate any of his many charges, he was still given credence by some board members. Francis White wrote Barton that Blome's suggestion that the trustees take a definite stand on the matter of the abuse of academic freedom was "correct," that it should "be fully discussed, both in general terms and as it applies to Mr. Lattimore in particular."[32] With tenacity and often farfetched accusations, moral entrepreneurs took their toll.

Lattimore kept himself in the public eye. He continued to travel the country and express his views on foreign policy issues and other matters. He had hardly been intimidated by the Tydings committee hearings. Indeed, his style was intentionally confrontational: "In the Chicago speech, seeing it will be right under the nose of the *Chicago Tribune,* I intend to come out swinging."[33] In spite of warnings from friends ("I have heard in our best circles that it is too bad you have had to be so 'vituperative' "[34]), he was convinced that he would reduce the damage from attacks by the moral entrepreneurs by answering in kind. As it turned out, this assumption was incorrect.

Spring 1952

In early March 1952 after he began giving testimony to the McCarran committee, there was a significant increase in the amount of mail regarding Lattimore to administrators and individual members of the board of trustees of Johns Hopkins. The criticisms of Lattimore were now more bitter. The facade of resolve by officials and faculty at Johns Hopkins not to back away from an uncompromising defense of Lattimore began to show cracks. There was a sense on the part of a significant minority that by setting himself against the senate committee Lattimore had done something terribly wrong. They gave him little credit for testifying fully, for directly denying the charges against him. Some seemed not to understand why he might be angry by the attacks on his character, judgment, and competence.

The Academic Council, which operated somewhat like an executive committee of a faculty senate, very much aware of the unfavorable impression that Lattimore's aggressive language and method had on the public during his appearance before the McCarran committee, in early March established a subcommittee to formulate a statement of its position on the matter to present to the board of trustees. Although the members of the Academic Council agreed with Lattimore's critics that his behavior before the McCarran committee left a great deal to be desired—it lacked "the restraint and dignity that should be expected of a scholar"—they wanted to remind the board that he had the right to defend himself in the best way he saw fit. They noted that Lattimore "had a good deal of provocation," and recommended that that university take no action or make no statement against or for Lattimore. The feeling was that the former would be misunderstood as a categorical refutation and the latter as unqualified support. They invoked themes often used by faculty: they were most concerned that the board of trustees not do anything that

> . . . would split the faculty into factions over various aspects of the controversy which the faculty has hitherto refrained from discussing in public and would have a serious effect on the academic reputation of the university. While the Council fully appreciates the grave difficulties facing the trustees, it believes that the only course at the moment is patient and watchful silence.
>
> . . . But it would seem suitable at a future date—when calm judgments can be reached—for an appropriate academic body to be requested to consider whether the evidence produced indicates unfitness as a scholar.[35]

The statement was hardly a vote of confidence for Lattimore. The political attacks on Lattimore had succeeded in planting in some people's minds enough doubt about his competence that it seemed fair to examine the matter. For some, a person's politics were less important than his manners. Being irascible might not necessarily mean that a person was wanting as a scholar, only that the question would merit consideration.

Time still had not run out; the failure of the trustees to act was not in any way a sign that they were devoid of interest.

Taking the Initiative

Within a few days after Lattimore had completed his testimony before the McCarran committee, Donaldson Brown and other board members met and came close to consensus on a draft of a policy statement regarding Communists on the Johns Hopkins faculty. The new policy was formulated as a resolution to be conveyed to the faculty through the president.

Brown and his colleagues on the board began with the premise that because communism constituted "the greatest menace in the world today" and was a particular threat to individual freedom, new regulations were long overdue. Like board members at nearly all other institutions of higher learning across the country, they were convinced that membership in the Communist party automatically rendered someone unfit to hold an academic appointment. They noted a pattern of abuse of privileges (undefined) by faculty protected by academic freedom and tenure and felt that this weakened the American constitutional system, a system in which all members of the board of trustees "profoundly" reiterated a belief.

Given the threat of communism to personal freedom, they were also convinced that faculty must unequivocally accept the principle of constitutional rights for individuals and reject all totalitarian doctrines. The academic freedom of an individual faculty member could be protected only insofar as he refrained from all disloyal behavior.

The document went on to caution faculty that they must always be objective in their teaching and research, especially if they were teaching something incompatible "with the requirements of our form of government." It was concluded that the university was under no obligation and, in fact, should not employ or retain anyone who the board of trustees was convinced advocated a system of government that would destroy individual liberty in America. These principles were quite similar to those being adopted by many other colleges and universities around the country and those promulgated at about the same time by the Association of American Universities, an organization representing the administrations of thirty-five of the nation's leading graduate centers.

As Lattimore was completing his testimony before the McCarran committee not only did the board take its first step to serve notice on faculty that they could not be members of the Communist party or further its interests, but it also warned that if anyone taught about communism he should have "a clear display of the facts" or he would put his appointment at Johns Hopkins in jeopardy. Lattimore and all faculty at Johns Hopkins were being warned that they were forbidden from advocating "a form of government that denies such [individual] freedom to its citizens." One would have to take care that any positive observations made about China or the Soviet Union could be verified by evidence that the board accepted as factual. One could not even give the impression of supporting an experiment in Marxism for the United States.[36]

At the same time that the board's position on communism was being finalized, a shorter four-paragraph statement, which was more of a direct threat to Lattimore's tenure at Johns Hopkins, was being drafted by a second group of board members led by Francis White, the namesake of a member of the first board of trustees of Hopkins who had spent many years in the diplomatic service in Peking, Teheran, Buenos Aires, and Madrid and was later to serve as ambassador to Mexico and Sweden. This statement began by noting that Lattimore had caused the university "much harm and embarrassment for over two years." It faulted him for failing to show an understanding that freedom and privilege carry corresponding responsibility and obligations, and for lacking a sense of loyalty towards the university and his colleagues. It noted that not only had he done nothing to disassociate himself from the university as the controversy swirled around him, but he had invoked the prestige of the institution by, for example, holding press conferences in his office and using university letterhead for these nonacademic matters. Moreover, he did not consult the administration for advice "as to how he might alleviate the embarrassment and harm he was causing" or even to express his concern or regret. All of this was in contrast to what the university authorities saw as the "full freedom and latitude" they had given to him.

Echoing the McCarran committee, the charge was made that Lattimore had acted shamelessly in not giving "calm, temperate and factual testimony." There was no justification for him to have acted so "flagrantly defiant." The belief was expressed that his behavior unequivocally disqualified him from holding an academic appointment at Johns Hopkins. His injudiciousness vitiated any claim which he might make that he was an objective scholar and patriotic citizen. He was not qualified to hold "a position of trust and honor" at the university. As far as those who drafted this indictment were concerned, Lattimore's behavior before the McCarran committee demonstrated that he lacked a sense of academic responsibility and reflected on his competence. The statement concluded:

> His conduct is so at variance with all the traditions, precepts, and tenets of the university that the trustees have found themselves under the inescapable necessity of dismissing him. Mr. Lattimore will be paid his salary for the rest of his academic year and for one additional year, but his connection with the university is terminated as of today.[37]

Donaldson Brown had become convinced that the university was not showing the necessary leadership in taking a public and firm stand renouncing communism on campus. He and his committee had prepared an unambiguous compact which, as he saw it, was languishing. It was time that the board endorse it. It was wrong for a university to teach communism or have Communists on the faculty; it was a board's obligation to see that this did not occur.

The fact that the administration and other board members saw the matter as less urgent frustrated Brown. As far as he was concerned, further delay was unacceptable. World events were too compelling. He wrote to President Bronk laying out his philosophical views, demanding action by the board and threatening to resign if it did not exercise its prerogative and wisdom.

> Dear Det:
>
> We had a brief discussion last Friday regarding my desire to seek adoption by the board of trustees of the Johns Hopkins University of a resolution aimed towards a constructive treatment as regards the problem connected with academic freedom. When in January I submitted to you a tentative draft of a resolution of the kind, you indicated full sympathy with my objective, as you did again at the time of our last meeting. Then, you had some reservation as to whether this is an opportune time to proceed in the intended course, having in mind the Lattimore situation, and were to communicate with me after giving the matter further thought.
>
> I have very strong feelings on the question after having given it a great deal of thought over the past two or three

months. Von Mises says " . . . the real problem in our universities is not that so many teachers are committed to the collectivist fallacies of Keynes and Marx, but that these 'progressives' virtually monopolize the teaching profession." Certainly I know that many citizens of the country who hold to fundamental beliefs such as you and I do are gravely concerned over the situation. Among them are those who can be looked upon as representing the chief source from which financial aid might be found to assure the protection of our universities against governmental domination; thoughts such as expressed by von Mises are gaining ascendancy progressively and there is no denying the fact that the preservation of our privately endowed institutions of learning is seriously threatened, by the growing tendency to say "what's the use?"

There is no need for me to enlarge upon the subject. You are no doubt as conscious as I am of the threatened financial difficulties, and are far more familiar with the problems that have to be coped with in the academic field. I would like, however, to register with you the position I have come to.

A good many years ago, primarily for sentimental reasons, I accepted an invitation to go on the board of the Johns Hopkins University. I have felt that I could contribute very little, as a trustee, and in accepting the responsibility of such it is fair to say I violated a principle that I have tried to adhere to. I don't think of another instance where I have accepted a directorship without feeling I could make some contribution measuring up to the responsibilities assumed. As a trustee of Johns Hopkins I do not hold that I have any responsibility with regard to the academic side of the institution other than on the score of fundamental policy. I do feel that I have responsibility in connection with the financial and general management aspects. Furthermore, I would not be content to remain identified with any university that could be considered open to the charge such as that leveled by von Mises as quoted in the second paragraph above. I know that your philosophy does not differ essentially from mine on this score. Irrespective of the difficulties and problems in the way of implementing a policy such as I am proposing, I could not be happy to continue as a trustee unless the board, with your sympathetic acquiescence, is willing to face up to the issue in this manner.

I hope you will accept this letter in the spirit in which it is intended. There is no implied criticism of you, regardless of what your conclusion may be. I would have to admit that you are far better able to weigh the practical considerations in the case than I am. If an attack on the problem such as I am urging is deemed to be impractical then, as I say, I would simply wish to retire from the scene. My resigning from the board would, of itself, impose no threat to the future of Johns Hopkins and the university and hospital will have my continuing best wishes.

So, may I hear from you as soon as can be convenient?

Yours sincerely[38]

President Bronk responded to the ultimatum without delay, and the document drafted by Brown and his committee was prepared for the board's consideration.

President Bronk was able to incorporate various suggestions into a revised draft before final action by the board of trustees. For the board, this was important as "the sympathetic acceptance of the principles by university administrative officers is necessary to the successful indoctrination of university personnel and to the compliance of personnel with the principles enunciated." By the time it reached the full board, the document had also been shown to some senior faculty, "all of whom concurred in the belief that the statement [was] sound as definitive of basic policy."

When formally presented to the full board in the early summer, the resolution denouncing communism on campus was characterized as something that would show the board of trustees as "again taking leadership in a critical situation."[39] It passed by a unanimous vote, with one member recorded as not voting. The board agreed to defer publicizing its adoption until the university administration devised a way of presenting it to the faculty in the best light.

When taken up officially by the board, the second statement that had been drafted by some members of the board, the proposal to terminate Lattimore, underwent considerable revision. Its general tone was made less harsh; it was less critical of Lattimore. It noted that after some members had expressed "grave concern," Lattimore had asked for a hearing before the board. Still, it was far from conciliatory. Its central point was that Lattimore lacked the "sense of responsibility" to resign or to request a leave of absence. It noted that it was therefore necessary for the board to take it upon itself in "the best interests of the university, and fairness to his colleagues as well as to Mr. Lattimore himself" to suspend him indefinitely. It promised that after the investigation by the government was complete and the notoriety had subsided, Lattimore's academic work and other activities would be looked at by university authorities and his permanent status would then be determined.

The intention was no longer to terminate Lattimore, he would merely be placed on leave, with pay. From this action, it would be difficult to impute prejudice to Lattimore or to Johns Hopkins. It was, in fact, explicitly noted in this new draft that the board would not be taking a position regarding Lattimore's troubles with the McCarran committee. That was a matter that would be settled by civil authorities.[40] Still, this more moderate, less punitive plan was not approved by the full board, and no steps were taken to change Lattimore's appointment until he was formally indicted at the end of the year.

A New Issue

As more and more letters condemning the university's failure to take decisive action against Lattimore were received by the administration and the board or published in the press, fewer and fewer trustees seemed firmly committed to a position of neutrality.

By early April, individual board members were openly stating that they were "embarrassed" by the Lattimore affair, by what he had said while before the McCarran committee and what it had said about him after his testimony. He had been irreversibly labeled as irresponsible. It was taken for granted that he was an encumbrance to the university. The authorities at Johns Hopkins were not necessarily opposed to the content of Lattimore's remarks about China or about his more general views of American foreign policy; however, his wide-ranging comments had clearly offended others and they had come to view the university less favorably. There was little question that the growing opposition to Lattimore by the Johns Hopkins authorities was less a matter of principle than of public relations.

As many saw it, Lattimore had a duty to the welfare of Johns Hopkins. Since in any conflict between his rights and the interests of the university he as a single individual was less important, the institution obviously must first be protected. The university's commitment to Lattimore had to be weighed against its overall health in an uncertain political climate.

Copies of Senator McCarran's long statement criticizing Lattimore, chastising him for being contemptuous and untruthful, were everywhere on campus, having been anonymously placed in the mailboxes of most faculty members. There was no explanatory message as to why the material was sent, yet one was hardly needed. It was clearly an attempt to embarrass Lattimore. The distribution was a deliberate and undisguised attempt to cause him more difficulty with the administration and faculty at Johns Hopkins, and it, in part, succeeded. The case now absorbed the interest of nearly everyone on campus. It became a subject of debate; it became a distraction.

Another matter that held the attention of faculty was the public accusation by Lattimore that George F. Carter, a professor of geography and chairman of the Isaiah Bowman School of Geography at Johns Hopkins, had given what Lattimore and his allies characterized as patently false information to Senator McCarthy. Carter allegedly told Senator McCarthy that while at a picnic at Lattimore's home in 1945 he had seen government documents spread out on a bed. Lattimore explained that the papers were galley proofs of a book that he was helping one of his guests to correct. He publicly denounced Carter as "an informer."[41]

Carter did not deny the charge that he had given testimony damaging to Lattimore and at first would not comment on the matter. When the McCarran committee's report was published, he felt it was damaging enough to Lattimore to urge his colleagues to read its conclusions. He believed that the fact of the case vindicated him.

At this point the Johns Hopkins University faculty were far from being totally united behind Lattimore, although, of those who made their views known, the majority sided with him. Under the auspices of the Johns Hopkins chapter of the American Association of University Professors, twenty-nine faculty wrote President Bronk praising the board and the administration for their "judicious restraint" and urging that the "same temper continue to prevail."

> We take this position because we believe that the good reputation of our university and the security of a great tradition in which we share are at stake, and that the issue is of more than local or even national significance. The attention of educated people throughout the Western world is temporarily focused upon us because the Johns Hopkins is a university of international reputation, Mr. Lattimore is a scholar of international repute, and the issues under congressional investigation are of immediate concern to the whole world. Our friends at home and abroad who cherish and guard our tradition do not expect that it shall be used to shelter a man duly convicted of serious offense against our laws. But they do have a right to

> expect that this tradition shall protect a scholar while he pursues his own studies, comes to his own conclusions, and expresses them openly, even though they may be unpopular.

The twenty-nine urged the board of trustees not to move against Lattimore unless there was valid evidence of serious misconduct. They asked that faculty be consulted about any action the board planned against Lattimore "in order to forestall unfortunate cleavages" and minimize harm to the university's academic standing.[42]

To more and more people, Lattimore's stridency and lack of self-restraint before the McCarran committee had become the most vexing problem. Issues were being reframed. The question of whether or not he had Communist ties was no longer what was being debated; it almost became a secondary issue. Style, as much as substance, can affect opinions about someone or something. Indeed, it is not unusual for extraneous considerations to influence judgments and detract from the veridical assessment of individuals and events. Focus can be lost. Issues can readily become obfuscated. By spring 1952, Lattimore seems to have become a victim of this process. To many, the question of the alien ideology that may have informed the advice he had given government officials was not as important as his disrespect to Senator McCarran and members of the Internal Security Subcommittee. To many, Lattimore's behavior was an obvious sign that he was not rational and in control of himself. He appeared to be unbalanced. It could even indicate that he had something to hide and was bluffing.

Lattimore's stinging counterattack on his accusers was beginning to exact a heavy price. He was seen as obdurate and indiscreet. Members of the board now began to feel free to express their concerns publicly. Board member S. Page Nelson was one of the first to be quoted in the press: "The situation is very embarrassing," he admitted, "none of us wants to do the wrong thing."[43] Not unexpectedly, there were rumors that the board of trustees was planning to meet to consider Lattimore's status in the university. It appeared that the publicity-conscious board was on the verge of finding a politically expedient solution to placate an unmeasured but very vocal segment of the public.

With a number of lawyers on the board of trustees, it is hardly surprising that it moved to examine its legal options. Yet, it moved cautiously. Its president, Carlyle Barton, wrote to provost Macaulay asking to see a copy of Lattimore's letter of appointment to the faculty and for an authoritative definition of "indefinite tenure," the type of appointment given to Lattimore in 1939. Barton told

Macaulay that he found the commonly accepted meaning given to "academic freedom" unsatisfactory, since it implied that it was up to the individual faculty member to judge the propriety of what he said or may wish to say. Barton believed that under some circumstances the board should have the authority to terminate faculty. This, after all, was its right and responsibility. He thought that this might be one time that such an action would be appropriate. It was quite possible, in fact, that "book writing and other entirely private affairs" were interfering with Lattimore's ability to perform his institutional duties. Barton also wondered why Lattimore did not at least pursue what to his mind was the proper course of temporarily interrupting his relationship with the university until matters were cleared up. By doing so, he would avoid letting, as Barton saw it, his personal problems continue to cause damage to Johns Hopkins.[44]

Macaulay responded that to his knowledge there was no explicit mechanism in the university's rules and regulations for terminating a tenure appointment for cause. He also reminded Barton that the university had no formal statement regarding legitimate grounds for dismissal and no mechanism for judicial hearings as suggested as appropriate by the American Association of University Professors.[45]

Given the board's new posture and inclination to give way to the demands of those applying pressure on the university, there was an unmistakable rumble that occasioned a sudden wave of letters backing Lattimore.

Someone from Ann Arbor, Michigan, wrote to Board President Barton, with a copy to President Bronk, saying that she was saddened that he as a board member had told the *New York Times* he was embarrassed by the Lattimore controversy. She knew Lattimore as an able scholar and courageous fighter; to her mind he had "demonstrated in every way his belief in and adherence to the principles of good American citizenship." She also told Board President Barton that she disagreed with his observation that "there is nothing to be done."

> [O]n the contrary, there is a great deal to be done, and I believe, furthermore, that it should be done quickly. Johns Hopkins can preserve its place as one of the country's finest universities only if its officials rise to the defense of academic freedom and positively support Professor Lattimore in his right to express the views he has arrived at by years of study and honest observation.
>
> If leadership in restoring our basic commonsense does not come from the universities, I fear it will be a long time in

> coming. I beg you, for the sake of all our American liberties, not to fall into the trap set by those benighted protagonists of totalitarianism: Budenz, McCarthy and McCarran. Those forces supporting Budenz and his cronies seek to overthrow all free inquiry and expression. What dictatorial regime they intend to set up in a new Dark Age one shudders to imagine.
>
> I urge you as custodians of our future to seize your unique opportunity to support American freedom and to set about actively defending the rights of Professor Lattimore and all others whose opinions are currently unpopular. By your so doing, perhaps we can save a modicum of those civil liberties which subversive, un-American forces in our country are warring against.[46]

The greatest pressure to take Lattimore's side again came from within the university. A number of prominent faculty made it quite clear they believed that the administration and the board of trustees had a responsibility to shield Lattimore from what to them was little more than politically motivated frenzy. Although their letters were polite, and they did not make demands or issue ultimatums, it is apparent that they expected the administration and board in their deliberations to take their views seriously.

Helen B. Taussig, the eminent cardiologist who had been doing important and internationally acclaimed research on congenital malformations of the heart, wrote Board President Barton defending Lattimore, insisting that he had acted as every scholar should, namely to investigate all sides of a problem. It appeared that Lattimore had "nothing to hide." What he had done should "be permitted in a free country."

> He is not a Communist and he has not been engaged in subversive activities. All of his answers were not tactful and some of them may have been inconsistent, but could any of us be questioned for eleven days on the minute details of his activities during the previous ten years and never contradict himself?[47]

She sent a blind copy of her letter to President Bronk.

Prominent faculty from other universities also urged the Hopkins administration to defend Lattimore more forcefully. Most were individuals who did not usually identify with political or social causes and were certainly not left-wing activists. They were, in fact, academics very much in the mainstream who saw one of their own under attack; they expected that the academic world would, in defense, close ranks. Some had long-standing friendships with the

Hopkins authorities. Their letters were cordial and direct. They were giving what they believed was useful advice.

> Dear Det:
>
> I have been hoping I would see a good strong statement from you in support of Owen Lattimore. From all I have been able to determine, all of us should have nothing but admiration for his fearlessness and honesty. Certainly, his interest was no more than General Stilwell's; namely, in a Chinese regime which would establish a nation independent of Russia, or perhaps a regime similar to Tito's. It did not appear to me that Lattimore went even as far as General Stilwell in this direction. I believe it is a great opportunity for a university president to speak out for freedom of thought and speech. You certainly now have that chance. Perhaps you have done so already and I just have not seen it.
>
> It is always a great disappointment not to see you at our Sydenham Coterie every month, as formerly. We all miss you a great deal but fully realize why you cannot get there.
>
> With best regards,
>
> Sincerely,
> Joseph Stokes, Jr., M.D.
> [Professor of Pediatrics, The School
> of Medicine, University of Pennsylvania][48]

A Call for Leadership

Edwards A. Park wrote to both Board President Barton and President Bronk. In his lengthy letter to Board President Barton, Park acknowledged that he knew Lattimore well and was certain that he was not a Communist. He claimed that Lattimore was one of the finest men he knew, "as patriotic a citizen as this country has, although I should think that now his ardor might be dampened." It was his opinion that Lattimore was being persecuted only because he was an outspoken liberal. Since Lattimore's ideas were so different and unpopular and in an area supercharged with conflicting views, they were particularly liable to criticism and attack.

Park reminded Barton that Lattimore's primary accusers were from the "lowest stratum of our political life." They were disaffected outsiders. It was his impression that their animus was not really directed at Lattimore, but that those on the attack were attempting to discredit the Truman administration by discrediting Lattimore. In effect, Lattimore was an accidental victim of large-scale political intrigue. Senator McCarran's predetermined objective was to damage the State Department.

Park also told Barton that two individuals who were present at the hearings in Washington, who did not know Lattimore, assured him that he had been treated harshly and unfairly, and that he had had "no chance." It seemed obvious that the committee was more interested in tricking Lattimore than learning the truth. It also seemed obvious to him, and he hoped to others, that Lattimore's small misstatements were exaggerated or distorted so as to appear to be evidence of deception or guilt. The entire proceedings were an attempt at defamation of character on the principle that if Lattimore's character were destroyed he would be defenseless even if there was no evidence of guilt.

Although Park felt that Lattimore had acquitted himself well during his testimony, he allowed that he was at times injudicious. His abrasiveness prejudiced his case as it was reported in the press and negatively affected public opinion. Park believed that this lack of discretion was merely the result of Lattimore fighting back and adopting the language and methods of his inquisitors. This was the only basis of criticism of Lattimore, "and after all is not in itself so important." The background of this unfortunate series of events—being suddenly named a Communist agent and not being given an opportunity to confront Senator McCarthy who was hiding behind congressional immunity—which caused him great frustration should not be overlooked in assessing his behavior.

Park believed that the behavior of George F. Carter, who provided Lattimore's enemies with information that turned out to be false, was more "scandalous" than anything Lattimore had said or done. He was convinced that the circulation of the McCarran report to the university faculty was a "planned effort" to destroy Lattimore. The fact that it was done anonymously made it obvious to him that the motivation was evil.

Barton was warned that if Johns Hopkins fired Lattimore, not only would it become "an innocent accessory in a plot to destroy" him, but that the act would have greater implications: "McCarthy could receive no better endorsement of his methods and ethics and no greater aid in his political career than if the university should dismiss Lattimore."

Park also said that he believed the university's failure to take a strong position in support of Lattimore when he was initially attacked by Senator McCarthy had harmed Lattimore and the university. After all, Lattimore was "one of the greatest scholars the Johns Hopkins University has possessed," and he had strong backing from his colleagues. The university should make every effort to set things right. There was still "a great opportunity" for it to use its prestige and authority in support of the rights of freedom of thought and expression with fear and intimidation. It, in addition, should condemn the widespread hysteria abroad leading to repression of thought and conformity.

He closed his letter emphasizing the suggestion that it was the perfect time for the university to take the initiative in support of intellectual freedom. If it did, he was sure its leadership would be acclaimed by liberal-minded people, the liberal-minded press, and other universities:

> Is not the present perhaps the psychological moment for success on the grounds that there is a widespread revulsion of feeling among better people against McCarthy and his methods and influence which needs some bold leadership in order to find expression? As one who is particularly devoted to the Medical School and university and grateful to it for its many benefits, I feel as if I would scarcely bear it if the McCarthy influences affected even unconsciously the policies of the university.[49]

Park's letter to President Bronk was considerably shorter than the one he sent to Board President Barton. He pleaded to the president to go on the offensive in the matter of Lattimore: "Oh that I could be instrumental in persuading you and the university to come out with all your power for the right of the individual to think and speak without fear or intimidation." He again expressed the belief that if the university, and the president in particular, exercised leadership the "wave of hysteria" sweeping the country would come to an end, and "American traditions" would be restored.

Park was convinced that this was the time to move; the country was in need of a leader. He was sure that thousands of people were waiting for someone willing to take chances to come forward and stand firmly on the side of intellectual freedom. Using language from his letter to Board President Barton, Park closed this handwritten appeal with the same emotion and fervor with which he had begun.

> A wonderful response would come from the other universities and the learned societies and liberal-minded people everywhere. I wish I could make you and the trustees perceive

> the wonderful chance to convert an apparent debacle into a victory and JHU would win friends by this bold positive action which would more than compensate for the losses being sustained now.
>
> P.S. I believe the McCarthys, the McCarrans and the foes of liberty have overstepped themselves and that this is the psychological moment for a counterstroke by a great university and its president.[50]

These eloquent arguments in defense of Lattimore and academic freedom could not be easily ignored. They were a succinct summary of the refutation Lattimore and his advocates had been making for months. They were being made by influential people, people as influential as those most vigorously pressing for Lattimore's dismissal. The standing of those who made the arguments gave the ideas a credence that they heretofore may have lacked when made by those on the margin of power. Important people were taking a stand.

Given the contradictory nature of the advice it received, the board was brought to a full stop. No satisfactory solution to the dilemma was apparent. Hesitation brought criticism; decisiveness—moves to punish Lattimore—would clearly bring the same, only from another source. Whatever action the university took would surely offend someone, someone it would prefer not to offend. The situation was corrosive. One of the few things everyone agreed upon was that Lattimore was at the center of the problem. This made him a logical and available target for teeming frustration.

Illustrations

1. The Johns Hopkins University, aerial view looking west, 1956. (Courtesy of the archives of the Johns Hopkins University.)

2. Owen Lattimore, 1950. (Courtesy of the archives of the Johns Hopkins University.)

3. Owen Lattimore before the Tydings committee with two of his attorneys, Abe Fortas (to his right) and Paul Porter (behind Fortas), and the principal witness against him, Louis F. Budenz (with briefcase on lap). (Courtesy of Life Magazine, Michael Rougier photographer.)

4. University President Detlev W. Bronk speaking at commencement, 1950. (Courtesy of the archives of the Johns Hopkins University.)

5. University President Lowell J. Reed, 1953. (Courtesy of the archives of the Johns Hopkins University).

6. Professor George F. Carter, 1949. (Courtesy of the archives of the Johns Hopkins University).

7. Professor George Boas, 1940. (Courtesy of the archives of the Johns Hopkins University.)

8. Trustee Carlyle Barton, with University President Milton S. Eisenhower and Provost P. Stewart Macaulay, receiving honorary degree, 1958. (Courtesy of the archives of the Johns Hopkins University.)

9. Trustee Charles S. Garland, 1955. (Courtesy of the archives of the Johns Hopkins University.)

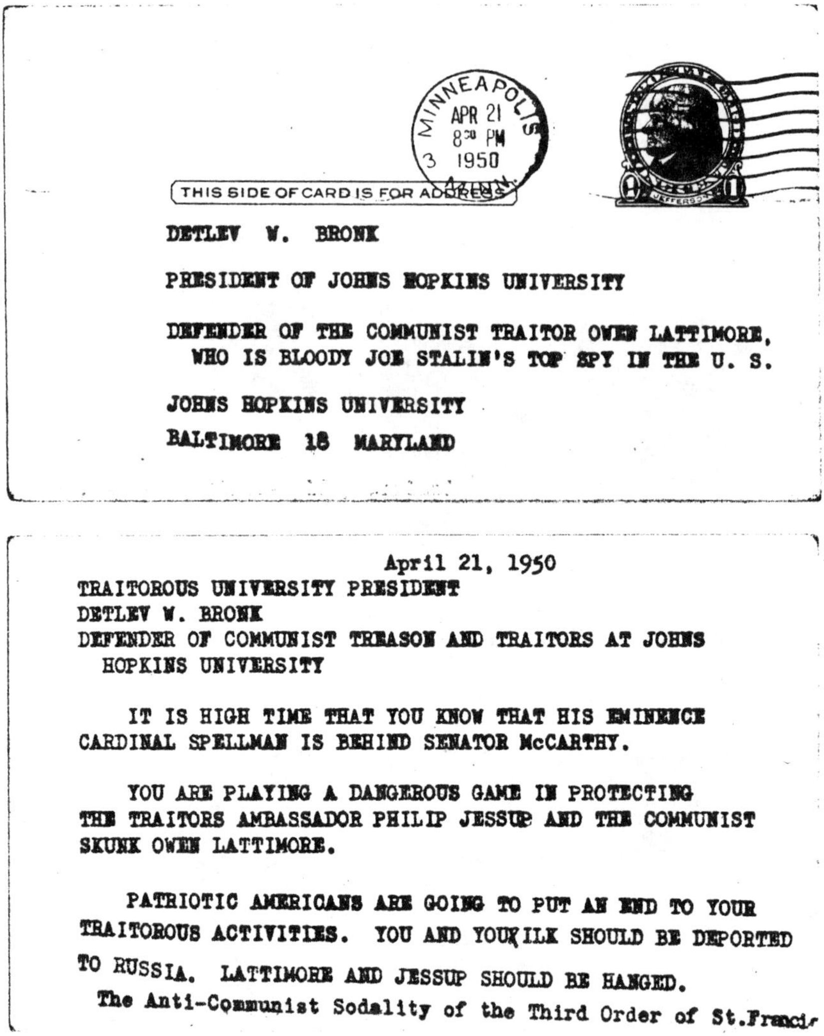

MINNEAPOLIS APR 21 8³⁰ PM 1950 MINN.

THIS SIDE OF CARD IS FOR ADDRESS

DETLEV W. BRONK

PRESIDENT OF JOHNS HOPKINS UNIVERSITY

DEFENDER OF THE COMMUNIST TRAITOR OWEN LATTIMORE, WHO IS BLOODY JOE STALIN'S TOP SPY IN THE U. S.

JOHNS HOPKINS UNIVERSITY

BALTIMORE 18 MARYLAND

April 21, 1950

TRAITOROUS UNIVERSITY PRESIDENT
DETLEV W. BRONK
DEFENDER OF COMMUNIST TREASON AND TRAITORS AT JOHNS HOPKINS UNIVERSITY

IT IS HIGH TIME THAT YOU KNOW THAT HIS EMINENCE CARDINAL SPELLMAN IS BEHIND SENATOR McCARTHY.

YOU ARE PLAYING A DANGEROUS GAME IN PROTECTING THE TRAITORS AMBASSADOR PHILIP JESSUP AND THE COMMUNIST SKUNK OWEN LATTIMORE.

PATRIOTIC AMERICANS ARE GOING TO PUT AN END TO YOUR TRAITOROUS ACTIVITIES. YOU AND YOUR ILK SHOULD BE DEPORTED TO RUSSIA. LATTIMORE AND JESSUP SHOULD BE HANGED.

The Anti-Communist Sodality of the Third Order of St.Francis

10. Postcard, front and back, example of angry correspondence regarding Owen Lattimore received by administration of the Johns Hopkins University, 1950–55. (Courtesy of the archives of the Johns Hopkins University.)

5

Inaction, Reaction, and Action

Most of 1952, from the time when Lattimore testified before the McCarran committee in the early spring until he was indicted in December, was a time of frustration for the board of trustees of Johns Hopkins. While there were more and more bitter words, there were fewer and fewer options to move the problem toward resolution. Many trustees felt that Lattimore should be disciplined, but the board as a whole felt its hands were tied. The imperatives for a hastily charted solution were great, but the background of many trustees made them cautious, too cautious to move contrary to the recommendations of the administration and against the judgment of most faculty. The board could only wait and fret.

The Board's Dilemma

As matters stood, the choices open to the board of trustees were limited and in various ways unattractive: the risks in changing its official and public position regarding Lattimore as it waited were at least as great as in holding to it—at least temporarily. At the conclusion of the investigation of the Institute of Pacific Relations and after discussing the problem with the administration, it released a two-sentence communique stating that since it would be premature and inappropriate to take any action in the Lattimore case before the McCarran committee published its conclusions, it was not contemplating doing so.[1]

It was becoming increasingly obvious, and the fact could hardly be ignored, that Lattimore had greatly alienated and with his obduracy continued to alienate many people. Not least of these was an increasing number of the more prominent members of the board who had become convinced that he had abused his position and was injuring the university, which was seen as quite vulnerable. In an effort to bring the issues back into focus—to mollify these critics and reduce his own vulnerability—Lattimore wrote to President Bronk asking if it would be possible for him to meet the board to explain matters as he saw them. He felt through no fault of his own he had become a lesson and a story. A face-to-face discussion about his loyalty and his testimony might make him seem a more plausible human being. He recognized, given what he saw as the unbalanced and sensational manner in which the press reported the McCarran committee hearings, why a number of board members might be "disturbed."[2]

Some trustees were eager to meet Lattimore. The executive committee of the board agreed to call a special meeting within two weeks in order to give him the opportunity to appear before the full board. Before the meeting, however, one board member lobbied others to convince them that they should not hear Lattimore, "that the matter should first be dealt with through regular administrative channels." It was argued that such a discussion was outside of the board of trustees' proper function. The point was also made that the executive committee of the board had already voted to authorize President Bronk to appoint a faculty committee "to consider the Lattimore situation" and to make a recommendation to the full board. The committee was charged with making "inquiries here and in other institutions as might seem appropriate." A meeting before it had completed its work would undercut its mandate.[3] In the face of these arguments and facts, enough board members were convinced that they should withdraw their invitation, and that Lattimore should instead meet with the duly appointed faculty committee. Perhaps it would be possible to meet with the board at some later date.

The afternoon that Lattimore was to present his case to the board, President Bronk wrote to him canceling the interview and informing him the board now felt that it would be inappropriate for him to come before it.[4] It appeared that those who wanted to keep or even to increase the distance between Lattimore and the board—who wanted Lattimore isolated—had prevailed.

The Faculty Committee

The eight faculty members (called by some the Bard committee, after its chairman the physiologist Philip Bard, who was later to become dean of the School of Medicine) President Bronk appointed to consider Lattimore's testimony before the McCarran committee and the unfavorable publicity it had generated for the university completed its work before the end of May. The report it submitted to President Bronk was brief and unanimous.

One committee member drew up a statement on academic freedom and faculty responsibility that guided its discussions and the drafting of the report. The premise that informed the committee was simple: academics cannot pursue their research without complete freedom of inquiry and freedom of expression. This point was followed by the observation that a university need not take any position with regard to the actions or speech of a faculty member who is said to have violated the law. That is a matter that is best handled by civil authorities. A university should assume that a faculty member, like any other citizen, is innocent unless proven guilty in a court of law. Should guilt be proved, a university, of course, would have to take action commensurate with the seriousness of the offense.

The statement was also informed by another central tenet, namely that there is such a thing as academic law, that there is a set of principles which calls for honesty of purpose, gentlemanly conduct, and the restriction of scientific pronouncement to one's own subject. It was argued that this code transcends national ideologies, and that faculty must assume collectively the responsibility for determining and applying academic law, for seeing to it that it is not violated. The narration concluded with the assertion that "mankind's development" cannot be assured unless faculty rights are guaranteed; sanctions should be applied only in the most serious and clear-cut cases. The premise of the committee—which was held by more administrators and faculty at Johns Hopkins than their counterparts at most American universities—was that power and authority in institutions of higher learning are not hierarchical as in the military or in business organizations. Power and authority also are not separately distributed, with a system of checks and balances, as they are in principle in the U.S. government. They are diffuse, and should be kept that way.[5]

Given this set of beliefs it is hardly surprising that the faculty committee was almost totally supportive of Lattimore. It began its report by arguing that since there were "adequate legal means" to determine subversion or perjury, both of which Lattimore had been accused, it would be unnecessary and improper to pass judgment on his guilt or innocence. Those decisions were matters for civil authorities. It added that the university must abide by the principle of innocent until proven guilty beyond a reasonable doubt. It noted that at the time it was deliberating Lattimore had not even been indicted, much less proven guilty.

The faculty committee commented on Lattimore's conduct before the McCarran committee, which it agreed lacked restraint and dignity, especially the restraint and dignity expected of a scholar. As many others had already done, it was careful to point out that the provocation was great. In any case, it felt that Lattimore's contentious behavior and lack of judgment as a witness were secondary to the basic rights that individuals were entitled to, mainly a proper trial in a regularly constituted court of law. The McCarran committee did not provide that opportunity. It cautioned that if the university administration were to take steps to punish Lattimore because of these secondary issues, this would be widely misinterpreted. Too many would believe this meant university authorities were convinced that Lattimore's politics were suspect and they were condemning him. It would be a mistake for the university to reprimand Lattimore.

It felt that the Johns Hopkins community should pride itself in not having taken any action that indicated prejudgment of Lattimore's innocence or guilt. It skirted evaluating Lattimore as a scholar. It held that if at some point the administration became convinced that it was necessary to investigate Lattimore's competence, this should be done by faculty qualified to make such a judgment and at a time when calm and fair judgment would be possible. It concluded that it would be in the best interests of the university to maintain its neutral stance with regard to Lattimore.[6]

The report notwithstanding, by late spring a growing number of board members had become convinced that Lattimore was a serious liability to Johns Hopkins. Francis White wrote to William C. Bullitt, who, after having served as ambassador to the Soviet Union in the 1930s, had become an avid anti-Communist and supporter of Chiang Kai-shek: "I am still hoping we can do something about the man [Lattimore]. You know all about the racket of academic freedom, I am sure. It is a hard union to overcome."[7] Although the most open, White was far from the only trustee to express cynicism and ambivalence with regard to academic norms.

The Board and the Faculty: Differing Views

The board had to consider issues that went well beyond the simple question of whether or not Lattimore might expose his students to dangerous ideas. After all, as one board member wrote to another during this period, we are "depended upon to do the needful in connection with the forward fundraising program."[8] The trustees spoke mostly of democratic ideals, but what they were often really concerned about was not letting the controversy surrounding Lattimore threaten the financial stability of the university. That this question was on their minds was hardly surprising. After all, the principal function of governing boards of institutions of higher learning is financial oversight.

Board President Barton wrote President Bronk at the end of the summer telling him of correspondence he had had from the assistant attorney general of the State of Maryland who was in charge of the enforcement of statutes relating to subversive activities. Although the letter was businesslike and did not even contain an implied threat, Barton was uneasy about the impending renewal of the annual state appropriation for the university, and he suggested that the president arrange a meeting with Lattimore: "I hope very much . . . when you see him, at his request, there will be an appropriate opportunity to discuss our problem." He did not hide the fact that he was becoming more and more anxious about the situation, and had become committed to finding an early solution "of this problem and the continued unpleasant publicity."[9]

On the other hand, many senior faculty felt that too much attention was being paid to fiscal matters and continued to express openly the view that the university had no right to apply negative sanctions against Lattimore. The university was something more than a business; considerations other than its solvency took precedence. Many faculty completely rejected the suggestion being openly expressed by some board members that it would be in the best interest of the university if Lattimore were dismissed or persuaded to resign. As they saw it, the fact that the Lattimore case was page-one copy was irrelevant—and had to be ignored. The faculty view was fairly well summed up by Leo Spitzer, a widely respected professor of romance philology:

> As long as nothing is officially proven, the man is not guilty. If a scholar happens to antagonize public opinion by his investigations, he must have freedom of thought and expression. . . .
>
> If a scholar in such a position as Mr. Lattimore's happens to cause a feeling in the public that results in damage financially to the university, the university should absorb this damage as a necessary consequence of the upholding of academic freedom.[10]

Given dissimilar interests, it is not surprising that board members and faculty saw the matter quite differently. Informal, amicable meetings between them changed very few minds; the exchange of views did little to bring the two sides closer together. Their perspectives were just too different. Each was convinced the other did not quite understand the depth of the problem, how an erroneous decision would do incalculable harm to the institution. Moreover, each believed the other's view to be too narrow, too naive, too superficial.

The board was not prepared to disregard faculty opinion and the principles, for example, academic freedom, that were being espoused, and was again forced into inaction. Many trustees had become convinced that there was a grave risk in firing Lattimore over the strong opposition of a substantial number of faculty, many of whom were eminent researchers and scholars in their respective disciplines. Some board members had to convince others that such an action would be too divisive. The board spent a good deal of time engaged in internal debate. Most trustees were eventually convinced that even if Lattimore were mildly punished there was a risk that some faculty would become angry and resign. This possibility stopped short any efforts to terminate Lattimore summarily. The threat of a divided faculty, of research interrupted by intramural bickering and resignations, worried the university administration and this fear was directly and repeatedly communicated to influential board members. Even the resignation of one faculty member, particularly someone visible in his discipline, would be inauspicious. There was a reluctance to upset the institution's equilibrium In this way faculty from all disciplines exerted influence over the administration and the board, and over Lattimore's career. It was the understanding of this fact that led faculty to be so deliberate and to exhibit such restraint.

The trustees were well aware that at other institutions governing boards had taken unilateral action in firing faculty, and that they had the legal right to do so. None wanted to be precipitous. Even those most publicly hostile towards Lattimore knew the board on its part must show restraint. There was a feeling, perhaps wishful thinking, that the administration "through effective missionary work" would eventually convince a substantial number of faculty to, as one board member wrote another, "accept the realities of the situation." The board would have to be patient; getting faculty to see matters from a different and new perspective would not come easily or soon. "I think personally that we will have to content ourselves with the lapse of some time (I hope this can be minimized) before the separation which we believe is necessary is effected."

The board was patronizing of faculty, but no more than the faculty was patronizing of the board. It was believed that faculty held the position that they did mostly because of a failure to understand "that the barrel can be spoiled by one rotten apple."[11] The board could do little to affect the thought and expression of faculty. By the same token, faculty had not changed the thinking of most trustees. Some seemed persuaded by faculty, but they might have been predisposed to support Lattimore. The likelihood that there would be a price, largely unknown, for firing Lattimore made the board wary. Lattimore was pugnacious and he surely would not go quietly; he could use the courts as well as his friends to forestall termination. It would have to wait for a more propitious time before it could act. That faculty could exercise such clear influence on trustees is noteworthy, and contrary to conventional wisdom—and the situation around the country during (and, it should be added, before and after) the Cold War.[12]

The independence of the thought and expression of Johns Hopkins faculty cannot be overstated. For example, George Boas, the professor of philosophy who was instrumental in organizing the dinner and reception for Lattimore in 1950, wrote a much discussed article for the May 1952 issue of *The Johns Hopkins Magazine* in which he described and lamented what he called the "new authoritarianism" sweeping the country. As Boas saw it, this authoritarianism was a symptom of "a creeping paralysis which has begun to infect our schools, our government, and the general public itself." While authoritarianism was thriving, individualism, which had traditionally been the dominant philosophy of America, had been weakened. The essay was clearly an apologia for Lattimore or particular events surrounding his case.

Developing a quite general theme, Boas began by noting that what made the United States unique was its "great tradition of freedom and adventure." Besides coming from its conspicuous and impressive wealth, the country's great strength could be found in its solidarity and ability to solve new problems with new solutions. Boas was concerned that in the political climate of the Cold War this strength was being eroded. He found it troubling that such positive values as hope and charity, which in the past had been beacons for Americans, were being superseded by fear and hate. America was being divided because too many people had become convinced that there could be only one interpretation of current events. What was passed off and taken as the official truth had become more narrowly defined; to question it had become both more unacceptable and more risky: "The protestant, with a small *p*, is out of step. One must conform, agree, goosestep, chant hymns to Order, Discipline, Tradition."

Boas believed that those most desirous of producing a highly structured society in which orthodoxy and heterodoxy were sharply defined were gradually getting the upper hand in America. This could be seen in the growing attacks on teachers and on all recalcitrant individuals—artists, scientists, reformers, philosophers—and on freedom of thought. Why this was occurring was quite understandable.

> Those of us who modestly attempt to contribute to the enlightenment of our fellows, who try our best to solve genuine problems, and not merely to repeat the solutions of the past, who are actually able to say "No" when "Yes" would be treachery to our conscience and to our intelligence, are now labeled traitors or, at the mildest, disturbers of the peace. . . . We are engaged in the search for truth and in its dissemination.
>
> Unfortunately the truth hurts. It hurts the feelings of everyone whose pet ideas it contradicts. Some of these ideas are sacred. Some have the prestige of tradition. Some are merely the ideas of men who hold positions of power in society.

Knowing what was happening and why did not make the problem any less a threat. It had the gravest implications for higher learning. This was why, Boas believed, the new authoritarians were the most "vicious" in making the academic profession their "pet targets." Those who led the attack were quite aware that silencing professors was an effective way to keep the rest of society in ignorance:

> There is no doubt that the authoritarians are right in seeing in the teaching body the greatest enemy to tradition as such. . . . We are all committed to the doctrine that our truths are on trial and must constantly be re-submitted to examination. If they cannot meet the test, they must go. Nor is free enquiry a respecter of persons or of dogma. . . . [13]

Few saw Boas' analysis as dispassionate. Some who had grave doubts about Lattimore and what he seemed to represent were outraged not only at how inflammatory and self-serving the essay seemed, but also at the barely disguised subtext.

The article served to rekindle interest in the issues raised by the controversy surrounding Lattimore. One well-placed attorney who, among other things, had been a college classmate of Provost

Macaulay and had actively worked in the Hopkins 75th Anniversary Fund, even initiated a campaign to have *The Johns Hopkins Magazine* publish a paper which "espoused the other side of the controversy."[14] More letters were sent to university authorities; more responses had to be written. With the greater effort, the level of apprehension of some trustees and administrators increased.

The board of trustees was thwarted by its inability to help bring the Lattimore case to some resolution. Not only was there faculty resistance, but the board of trustees was aware that a grand jury which had been asked by the McCarran committee to inquire into whether Lattimore had violated the law was in the process of doing so. There was no way of determining when the jury would complete its deliberations, and what it would finally decide. While the matter was in the grand jury's hands, the board could not take any action which might prejudice the course of the investigation. It was forced to bide its time.

The situation smoldered. Although some moral entrepreneurs were unflagging in their assaults on Lattimore (see excerpt from a speech by Senator McCarran in September 1952—between the time his committee recommended the indictment and the grand jury's action—Appendix J), for the general public, the matter receded from consciousness; there were significantly fewer signs of indignation. The university received fewer postcards, unsigned letters, and other communications from distant places. In the mail, there were fewer expressions of raw anger.

On the other hand, there was no leveling off in the correspondence from those with some connection to the Johns Hopkins University, most particularly alumni. They were just as interested. For these individuals, there was a feeling that the university should take decisive action; the university should make its disapproval of Lattimore's views and conduct quite explicit. It should go on the offensive. It should distance itself from Lattimore even if this meant firing him. It should be a step ahead of the grand jury. As matters now stood, it appeared that the administration and board of trustees were uncertain, indecisive, or too timid. It was beginning to look as if the administration believed that Lattimore had done nothing to merit censure, that it might even approve of what he stood for and his attacks on public figures. The university could not expect a solution unless it provided one. It was unrealistic to assume that the problem would disappear or that the situation would right itself. Why hadn't the board or the administration done something?

Administrative officers and members of the board were contacted by acquaintances and friends and urged to take action. Some individuals communicated with both administrative officers and members of the board, sometimes at the same time and sometimes sequentially. Most expressed impatience. Some warned that they might withhold contributions from the university. The angriest threatened to ask their friends to do the same.

Fund-raising

As the university's reputation diminished, it appeared that its ability to enlist contributors to its fund-raising drives might also diminish. Responses to a major campaign to the Baltimore community for $6 million as the first step in a national effort to raise close to $80 million ($3.5 million for buildings for the Homewood [main] campus, $20 million for additional endowment for university divisions at Homewood, $30 to $40 million for new construction and rebuilding of portions of the hospital, Medical School, and School of Public Health, and $20 million for the endowment of the medical institutions) were one indicator of how local support for the university seems to have generally eroded. *"Not a cent* to Hopkins while you keep *Owen Lattimore* and *15* card carrying Communists as teachers. Who they are, you can find out today, in Washington IF YOU WANT TO???"[15]

One wealthy attorney wrote the treasurer of the university and secretary to the board of trustees venting his frustration:

> In accordance with my expectation so to do, I am enclosing herewith my check to the order of the Hopkins Fund in the amount of $5,000.
>
> I send the check with great reluctance; I certainly will not send another one as long as the Lattimore situation remains as it is. . . . [16]

When President Bronk told Board President Barton of the letter, the latter solicitously responded, expressing his own disappointment about the turn of events and explaining the limited options open to the university. He reassured the donor that he and his fellow trustees closest to the matter were not "in the slightest degree sympathetic with the kind of activity in which Lattimore was engaged, as described before the McCarran committee, or with his personal conduct." He went on to point out that the board of trustees had the responsibility to do what was "best" for the university, and explained that being close to the problem gave board members an understanding of it that others not so situated might lack. He expressed the hope that "the presence of this man in one of the Hopkins departments" would not result in lessened support resulting in harm to the education and research programs of the university.[17]

The response to Barton's explanation and plea came quickly and was ominous.

> I feel and I am confident that the majority of those who have contributed and are currently contributing funds to the university feel the same way, namely, that we should not temporize with the Lattimore situation and that it concerns itself with the very essence of our civilization.

The letter went on to explain that it was wrong for the university to believe that it did not have to accede to any of the wishes of those who supported it and still expect them to do so. If the university could offer only unpalatable alternatives "there is only one answer and that is to refuse to make any further contributions; certainly I will not make another one and I am confident that if the situation as it exists today is known to potential contributors . . . subscriptions will be materially curtailed."[18] The problem faced by the board of trustees could not have been any clearer, or more unpleasant.

The 1952 Annual Roll Call, the Johns Hopkins University campaign for funds "to do some of the things"[19] not permitted within the budget solely from tuition, research grants, and endowment, brought the most discouraging responses—from wealthy and generous alumni, from modest but steadfast subscribers, from individuals not known to be supporters who pledged to give after Lattimore was fired, and from anonymous critics of Lattimore, the university, or the administration—all disgruntled:

> I received your letter of December 8 in connection with the 1952 Annual Roll Call and feel that I should pass on to you my reasons for not contributing.
>
> They can be rather simply stated as: communism, or suspicion of communism. Perhaps, to you in the East there does not appear to be as much stigma attached to these terms, as we in the Middle West seem to feel. . . . As I look back into my undergraduate days, I recall, I believe, a Professor Mitchell about whom we in the student body had serious questions in regard to his loyalty.
>
> I agree that any organization must protect its own, but in doing so it must make every effort to keep its house in order, and to present an unsoiled front to the rest of the world. . . .

> I, personally, am extremely sad that I should feel this way, but I am even more grieved that a university to which I owe so much, should make me feel this way.[20]

The responsibility for answering such letters largely fell to Provost Macaulay. He did this with considerable delicacy and patience.

> Your letter of December 15 addressed to Eli Frank deserves a straightforward answer and, belatedly, I am going to undertake the job. . . . I shall limit this letter, therefore, to two major points: the university's general position with respect to communism and its position specifically in the Lattimore case.
>
> You took your degree in '38 at a time when practically every campus in the country could count fairly large numbers of Communists or near-Communists or pseudo-Communists among the student body and, in some cases, among the faculty. Even in those more tolerant days, however, and even in the succeeding period of "friendship" with Russia, there was no tolerance on the part of the Hopkins faculties for men who used the classroom or their contacts with students to advance the cause of communism. Within a year or so of the time you took your degree, one member of the faculty was summarily dismissed because he thus abused his position as an instructor. At about the same time Broadus Mitchell, to whom you refer in your letter, resigned from the university under pressure by his colleagues, who disapproved of his views and particularly his insistence on advancing them in classrooms and lecture halls. These are only two cases; there are several others in the record. They combine to show, I believe, that there is not now, and has never been, any faculty support for persons known to be adherents of communism.
>
> I would be foolish to assert that there are no Communists on the faculty now, but I believe I can say with assurance that there are no *known* Communists and I have no doubt that any faculty member, electing to use his university position to spread propaganda for *any* political or social cause, would receive the same treatment from his colleagues as was accorded those referred to above. Let me make it quite clear, however, that the only way the university—faculty or administration—can identify a Communist is by his performance. We do not have an FBI within the institution, nor do we have access to the files of the FBI in Washington. It is quite possible that hid-

> den Communists exist at Hopkins, just as it is possible that some may be concealed within the Square D Company [the correspondent's employer].
>
> Against this background, let us look at the Lattimore case. Until the day Senator McCarthy's charges were publicized, Lattimore was just another member of the university staff. . . . He was a popular speaker both within the university and to such outside groups as the Rotary Club, the New York Alumni, and many others. His books had been widely read and his lectures widely attended and hundreds of persons of unquestioned loyalty had failed to read into them any intimations of Communist leanings. None of this is said in defense of Lattimore; it is simply a statement of the situation as it existed.
>
> You will recall that in his first appearance before the Tydings subcommittee, Lattimore voluntarily asserted under oath that he was not and never had been a Communist. It is this sworn statement that is one of the bases of the present indictment against him. . . .
>
> From that point on, it appears to me the university's position was clear. It could not intervene without prejudicing a case which, under the laws of this country, could only be judged properly in the courts. . . .
>
> For Hopkins to have acted otherwise than it has acted would have involved the usurpation by an extralegal agency of the functions of duly established investigative and judicial bodies. . . .
>
> Admittedly I have oversimplified a very complex situation, but in so doing I have tried to emphasize the single principle which has guided the university in its actions. I hope you may realize, from the content of this letter, that what may appear to be inaction on the part of the university is really the only action possible under the circumstances. . . . [21]

Macaulay's basic thesis that the solution demanded due process of law was generally well received.

When the chairman of the executive committee of the Annual Roll Call responded to a reluctant donor, he also talked about principle, but returned to the point of the whole exchange—the need for contributions.

> You appreciate that the board of trustees and the officers of the university share with you the desire that the

> university should always act patriotically and with justice towards all. You believe that the action of the university in granting Professor Lattimore a leave of absence with pay after he had been indicted was a mistake. Knowing the makeup of the board of trustees and of the officers, it is difficult to believe that this mistake should be attributed to sympathy with radicals or to any other form of bad faith.
>
> It must be remembered that under our American system the indictment of a grand jury means only that the state has been given permission to present charges against the person indicted and no more. . . . The action of the university after the indictment of Professor Lattimore is in accordance with the best American tradition.
>
> If the university had acted in any other manner, it would have been punishing Professor Lattimore for a crime of which he has been merely accused and might prejudice his defense in advance of trial. . . .
>
> I appreciate the frank and detailed expression of your position and the opportunity which it has given me to present to you the other side of the picture. If, on reflection, you still consider the action of the university a mistake, I trust that you will conclude that it is a mistake on a matter where disagreement with your position does not indicate lack of loyalty. If you come to this conclusion, I suggest that it is still proper for you to continue your loyal support of the university of which you are a graduate and that a contribution to its funds would indicate a confidence in the American principle of freedom of expression and in the procedures of American criminal justice.[22]

Sometimes liberal-minded and powerful alumni used their influence on the university's behalf on former classmates. Sydney Cone, of the textile family, became involved in such an effort.

> . . . [B]ut I am your friend and I write as a friend to tell you quite frankly that your attitude wounds me; it wounds me, yes, but it also wounds you, and I do not enjoy the picture of my friend Jim doing himself this damage. Looking at the matter from one aspect alone, what are you making out of your judgment, accurate, acute, authenticated though it may be? You are electing yourself judge, jury, advocate for the prosecution, all in one man, and insisting by pressure ($100.00 a year plus the example to others you hope to influence likewise) to carry out the sentence you have passed. That, my boy, is one hell of

> a "democratic process," and I don't believe you have thought of it in this light, or realized what company you are keeping when you put yourself in this position. . . . [23]

The university administration was naturally quite grateful for this sort of support.

> Dear Syd:
>
> I hope you will permit this informal salutation. Although you may not remember me, I do recall you quite well. . . .
>
> Under these conditions you will understand how much comfort I found in your straightforward exposition of the principles which many of us here have been trying to defend—and which must be protected if free institutions are to survive.
>
> I am going to keep a copy of your letter in my desk to read whenever communications of another sort persuade me that the world is filled with dangerous people. I wonder if I might also have your permission to use the letter (with names and other identifying marks expurgated, of course) in some of my contacts with alumni and others who need the kind of warning which you so clearly sound.
>
> Sincerely Yours,
> P. Stewart Macaulay[24]

Although the Lattimore case may have loosened ties that many alumni had with the university and with each other, this was generally done without great bitterness. In most cases relations were strained rather than broken. The consequences of the tension were short run. The detailed explanations offered by university officials appeared effective in more cases than not. They may not have changed anyone's mind, but they worked to mute the disagreement. After the administration made its case, few alumni pressed their demand for Lattimore's dismissal. It was more like a standoff. To be sure, those who expressed displeasure were not persuaded. They did not, however, rebut; they seemed satisfied or at least willing to wait. This result was no small success for the administration and board of trustees who felt under siege.

It is unclear whether or not the university actually was hurt financially during the time so many were insisting that Lattimore be terminated. Financial reports[25] for the years between 1948 and 1958 show educational and general income increasing every year but one. (Between 1951 and 1952 there was some decrease in endowment income, restricted gifts, grants and fees, and, most particularly, government research contracts.) At the same time, for the three years (1951–52 through 1953–54) for which record keeping was uniform and detailed comparisons are possible, contributions to the Johns Hopkins Fund decreased while the Annual Alumni Roll Call steadily increased. The pattern of contributions was the same for the university as a whole and for the Faculty of Philosophy and the School of Engineering, which would have been most affected if donations were being withheld to protest the administration's not firing or otherwise punishing Lattimore.

FISCAL YEAR	JOHNS HOPKINS FUND		ANNUAL ALUMNI ROLL CALL	
	Total	Faculty of Philosophy and School of Engineering	Total	Faculty of Philosophy and School of Engineering
1951–52	$725,417	$365,417	$108,737	$54,368
1952–53	$711,500	$353,600	$112,444	$56,222
1953–54	$708,820	$350,850	$121,975	$60,955

For four years beginning 1954–55, when the concern about Lattimore's continuing connection with the university was dissipating, the gifts for general purposes decreased in two of the years for the university as a whole, but only in one year for the Faculty of Philosophy and the School of Engineering.

FISCAL YEAR	TOTAL GIFTS	GIFTS TO FACULTY OF PHILOSOPHY AND SCHOOL OF ENGINEERING
1954–55	$580,813	$135,167
1955–56	$544,244	$130,748
1956–57	$557,383	$134,644
1957–58	$506,372	$136,900

The data are incomplete and murky, and the most that can be concluded is that the university did not suffer to a great extent financially by retaining Lattimore. No record could be found in which a senior administrator expressed the view that it had.

It was nonetheless apparent that as the case dragged on the potential for damage could only increase. With regularity, something was published or broadcast that added to Lattimore's, and to the Johns Hopkins University's, notoriety.

A November 1952 issue of *The New Leader*[26] reprinted a six-paragraph editorial about the Moscow Trials that Lattimore had written for *Pacific Affairs* in 1938. In the piece, unearthed by the McCarran committee, Lattimore expressed the view that the Moscow Trials were fair and that in the long run they would result in greater democracy in the Soviet Union. In the climate of the Cold War, these conclusions by themselves made Lattimore seem not only foolish or stupid, but dangerously pro-Russian. However, they were not reprinted by themselves, but were juxtaposed to a lengthy exegesis by the virulently anti-Communist philosopher Sidney Hook who characterized them as "one of the most extreme statements ever penned in their [the Moscow Trials'] defense." According to Hook, the detailed evidence available to Lattimore in 1938 "renders his own statements on the trials fantastic, a willful piece of question-begging and special pleading in favor of the Kremlin." In his broadside, Hook accuses Lattimore of not disapproving when "Stalin openly connived with Hitler to unleash World War II. . . ."[27]

In a newspaper column, Arthur Schlesinger, Jr., called Lattimore "a notorious and unabashed fellow traveler," a fact which "may render [his] character . . . distasteful." He went on to suggest that it would be easier to defend Lattimore against false or exaggerated charges if he candidly admitted that he had once been infatuated with the Soviet Union, rather than by making the "disingenuous" claim that he had always been "a stout anti-totalitarian."[28] Seeing this as a restatement of the principal count in the perjury indictment, Thurman Arnold wrote to Schlesinger pointing out what he was conceding to Lattimore's enemies and how damaging this was to any defense. He asked Schlesinger—with how much irony is unclear—to assist him in finding what it was about Lattimore's actions or writings which led some to conclude that he was sympathetic to Communist interests. He and his partners were having difficulty addressing the matter, and honestly did "not know just what we have to get." In view of the injury Arnold believed Schlesinger had caused, he felt that he owed it to Lattimore to provide a bill of particulars.[29]

Lattimore, his supporters, and the university barely had time to respond to each new assault. The cause and Johns Hopkins seemed to be sinking deeper and deeper in the morass. The university authorities understood that they had to act. The grand jury's decision to indict Lattimore finally made it possible for them to do so, and they moved deliberately but quickly.

The Board Meets and Acts

The same evening that Lattimore's indictment by the grand jury for perjury was made public, the executive committee of the board of trustees met with senior administrative officers to formalize the plan that had been prepared for this eventuality. President Bronk, who presided at the meeting, told the gathering that following the announcement of the indictment he had reviewed events with Philip Bard who had chaired the committee which had already examined and advised him about the Lattimore case. He then read a draft of a letter which he planned to send to Lattimore. After considerable discussion and some rephrasing, the meeting unanimously voted approval of the letter. The group of twelve also unanimously agreed that the letter should be sent that evening, that the president should notify Lattimore by telegram that it was forthcoming, and that he should issue a statement to the press that the letter had been sent.[30] The authorities at Hopkins were moving with nearly unprecedented speed and sound to disassociate themselves from Lattimore.

More interesting than the letter were many of the points raised by various individuals during the nearly two-hour discussion. Of most concern was what the university should do in the event that Lattimore was not found guilty. The board wanted to assure itself that the university would still be able to "take any action later on at the proper time" if it chose to do so. It did not want to make it appear that it had a commitment to Lattimore. Basically, it still wanted to retain the option of punishing him, even if he were found innocent. It was reiterated that the case had "been the talk of the country." Given the comment any action it might take would surely prompt, the board definitely did not want to imply that it would automatically reinstate Lattimore even if he were cleared by the courts. It wanted everyone to understand its position; it wanted to leave no room for misunderstanding. It was still very attuned to public opinion; there was a concern that it would have the option to deal more harshly with Lattimore if enough politicians and powerful people continued to demand it.

At the same time, apprehension was expressed concerning adverse faculty reaction if Lattimore were seen as being treated badly by university authorities. Uncertainty about what faculty might do without question moderated the position of the board. When comparisons with other institutions were made, considerable attention was paid to a case at the Massachusetts Institute of Technology where a physicist had been granted an indefinite leave of absence while the charge of contempt of congress was being resolved in the courts. The board wanted very badly to leave the impression that it was prudent, yet forceful. As one member said, "don't let's fumble now."[31]

The letter of suspension to Lattimore was brief and courteous:

> Because a federal grand jury, having considered evidence presented to it in support of certain charges, has returned an indictment against you, as a step in our established judicial procedure, I have as of this date given you leave of absence, with salary, from your university duties and official connections until a federal court shall have passed upon the charges.
>
> I have done this with the advice of a committee comprising members of the several faculties of the university and with the approval of the board of trustees.[32]

Lattimore responded within a week.

> Thank you for your letter of December 16 granting me leave of absence, with salary. It is a great satisfaction to me that your action, taken with the advice of a faculty committee and with the approval of the board of trustees, conforms to the request I had previously made of you, through Mr. Macaulay, when I was unable to reach you by telephone from Washington. . . .
>
> I deeply regret that there should unavoidably be unpleasant repercussions for the university in the prolonged political persecution of a member of its faculty.[33]

The suspension was a form of punishment; it removed Lattimore from campus and minimized the possibility that he would be able to protect himself from any adverse actions that the university might take.

The reaction to the board's decision to place Lattimore on leave was generally favorable. Few expressed the view that the university should have done less. There was some criticism that Lattimore would continue on salary.

> TELEGRAM
>
> Why don't you give Lattimore double salary during leave and further lower the regard of real Americans for the great institution that you at this moment had?[34]

While praising university authorities, those most favorable to Lattimore, such as the Johns Hopkins chapter of Students for Democratic Action, urged that no further steps be taken, as this might make his defense more difficult.[35]

According to a written account, the "Lattimore committee" of the Academic Council also did not feel that he should be terminated unless he were "found guilty in court." There was a general feeling that if he were acquitted on the charges of perjury he should be reinstated since he had tenure: "Whether that appointment is a mistake or not is immaterial. Other mistakes have been made and tenure cannot be revoked but for *good cause*. . . ." It was thought that it would be an error and a "flimsy excuse, only" to eliminate Lattimore's position, since nobody would believe that it was not done merely to avoid his return to campus. It was also recognized that although Lattimore's "conduct [was] deplorable," he was advised by his attorney to attack the McCarran committee and "he was quizzed mercilessly on events of ten and more years ago." The committee also wondered why neither Lattimore nor his counsel "could ask questions or verify other witnesses. . . . In spite of the statement that Mr. Lattimore was not on trial, he nevertheless was by implication."

The Academic Council statement closed with the view that the university should continue to pay Lattimore's salary regardless of how long the legal wrangling continued. There was agreement that faculty stand aloof from any "uproar" and limit "endless discussion and debate on the merits of the case."

> . . . [I]t is utterly important to avoid splitting the campus in the same manner as the country has been divided on the same issue. Above all the *integrity of the university must be preserved* and measured against that fact; our own welfare is second in order of priority.[36]

Few were convinced by the assertions of Lattimore and his close friends that there was no substance to the case against him, that it was all only a political inquisition. There was a sense that Lattimore was guilty of much more than what he had been charged with in the indictment. There was a widespread perception that someone who was truly innocent would have, after so many months, been able to prove it. The federal government certainly did not wantonly make accusations against innocent people. Some critics put it simply: "Where there is so much smoke, there must be some fire."[37] Others, making the same argument, were less direct. A letter from Vannevar Bush, a board member and president of the Carnegie Institution of Washington, to President Bronk a week after the executive committee took its action shows how pervasive this line of thinking had become.

> I think the action of the executive committee in the Lattimore case was excellently handled. This is undoubtedly the action that should be taken, and the fact that you had the principle understood before the event helped to do the job promptly and effectively.
>
> Beyond that we can merely see what occurs. I doubt if the grand jury would have indicted if there had been no more to base the indictment on than has appeared in the newspapers. In fact the various statements of Lattimore which are held up as the basis of a charge of perjury seem to me to be mostly the sort of thing that a court would regard as a matter of carelessness rather than intent to deceive, particularly because the court will be reluctant, I am sure, to attribute an attempt to deceive congress unless there is a good deal of background evidence. Thus I think, since the indictment has been brought, we will in due time learn a good deal. Certainly if there is conviction our skirts will then be clear. I also feel that if there is no conviction it will be because nothing much has been presented except hearsay and innuendo, in which case we have no basis for action except reinstatement. But I think we are going to hear a great deal or the indictment would not have been brought.
>
> At any rate I will be glad to talk the whole thing over when I see you next, and I am glad we took no action until there was a definite basis for it.[38]

The board of trustees itself was very much relieved that Lattimore was finally, at least, at arm's length. Board members most sympathetic to Lattimore believed the prodding that they do something would now abate, and the university would be temporarily out of the limelight. Board members less tolerant of Lattimore hoped that this was only the first step in permanently removing him from the university. All but perhaps one or two believed that the university was long overdue in taking action. A board member wrote to a General Motors executive:

> . . . [T]he trustees of Johns Hopkins have been extremely hot and bothered over the Lattimore situation. . . . The fact that nothing was done prior to this time is a long story which I will not undertake to go into. For many months the trustees unanimously were insistent that something be done to effect the separation of Mr. Lattimore but were unable to bring the administration and the faculty around to where they were willing to step up to the situation. . . .
>
> Certainly we can be happy that Eisenhower won in November, and as time has passed I have become growingly encouraged and heartened over the appearances that we may have an opportunity of getting back to fundamental principles in our form of government and way of life.[39]

These "fundamental principles" were surely somewhat different from the "true American traditions" referred to by Edwards Park in the last chapter. Whatever they were, the conclusion seemed clear: it would undoubtedly be easier for the country to get back to them if there were fewer heretics teaching in American universities.

The Lattimore Defense Fund

In early January 1953, with the impetus of, among others, George Boas, a defense fund for Lattimore was begun. In a letter of solicitation to the faculty of Johns Hopkins signed by Boas, the organizing committee explained that its goal was to collect $40,000 to cover Lattimore's disbursements and other legal expenses which Arnold, Fortas, & Porter had been providing *pro bono*.

Not surprisingly, the reaction—both on and off campus—to another highly visible effort on behalf of Lattimore was mixed. Many faculty, of course, ignored the appeal. Yet, a good number, agreeing with the premise of the defense fund committee "that the issues of academic freedom and free speech are on trial"[40] subscribed. Others, disproportionately from the Medical School, were infuriated that there was again the appearance that the university was siding with Lattimore. To some faculty, Lattimore was "notorious," not someone who should be lionized, helped, or given any special treatment whatsoever.

The gist of the opposition to the defense fund was that it was "in poor taste" to appear to support Lattimore while ignoring the fact that there were serious charges against him. Any fund-raising, before "evidence vindicates Mr. Lattimore's present position," was most certainly premature. Lattimore must first be cleared. "[T]hen I believe the university should come out strongly in his backing. Then and only then, it seems to me, financial assistance should be offered."[41]

A number of people complained that the request for contributions was ambiguous enough so as to give the impression that it was sponsored by the university. Many of those for whom this was an issue charged the defense committee with deliberately wording the solicitation to imply that it was acting with the full knowledge and sanction of the board of trustees. At question was a reference in the letter to the board of trustees' decision not to terminate Lattimore and instead to put him on a paid leave of absence, with the board being characterized as having "acted in a generous spirit consistent with the Johns Hopkins tradition."[42] It was thought the phrasing was intended to leave the impression that the defense fund had been initiated by the university. As one incensed professor put it:

> I was distressed to receive the letter soliciting funds for Mr. Lattimore, especially one apparently indicating that the board of trustees has taken some action already in this matter. I have talked to a number of other men on the faculty about it and find that many are disturbed about this course of action.[43]

Lattimore had again become a focal point of controversy. Most galling to some was that the putative neutrality of the university had again been seemingly compromised.

From the beginning it had been an article of faith of many that the university must studiously avoid any activity that would suggest support for Lattimore. Feelings on this matter were quite strong. One angry letter to President Bronk stated outright that if indeed the university had prior knowledge or had given approval to the committee's plan "then I here and now tender my resignation from the faculty of the Johns Hopkins University to take effect as of this date, as I will have no association with such an attitude, either expressed or implied."[44]

A number wrote directly to Boas, or to others on the defense fund committee, to express their displeasure. Some were quite angry.

> Permit me to say that I believe your statement that Mr. Lattimore's "cause is ours" is an affront, if not a gross insult, to most of us. If Mr. Lattimore's sympathy for Russia and the Communists is as great as I have every reason to believe it is, his cause may be yours but it is certainly not mine, and I do not believe it is that of the great majority of our colleagues on the faculty. . . .
>
> Spengler in his *The Decline of the West* comments on the part played in public affairs by such philosophers of the past as Confucius, Pythagoras, Goethe, Hobbes and Leibniz, and contrasts their thinking and achievements with those of the present day. Of the latter variety he has the following to say: "Turning from men of this mould to the philosophers of today, one is dismayed and shamed. How poor their personalities, how commonplace their political and practical outlook! . . . And this insufficiency indicates, not that they possess inwardness, but simply that they lack weight."[45]

Of course, not everyone on or off campus disapproved.

> My dear *Collega:*
>
> You don't know me; neither have I ever met you personally. The same remoteness of acquaintance exists between Prof. Lattimore and myself. How, then, am I to pass judgment on Prof. Lattimore's character or, for that matter, on yours; or how are either of you to pass on mine, if you cared?
>
> It is a sad condition of our judicial procedure that so much money is required for a man to prove his innocence, and that the lack of money may bring about his conviction in spite of his innocence. I should happily make a contribution to a well appointed effort towards elimination of this ugly situation in our courts.
>
> Now, the mail has brought me from the American Legion a reprint of some blabberings of a radio news-huckster which, with the frequent use of the miserable adjective "alleged" and blaring underscorings, tries to make Prof. Lattimore *look*

guilty before the trial has found him innocent, as we hope him to be. . . .

So please accept my contribution for the Lattimore fund.

It will please me if we should meet at some time, even though it be in jail.

Very truly yours,
Paul Hessemer
Assistant Professor of Civil Engineering[46]

Dear Professor Boas:

Enclosed please find my check for $10.00 for the Lattimore defense fund.

I am sorry not to have enlisted any of my friends here at Beloit in the cause. But I shall continue to make known the objective. We need to rally support not only for Lattimore in this trial. . . . [47]

As is obvious from the minutes of their meeting the week after the defense fund committee was formed, the board of trustees was, not surprisingly, far from pleased with this new initiative.

Mr. Francis White raised questions in connection with Dr. George Boas' appeal for funds to aid Mr. Owen Lattimore in his defense. Dr. Bronk replied that Dr. Boas had been advised that he could not use the university mailing list for the solicitation. Dr. Bronk added that he saw no way of preventing Dr. Boas as an individual from making the appeal. No action was taken, but it appeared to be the consensus of opinion that the appeal was unfortunate.[48]

All that the university could do was to move to disassociate itself from the defense fund; it again moved quickly. It was immediately announced that not only had university facilities not been used to promote the defense fund, but the administration knew nothing about it. Provost Macaulay publicly stated that the administration had taken "no position in this matter."[49]

A reference in the solicitation letter to "several members of the faculty" was also widely misconstrued to mean "all of the faculty" and therefore to mean that the campaign was a faculty project. This interpretation resulted in additional protests.

There was pressure from the administration on the Academic Council to meet to deliberate a resolution "questioning the propriety" of Boas' letter on behalf of the defense fund. In the strongest language and with detailed objections, the text of the motion disapproved "the form in which the letter is couched."

> 1. The Council questions the propriety of Professor Boas' action in sending out such a letter in his private capacity to faculty members, many of whom are associated with the Group Council of which he is chairman. Such an ambiguous role is calculated to create misunderstanding.
> 2. It is both misleading and in poor taste to identify the faculty of this university with the cause of a faculty member who stands indicted for perjury, no matter how respected that colleague may be, until a court of law has acted on the indictment.
> 3. The Council objects to the reference to the action of the trustees, which is so worded as to suggest that payment of the salary of Mr. Lattimore during his leave of absence indicates an expression of confidence in Mr. Lattimore.
> 4. The Council objects to the implication of the last sentence of the letter to the effect that Mr. Lattimore's impending trial necessarily involves the issue of academic freedom.[50]

The fact that such a proposal was given any consideration, and the inimical wording, makes it obvious that the activities of the defense fund committee were divisive to a community already strained by what was beginning to look like a permanent problem.

The Academic Council appointed a subcommittee to consult with Boas about clarifying the fact that the fund was "a purely private venture and [had] nothing to do with the university."[51] A new letter would make it clear that the defense fund had no connection to the university or the faculty. In the words of Provost Macaulay, Boas agreed to do so "willingly and voluntarily."[52]

> It appears there was confusion in the minds of some concerning the origin of the movement to obtain funds for Mr. Lattimore's defense. . . .
>
> [Boas] agreed to send out another letter, to the same people to whom the first letter was sent, explaining that the

> Lattimore fund was his own individual project and was not a faculty enterprise.

Macaulay added that the Academic Council was in no way attempting to discipline Boas or to influence his thoughts or actions.[53]

It seemed to many faculty that the university had to do more to protect its good name and correct the false impression created by the Lattimore defense fund. President Bronk and other administrative officers were advised by more faculty than had previously volunteered their counsel on the Lattimore case to issue an immediate and forceful public disclaimer on behalf of the university.

An increasing number of faculty were by now openly expressing their unhappiness about the undue attention directed at the university. Their arguments had begun to sound much like those heard from members of the board of trustees. They were concerned that Lattimore's name was too often in the press, and invariably identified with Johns Hopkins. In their minds, Lattimore was fully to blame for this. A not insignificant number of the public had become convinced that a not insignificant number of faculty were left wing and involved in left-wing politics. Not only was correspondence directed to the administration, but the defense fund committee was also cautioned: "When you mention that you hope this fund would serve as a nucleus of a national fund, I am fearful that even more harm may be brought to the university by this publicity." Some faculty obviously felt that working in such a visible manner on behalf of Lattimore was not a proper faculty function: "I do hope you have discussed this matter with President Bronk."[54]

It was immediately evident that the effort to help Lattimore financially was far from universally popular on campus; a significant number found something about it—from its conception and design to its execution—to which to object. Although a success, which in the end came close to reaching its goal with over 1,600 contributors, a large number of whom were faculty, the tension it produced unnerved both its sponsors and critics.

The creation of the defense fund became news across the country, and it elicited a new wave of letters and postcards to the administration, to the committee, and to Boas.

> He and the rest of the Communists who have been sheltered by your faculty, have brought disgrace to the Johns Hopkins University.

> Having such men as Lattimore, Boas and many other Communists in that university just waiting to overthrow our government by violence should, as Senator McCarthy said, be investigated.[55]

> You are another pro-Communist [group] infiltrated into our country's educational system, a comrade and a buddy to that proven traitor and Communist, Lattimore. . . . One traitor helps another. You will be under investigation.

> Many thousands of sensible and loyal people have known for a long time that the Hopkins faculty is loaded and lousy with "Reds". . . .
>
> It is hoped that enough of you birds . . . to clear you all out, fumigate the university, and start all over with a clean, loyal faculty. . . . Even your facial expression and appearance has "Red" stamped all over it.[56]

More letters than not contained a metaphor, threat, or argument assuming or concluding guilt by association.

The moral entrepreneurs who, with the indictment, seemed on the verge of success launched another offensive against Lattimore. Notwithstanding the claim of the defense fund, they argued, Lattimore's freedom of speech and academic freedom were not being threatened. Boas and his associates were focusing on an irrelevant issue. In a nationally syndicated column, the reactionary journalist Fulton Lewis, Jr., explained it this way:

> It may be news to Owen Lattimore and his fellow faculty members of the Johns Hopkins University, but neither the school nor academic freedom is on trial as a result of his indictment by a federal grand jury.
>
> Lattimore was indicted for allegedly lying to the Senate Internal Security Subcommittee, on seven occasions, including one in which he denied ever promoting Communist party causes. The seven alleged lies are the only issues involved. . . .
>
> However, it should be made clear that free speech and academic freedom have nothing to do with a perjury trial, least of all this one.
>
> To my own personal knowledge Lattimore has uttered several million words since he was first called as a witness before the McCarran subcommittee of the senate. . . .[57]

Other columnists with an audience coast to coast (e.g., David Lawrence) and editorial writers around the country echoed these sentiments. This resulted, not unexpectedly, in letters to the university and the newspapers reiterating Lewis' point:

> *Attention—the President*
>
> Gentlemen:
>
> It is a shocking and terrifying thing to learn that even one member of your faculty would dare to defend a man like Owen Lattimore. It is even more shocking that any person of his caliber would be permitted on the faculty of any one of our universities, or our public schools. . . .
>
> The issues of academic freedom and free speech are not involved in our case against Owen Lattimore, Alger Hiss, and others like them. The issue is *freedom* for all of us, and these men have assigned themselves the task of taking our freedom from us, as they took freedom from China, and I pray God that soon our schools and universities will be rid of these so-called intellectuals. We thank God that they are a small minority. We have thousands of real intellectuals who also have *brains,* God bless them.[58]

> To the Editor of the *Evening Sun*—Sir: Dr. George Boas, a member of the faculty of the Johns Hopkins University, has started a movement, by means of a mimeographed letter, to raise a fund for the defense of Mr. Owen Lattimore in his approaching trial. . . .
>
> What are the facts in this matter? Mr. Lattimore requested permission of the McCarran committee to testify before it. The committee was of the opinion that in his testimony Mr. Lattimore was guilty of perjury and recommended that he be indicted.[59]

The contention that academic freedom and free speech were not in any way involved and that it was dishonest to suggest that they were—Lattimore was accused of perjury; nobody was attempting to muzzle him—was accepted without question with those predisposed to that view and was ignored by those who were not.

Boas was also involved in an effort to end the continuing and acrimonious debate over whether Lattimore was a reputable scholar or whether he was merely a clever propagandist. By 1953, the argument advanced by detractors of Lattimore that without

Besides this very public action, there were a number of reported "threatening" telephone calls to Harvard officials. In the end, another speaker shared the platform with Lattimore, and the forum itself seemed almost anticlimactic.

Closing the Page School

At about the same time Lattimore was indicted, the Johns Hopkins administration decided to proceed with a plan to close the Page School of International Relations and the Bowman School of Geography. The official explanation for this change was that it would simplify the academic structure of the Homewood campus; the closing was said to be part of a general reorganization incorporating institutes into academic departments. In trying to deflect any suggestion that there was a connection between the Lattimore case and discontinuing the unit which he directed, it was pointed out that the previous year the School of Business had been abolished and also noted that other plans to reorganize the university were being studied.[66]

The Academic Council appointed a special committee, consisting of representatives of the administration and faculty, to formulate recommendations regarding if, when, and how the Page and Bowman Schools should be eliminated. Working closely with Provost Macaulay in drafting his recommendations, the committee readily agreed with the administration's view that both units should not be continued as separate schools. It was felt that the Page School functioned more nearly as a research institute.

The statement in the committee's brief signed report explicitly stating that Lattimore would continue at the university as a "lecturer on Inner Asia with no other change in his status" was deleted in the proposal voted on by the board of trustees; it was "deferred," being "thought inappropriate" in light of the fact that he had been officially given leave until the question of his indictment was resolved.[67]

Not surprisingly, the university administration was very much concerned with how the action would look to the public, particularly with reference to the status of Lattimore. Accordingly, two days after the board acted Provost Macaulay wrote the university officer who dealt with such questions:

> I think the following would be an appropriate reply to the question "Where does this leave Lattimore?": The decision to

> abolish the Page School obviously abolishes the directorship. Since he came to the university, Mr. Lattimore has had the additional title of lecturer and his status with respect to that title is the same as that indicated in President Bronk's letter of December 16 to Lattimore.
>
> In accordance with our conversation, will you draft a preliminary statement for the press, letting me see it before it goes back to your file for possible use.[68]

It was over two months before the closing of the Page School was publicly announced. President Bronk's statement did not focus on Lattimore except to note that he "was informed some time ago that these changes were contemplated." Press reports reviewed in some detail the events that led to his indictment and the university's decision to place him on leave. As a matter of fact, these questions were given more attention than the closing itself.

As for Lattimore, shutting down the Page School was expected and not terribly upsetting, although certainly he forfeited some of the ease of access and information that heretofore he had enjoyed within the university. In response to an inquiry from a relative of Mark Twain, Cyril Clemens, whether "the closing of the school has particular significance" he responded:

> The closing of the Page School was something that had been contemplated for some time. It has never, in fact, been a school in more than name since there were not enough funds to provide a permanent staff of more than two. Nevertheless, the timing will of course be very widely taken as indicating a hand washing act by the administration of the university.[69]

The Price

The names of Lattimore and Johns Hopkins had for so long been so closely linked that the university at times received as much—or more—attention from the moral entrepreneurs, public, and press as he did. It was as if Johns Hopkins was under suspicion for aiding the Communist cause, had offended a congressional committee, had been accused of dishonesty, and must as a consequence face trial. More and more frequently the university was viewed as dangerous, as an institution that encouraged and committed wrongdoings, as a haven for disreputable persons. No one expressed the firm belief that Lattimore had done what he had done because he was at Johns

Hopkins or that Lattimore's misdeeds were the university's misdeeds, but other damaging misjudgments were current.

A lengthy editorial in the *Tulsa Tribune* in May 1953, for example, began by calling Lattimore "an infamous liar" who had been identified as such by a congressional committee and a grand jury. But it hardly concerned itself with Lattimore and what he had reputedly done. Its real subject was the Johns Hopkins University and its failings: "we have long contended that one of the things this Nation needs most is the injection of courage and the elimination of cowardice in our college presidents and trustees."

In great detail the editorial faulted the weakness and irresponsibility of the university's administration and board of trustees. Although they professed intellectual honesty, they were "timid and stupid." The academic profession as a whole was characterized as misguided, lacking rudimentary common sense. The editorial concluded with the charge that America has been betrayed by the professoriat:

> Our colleges are wonderful in their biological and chemical laboratories. They are heroic in their battles with the bugs. But when it comes to human betrayers, enemies of society, traitors to our country, they are cowardly and incompetent. They have developed the childish notion that the collection of academic degrees makes any man wise and worthy. . . .
>
> The indictment of Johns Hopkins' Lattimore is bringing the American public to a realization of how inadequate have been our pretentious colleges. . . .
>
> There was not one college president in the country, at Harvard or Yale, Johns Hopkins or any one of the great state colleges that was smart enough and brave enough to find the agencies of treason as McCarthy did. . . .
>
> In our colleges we have endowed consummate cowards and incompetents. And a lot worse than incompetent. . . .
>
> What is Detlev W. Bronk thinking of? Or is he thinking? He is president of Johns Hopkins. He is supposed to be the captain of the college. He and his trustees have retained this indicted liar on the college payroll. . . . [70]

Across the country the drumbeat of denunciation became shriller and more personal. The good name of the university had been severely and obviously tarnished. What was happening to the authorities at Johns Hopkins was instructive to administrators and governing boards at other colleges and universities: the reputations of the institution and its leaders were being damaged. For some, efforts at fair-mindedness and a reliance on due process were little more than evidence of moral failures. Holding to a principle had become a provocation or invitation for vilification. In light of this, it is hardly surprising, although no more defensible, that at the overwhelming majority of American institutions of higher learning during the Cold War years academic authorities decided not to stand by faculty who were under attack because of their political beliefs or activities.[71] It was certainly more expedient to capitulate. Anticipatory acquiescence—the punishment of controversial faculty even before politicians, the press, or the public demanded it—was even more effective.

The Lattimore case at Johns Hopkins was apparently teaching academic administrators at other colleges and universities a valuable, but perhaps unjustifiable, lesson: It might be costly to listen to faculty who are out of touch with the feelings of the American public and are impractical. Their advice serves the interests of an institution poorly and does not take economic realities into account. They might shortsightedly defend one of their own at the expense of the welfare of the institution. Not necessarily dispassionate, too many of them are too far to the Left and have an unhealthy proclivity for dissent. They can cause an institution problems which plague administrators. Their good will may be less valuable than the good will of a nationally syndicated columnist, a wealthy donor, or the local elite. While the displeasure of faculty is an irritant, the displeasure of a nationally syndicated columnist, a wealthy donor, or the local elite can be a danger to one's career. Look at the heavy price the authorities of Johns Hopkins are paying for not dismissing one individual, an individual of questionable morality, an expert in misdirection. Fair-mindedness and the reliance on due process may not have seemed worth it to the administration or the trustees, or to the university.

6

Restoration and Leave-Taking

Only true Lattimore partisans had not been worn down by his doggedness. The authorities at Johns Hopkins were not only weary but also skittish. They were not looking forward to another encounter with the moral entrepreneurs. When the final major point of resolution came, when there were no more obstacles to Lattimore returning to campus and the classroom, their reaction made it plain how, at least in their eyes, badly tarnished Lattimore's reputation was and how weakened his position on campus had become. Thus, in spite of the fact that the mood in the country was different in 1955 than in 1950, that events—Stalin was dead, the Korean War was over, a Republican was in the White House, Senator McCarthy had been censured by his colleagues—had lessened Cold War tensions and university officials had less need to be cautious, they vacillated and kept a comfortable distance from him. He was never given the benefit of the doubt. They were cool and formal. They induced him, but did not ask him, to leave.

The Question of Lattimore's Return

In June 1955, the circuit court of appeals, dividing evenly four to four, sustained Judge Youngdahl's decision that the amended counts of the indictment against Lattimore were too vague and indefinite to require him to stand trial. Less than two weeks later the government decided that it had pressed the issue far enough and dropped the remaining, minor charges. Lattimore was technically free to take up his academic duties at Johns Hopkins. The fact that Lattimore had not been found unambiguously innocent, the many questions that not actually having gone to trial raised, occasioned uncertainty about his culpability. The shadow over him had not disappeared. The response from the university was vague and reserved.

> [The] Johns Hopkins University officials yesterday had no comment to make on the decision of the federal government to drop its charges of perjury against Owen Lattimore.
>
> P. Stewart Macaulay, provost of the university, issued a "no comment" statement in the absence of Lowell J. Reed, [now the] university president, who is out of town. Carlyle Barton, President of the board of trustees, concurred.
>
> Mr. Lattimore was given leave of absence from his duties at the university on December 16, 1952.[1]

If there was a feeling of relief or elation on the part of any university official, it was not being made public. Quite the contrary.

What "to do with the status of Mr. Lattimore" once again became a signal problem at Johns Hopkins. The administration and board of trustees were no closer to extricating themselves from the problem and the unfavorable publicity than they had been five, or three, years earlier. The fear that Lattimore's return to campus would stir the moral entrepreneurs to action now haunted many more administrators and trustees. Events since Lattimore had been indicted had made university officials considerably more timid. During the senate hearings in 1950 and 1952 most did not fully realize how aroused some segments of the public would become, how aroused they could become. Few anticipated how much the university had stood to lose. Now there was an overriding desire to avoid the hue and cry and additional criticism. Trustees and others who had never supported Lattimore or who had been ambivalent about his remaining on the faculty were clearly less patient, most on edge, and were most likely to grumble publicly and sometimes loudly. They were not concerned that they might cause Lattimore pain; they seemed to believe, falsely, that what they said would not redound on the university. As they saw it, Lattimore had long ago worn out his welcome.

However, those convinced that it was time for Lattimore to leave the university had no blueprint for action. There was no consensus that he be terminated, and it was unlikely one could be forged and that this would happen. Moreover, it was not at all clear how to minimize faculty opposition and other unfavorable consequences should the university demand his resignation. There was much doubt regarding what would be the most appropriate steps to take and what might possibly happen. There was now significant dissatisfaction about what seemed to be an endless series of inauspicious events. There were many signs of frayed nerves. The only thing certain was that Lattimore would not be receiving the homecoming of someone who had been vindicated. His victory in the courts had not been decisive enough. His case had not really been heard. There was a widespread perception that he had avoided a trial due to legal technicalities. Those who had long pressed for his resignation from Johns Hopkins and those who had reached the conclusion that the university was regrettably stuck with him had now become a substantial majority.

The first matter of concern to university authorities after the news that Lattimore was no longer under indictment was how over the summer they should respond to inquiries from the press and others regarding his status. The decision by Board President Barton was that they would "give completely noncommittal answers to any questions which may be addressed to us."[2] The university would be very cautious.

In the days that followed, those who were to speak for the Johns Hopkins administration seemed to feel, and thought it important to convey the idea, that the university was free to take whatever course it felt was necessary and desirable. The university's position was that Johns Hopkins had no particular commitment to Lattimore, and that he had no legal hold on it. If it wanted, the board could reinstate him; however, it could decide not to do so or could take other steps. The university did not want to foreclose any options. With the summer recess to consider what would be in the best interests of the institution, the inference was that the university would, at least in part, let public opinion dictate its actions. The university seemed to be inviting more letters. Pointing out that they had the well-being of the university in mind, the authorities attempted to convey the impression that they would do what was necessary and appropriate, that the situation was well under control. Lattimore, of course, had a tenure appointment, although, judging from their comments, this did not seem to be material to a number of trustees. Others, however, understood that there were risks in terminating a faculty member holding a permanent appointment without cause. Even if a dismissal could be shown to be justifiable, hearings—and more public attention and unfavorable publicity—could not be avoided. Lattimore's tenure ensured that the university would not move against him unless it was prepared for a new fight with those committed to the principles of tenure and academic freedom.

Given that there were so many people away from campus over the summer and Board President Barton's belief that there would be no immediate unsettling new developments in the case, it was determined that it was not necessary for President Bronk's successor, Lowell J. Reed, to interrupt his vacation and return to Baltimore.[3] Reed, not as eminent a scientist as Bronk although credited with having developed with Raymond Pearl the mathematical formula for the logistic curve used in studying the growth of populations, was well trusted by the board. Since his first appointment at Johns Hopkins in 1918, he had been head of the Biostatistics Department, dean and director of the School of Hygiene and Public Health, and vice president in charge of medical activities. He would surely be able to monitor events from his summer home in New Hampshire, and would know what steps, if any, to take. If the university was pressed for information, the public would only be told that the board of trustees would act in due course. Despite the posturing, no one in authority seemed much interested in tackling the issue or making a decision. They only wanted to leave the impression that they did not lack the capacity to do so. Things would have to wait.

Lattimore had heard that the government intended to drop the case against him while traveling in Europe. Not expecting the Justice Department's decision so soon, he told the media that he was "very surprised and happy," although in true character added that the government "should have made the decision a very long time ago."[4] He had hardly been humbled by events.

Lattimore saw less need for caution than the university authorities, and immediately wrote to President Reed telling of his plans to return to the university before the beginning of the new term so that he might resume teaching. At the end of his letter he again emphasized that he would "be ready for teaching at the Hopkins at the beginning of October."

In the same letter, Lattimore suggested to President Reed that he could very possibly arrange an exchange with a scholar from Cambridge University.[5] It would thus be possible for him to extend his stay in England for a semester. A similar proposal had been made earlier, but had been rejected by university authorities on the grounds that Lattimore at that time had no official connection with Johns Hopkins, beyond continuing to draw his salary.

President Reed promptly responded, explaining to Lattimore that he was mistaken in assuming that he would automatically be reinstated in the fall. He reminded Lattimore that in an earlier conversation he had carefully pointed out that the board of trustees had placed him on leave and that it would have to decide if and when he could return to the faculty. Reed believed that the question would come up at a board meeting in the early fall, but made no promises or predictions about the outcome. He also coolly rejected the possibility of the exchange, reminding Lattimore that his status had in no way changed since this proposal had previously been rejected.[6]

President Reed telephoned Board President Barton, informed him about the letter he had received from Lattimore, and read him his reply. As an indication that he was being as firm with Lattimore as some board members wished, he immediately followed this up with a letter to Barton and to at least one other trustee, reiterating what he had said on the telephone.[7] As the university administration and board of trustees saw it, it was self-serving and presumptuous of Lattimore to believe that he could simply begin teaching without them first acting, without being invited to resume his academic duties. Yet, it would not be inconsistent with his style just to show up at the beginning of the semester and challenge them to resist his attempt to do so. Such a possibility became an overriding concern. As one board member put it:

> [I]t would be entirely characteristic of him to take all this for granted rather than to feel that the formal action of the trustees must be rescinded before he would have the right to return.[8]

It was now becoming clear to the entire board that it could create as much of a furor to respond negatively as positively to Lattimore's wish to normalize his faculty appointment.

Some of the worst fears of those suspicious of Lattimore's motives seemed to be realized when it was falsely reported in the press that he had been publicly stating that he expected to be lecturing at Johns Hopkins in the fall. This news perturbed and angered not only university authorities, but a number of alumni, benefactors, and people across the country who believed that his innocence had not in any way been established, and that his association with the university blackened its reputation. Many were convinced that his insistence that he continue teaching at Johns Hopkins was perverse. Why didn't he just go away? Why did he persist in making the claim? Surely, he must realize how much trouble he had caused—and would continue to cause. He was badly hurting the university, and if he cared about it, and not only about his own welfare, he would not want the association to continue.

The Johns Hopkins authorities stood firm to the oft-repeated position that Lattimore's suspension was indefinite, and intentionally so. The university had wanted to know how the case would be resolved in the courts; there was now a feeling that it had not really been resolved. The board was determined that it alone should decide if and when Lattimore would return to his normal duties. It was made more resistant and resentful by the assumption that it should drop the matter as had the courts and the government. There was some pressure on the administration that Lattimore's leave of absence be ended so that he could take up his normal duties.

TELEGRAM

> President
> Johns Hopkins University
>
> I am waiting along with all Americans of good will and understanding the announcement of Mr. Lattimore's return to your faculty which will bring added honor to you and Johns Hopkins.[9]

It was not, however, overwhelming, and it was generally ignored. The authorities would not be stampeded, at least not by Lattimore's supporters. They would not be coerced; some were indignant and they most fiercely resisted such efforts.

Few board members believed that the university owed Lattimore anything; there was little evidence that he had ever acted with its interests in mind. Even his defenders acknowledged that he had not shown particular loyalty to the welfare of the university in the past. More than a small fraction of the members of the board had come to believe that Lattimore was self-centered and arrogant, that he was totally selfish. The fact that he had not resigned and saved the university from no end of difficulty seemed proof enough to support this conclusion. The fact that he was shamefully attempting to force his way back in before being asked was additional support. He could not see beyond his own wishes. More and more university officials were blaming Lattimore for being asked to defend his loyalty.

The Board's Decision to Meet

To avoid a showdown and unfavorable publicity, it was decided that the matter of Lattimore's reinstatement should be taken up by the full board at a special meeting at an early date, preferably well before its regularly scheduled October meeting. It was quickly agreed that the board could meet in September prior to the start of classes "so as finally to dispose of this troublesome problem."[10]

Board President Barton was circumspect in his replies to letters suggesting what course the board should take. He said little or simply that the university had persuaded the newspapers "not to quote any university officials as to the future relations with Mr. Lattimore." Even after he knew of the newly set time for the board meeting, and that the matter would be decided that day, he told those to whom he wrote that the next meeting of the board would not be until late October.[11]

The purpose of the special board meeting was never made public. Initially, the business at hand was not even disclosed to some members of the board. A story was put out that the meeting was called to discuss the expansion of the physical plant. Even in the announcement of the meeting, the agenda was not specified, it was only said that "[t]here will be several important matters which the board of trustees should consider."[12] On August 25, formal notice of the meeting was mailed. There was still no mention of the "main business . . . [what] to do with the status of Mr. Lattimore."[13]

> Dear Dr. Reed:
>
> The president of the board has called a special meeting of the board of trustees of the Johns Hopkins University for Friday, September 9, 1955 at 2 p.m. in the board room of Alex. Brown & Sons, Baltimore and Calvert Streets, Baltimore.
>
> This special meeting is called for the purpose of receiving interim reports from several committees of the trustees, and also for the purpose of considering and acting upon matters incidental to the financing and construction of the dormitory for the medical institutions, technical changes in the Applied Physics Laboratory and Operations Research Office pension plans, and other matters requiring attention in advance of the opening of the university for the fall term.
>
> I would appreciate it if you would return the enclosed card advising me whether or not you expect to attend the meeting.[14]

In preparation for the meeting, President Reed was asked by Board President Barton to determine "the views of some of the key members of the faculty" on the best course of action regarding

Lattimore so that he could report them to the assembled trustees. Reed was told that the board would also want his own recommendations, and that it would not "be seriously concerned" about the principle of tenure.[15] Barton related that one board member, reporting on conversations he had had with two or three faculty members with whom he was on close terms, had become convinced that it would be a serious mistake to terminate Lattimore. This annoyed Barton, who believed that it was a violation of the bylaws of the board for faculty members to communicate with trustees on university policy. If faculty had anything to tell trustees, they were to go through the university president.[16]

At the same time, Barton very much wished to avoid creating what he called "a faculty problem." Nonetheless, he was prescient in his belief that "whatever we do will cause a trustee problem."

In a handwritten letter to President Reed, the vice president of the board (Charles S. Garland) specified a number of items that he hoped would be explored during the discussion about Lattimore, and asked the president to begin compiling a wide array of information. Among the questions he addressed to the president were: "As he is not a professor, what kind of tenure does he have?" "Is it a fact that there exists a written agreement re: tenure and what is its legal force?" "How valid is tenure vis à vis incompetence, or internal administrative changes, etc.?" "What is your appraisal of [negative] tangible reaction—or positive tangible action—if he were to be separated?" "Would it [the reaction] be of long or permanent duration or the subject of immediate furor soon forgotten?" "If he were to be separated with full salary (say until July 1, 1956) would he, in your opinion, cause trouble, legal or publicity-wise, or would he handle it well?" "Just what was his status and status of his department five years ago versus today?" "If he were to leave, could [the] same courses be offered—and how vital are these courses to the whole scheme of things?" "Has he been a satisfactory—or brilliant—member of the faculty?" "How many students elect his courses, and has that number been increasing or on the wane?"[17] These were surely not questions that would be asked about a faculty member a university believed merited an appointment and was eager to keep. They were also not questions that someone who knew a moderate amount about institutions of higher learning, in general, or the Johns Hopkins University, in particular, would ask. They seemed posed with the intention of casting about for detailed information to justify a prejudgment. The answers could be used to support any decision the board was inclined toward or might actually take.

The inference that individuals should curtail their freedom of speech and freedom of association is but one indication that the

Lattimore case was making people on campus more peevish and was threatening to negatively affect heretofore mutually respectful relationships between faculty, administrators, and trustees.

Cross Talk

A number of distinguished and vocal faculty had as decided and strong views as those with formal authority on how the Lattimore case should be concluded by the university. As far as they were concerned, Lattimore should be promptly reinstated and the matter should just as promptly be closed. Not to do so would compromise the principles the university had stood by in not firing Lattimore in the first place—academic freedom, innocence until proven guilty, faculty autonomy and freedom of speech—and do irreparable harm to the university's reputation. The historian C. Vann Woodward, conveyed the thought that he was

> puzzled and apprehensive that a false step at this critical juncture might forfeit all the painfully earned good will and applause the university has received by weathering the five-year crisis and sticking by the man under attack.

Some faculty further believed that there was an obligation to someone who was in difficulty and in need of help. To their minds, the duty to Lattimore and the duty to press the university for an immediate and positive resolution were not in conflict. In fact, quite the contrary. Woodward asked the chairman of the History Department, Sidney Painter, if there were informed and influential faculty on campus during the summer who could "save the president and trustees from doing something stupid." The issue was quite simple, and no one better than faculty understood how a university should respond. The faculty had a responsibility to see that Lattimore received fair treatment, that is, that he be reinstated. Other tests were unnecessary. Other indignities were unworthy:

> If there are a couple of soreheads among the trustees then they will have to be told what the score is by someone with the courage to speak his mind.

If the university were to terminate Lattimore "a grave blunder will be committed" that would "reflect less credit and do more harm to the university than did the original affair."[18]

This groundswell prompted Painter to write to President Reed to clarify how faculty who had communicated with him viewed the situation, what they believed the university's needs were, and what they would like to see done. In his letter he urged President Reed to restore Lattimore "to active duty as quickly as possible," although, he noted, he had personally "disapproved" of Lattimore's initial appointment at Johns Hopkins and had found "various things" in Lattimore's testimony before the McCarran committee that "added to my doubts that Owen belongs on a university faculty." At the same time, he argued that Lattimore had been granted tenure, that no one had proved that he had done anything to justify dismissal, and that he had served the university well: "In short, Owen was given tenure and he seems to me to have fulfilled his part of such an arrangement." There were other considerations mentioned by Painter: "a failure to do this would have disastrous results to both the university as an institution and its prestige in the scholarly world." He also repeated his offer that the History Department would accept Lattimore as a faculty member with the rank of lecturer.[19]

Other faculty wrote directly to President Reed. Fritz Machlup communicated from Japan the observations that:

> The board of trustees gave Lattimore a leave when the government obtained an indictment against him; they [*sic*] ought to terminate the leave when the government asked for dismissal of the charges. The board was quite prompt in the first action; they [*sic*] ought to be just as prompt in the second action, regardless of vacations.
>
> I sincerely believe that a delay in the termination of the leave would be unfair to Lattimore, embarrassing to the faculty, and infelicitous for the reputation of the university in academic circles. The university has gained great respect among scholars when the trustees acted so judiciously in 1952 and avoided passing judgment on a member of the faculty. A delay in terminating the case after the government has done so might be interpreted, wrongly I trust, as implying that the trustees do have some hesitations and, thus, have after all prejudged the case.[20]

Others also had advice for President Reed:

> . . . and I presume Mr. Lattimore will return to "active duty" on the faculty in the fall. But it has occurred to me that, since

> the abolition of the Page School, Mr. Lattimore may find himself without a home base on the faculty. Speaking as one alumnus, therefore (with the well-known propensity of alumni for butting into university affairs), I should like to suggest that Mr. Lattimore be advanced to a professorship from his present anomalous status as lecturer, a professorship perhaps in Far Eastern history.
>
> In that way, the students of Johns Hopkins could again avail themselves of a noted scholar's knowledge of a crucial area of the globe. . . .
>
> Again, may I congratulate Johns Hopkins on its courageous stand throughout the *cause célèbre,* and on the happy result.[21]

The continuing debate caused Lattimore and his defenders considerable worry. One of his attorneys, Thurman Arnold, telephoned the AAUP national headquarters and requested an interview with its incoming general secretary, a professor of law at Indiana University, and its acting general secretary, who had the task of looking into incidents in which a faculty member's job might be threatened. Arnold was concerned about more than the resistance Lattimore was encountering; he suspected the "possibility [of] dismissal by abolition [of] his position."[22] Given the sense of urgency, arrangements were quickly made "to discuss the situation resulting from the withdrawal of legal charges against Owen Lattimore."

At the meeting a week and a half later, Arnold began by stating that he and Lattimore were "disturbed" that the curt reply to Lattimore's letter to President Reed indicating he would like to begin teaching as soon as possible "might forecast Lattimore's dismissal when the board meets. . . ." He wanted to know what action, if any, the AAUP would be willing to take. George Boas, who had been invited to the interview, felt that there was no reason for alarm, since the faculty committee appointed to advise university authorities on the matter was certain to recommend that Lattimore be retained and returned to duty. The others present were mollified by Boas' assurance that most of the trustees would be "disposed to this action." It was decided that the only sensible stand was to hold to the assumption "that Lattimore has a bona fide leave of absence, and that there is no question of his not returning to duty."

Arnold and Boas put forward a plan for soliciting contributions for the university in the "immediate future" as "a substantial symbol of the long-range advantage that would accrue" for its "courageous and academically correct course of conduct." This would presumably counterbalance the possible loss of contributions from those who might be enraged should Lattimore be reinstated:

> Professor Boas will write to those contributors to the Lattimore defense fund who stated that they would contribute again if necessary, and will suggest that, since contributions to this fund are no longer needed, money which would have been given for this purpose might be given directly to the university. Judge Arnold indicated that his firm would make a substantial contribution, and he and his partner, Mr. Porter, who joined the conference, agreed that they could and would communicate with other possible donors.

The discussion ended with the AAUP being asked if it could issue a statement of "appreciation" for support given to Lattimore by the administration of the university. It was pointed out that the officers of the organization did not have the authority to do so, and that no action could be taken until its council met, which would be some time after the Johns Hopkins board took a decision with regard to Lattimore. It was explained that the AAUP had no role to play unless Johns Hopkins took action adverse to Lattimore's tenure. Until his appointment was disturbed, the Lattimore case was strictly an institutional problem.[23]

As the date for the September board meeting approached, a range of arguments about Lattimore—from unqualified support to ominous predictions in the event of his not being fired—were heard from all quarters. No one body—faculty, administrators, or trustees—spoke with a single voice.

A common argument of those opposed to Lattimore was that he had not been acquitted and that the indictment alone indicated that he was not the sort of individual who should be on the faculty of Johns Hopkins. Correspondence to the university asked, among other things, how the board "in all conscience" could continue Lattimore on the faculty. The trustees were asked to transcend the difficulties in "taking the proper course of action" with "courage and acceptance of their responsibilities."[24]

Newspaper editorials pointed out that although the suit for perjury was withdrawn, Lattimore was still charged by the McCarran committee with being "a conscious, articulate instrument of the Soviet conspiracy" and giving false testimony. That question had not been adjudicated. The influential *Chicago Tribune* reminded its readers that Lattimore had in no way been exonerated:

> Thus Prof. Lattimore is today freed of all jeopardy so far as the courts are concerned. He will not have to stand trial for perjury. He is in no danger of being sent to prison for giving false testimony.
>
> But in another and much more important sense, Prof. Lattimore will not escape judgment. The record is extensive. It is found in the 14 volumes of testimony taken by the McCarran committee.
>
> Lattimore himself was on the stand for 12 days. The committee before which he appeared was composed of three Democrats and two Republicans and was therefore controlled by the party which had reason to defend the Democratic administration under which Lattimore had flourished. He was given greater latitude in his testimony than any witness within memory. He was permitted to denounce the committee and to answer evasively. Anyone who has read the record cannot but be struck with the contrast between the forbearance of the committee and its counsel on the one hand and the vituperative quality of the witness on the other.
>
> Lattimore will not go to jail for perjury, but the unanimous judgment of the committee about his role in the sellout of China to the Communists will stand for all time. . . . [T]hese conclusions are inescapable.[25]

The only matter everyone agreed upon was that it was all very exasperating. The patience of many had been thoroughly tested. As one trustee put it: "It will be a great relief to get this matter behind us for all time."[26]

At the same time, another trustee wrote President Reed about rumors he had been hearing that there might be plans to terminate Lattimore at the September meeting. He felt that there should be no action or even recommendation before giving Lattimore an opportunity to be heard. Reed was reminded that it would also be necessary to tell Lattimore what he was being charged with so that he could prepare a defense.

> I certainly would hope that no desire to attain an immediate objective would lead any responsible governing board of the Johns Hopkins University to take precipitous action which would ignore these fundamental principles of fair dealing. . . .

> I am writing you this letter because I am disturbed about the possibility of an ill considered runaway action which might either hurt the reputation of the university or result in an undue amount of unfavorable publicity, or both.[27]

Yet, before the September board meeting, this was probably a minority position among the trustees. Comments by the vice president of the board to President Reed seem better to reflect the sentiment of the trustees prior to the meeting.

> I believe this question [of Lattimore] must be discussed purely from an internal academic standpoint, with proper consideration to tenure, fairness, etc.—but, one man should not be permitted to affect adversely an entire university with all its ramifications, without full and just cause. . . .
>
> [A]s I sit here today, I am very much inclined to the position that our proper action is to find the means of having him separated from the university as painlessly as possible. . . .
>
> Last evening, Jack McCloy [the banker, (president of the World Bank and chairman of Chase Manhattan) and diplomat (High Commissioner for Germany)] and I spent several hours together and he gave me permission to say that in the absence of various data, he agreed with the conclusion expressed above.
>
> He feels more strongly than I do that the trustees must not be intimidated by tenure—we must do what we think is best for the university as a whole—and if a man has lost his effectiveness, some proper steps should be taken.[28]

One day before the September board meeting the eight-man committee, the Bard committee, which had been appointed in the spring of 1952 to advise the president on the Lattimore case unanimously agreed "that he should now be restored to the full exercise of academic functions." In its very brief report the committee also expressed the belief "that a very large majority of the members of the faculties of the university are of the same opinion."[29] This argument, rooted in faculty sentiment, was to prevail.

The Trustee's Action and Reaction

At the September meeting, Board President Barton stated that he had called the special session "for the purpose of having the trustees express their views as to the future position of the university as to Mr. Owen Lattimore." He added that the matter had not been mentioned in the notice "for publicity reasons."

President Reed reviewed the entire situation at considerable length and recommended that since the matter had originally been handled by the administration, the board should take no action other than refer it back. He related that he had discussed developments with a number of faculty and that they and he were of the opinion that the interests of the university would best be served in ending Lattimore's leave of absence and having him return to the History Department as a lecturer at his present salary. President Reed's proposal clouded the board's participation in the decision to reinstate Lattimore, and it strongly endorsed the recommendation with only two members voting in the negative.[30]

In a letter to one of the two dissenting trustees, Board President Barton agreed that Lattimore was not "fit" to be on the faculty, and allowed that a material reason the board was correct in voting as it did was the fact that the trustees would never have succeeded "in explaining to the public that we had let him go because of his bad manners and not because of our belief in the correctness of the charges which were abandoned." The management of public relations was what worried Barton the most:

> We would have undesirable publicity had the board of trustees exercised its legal power and insisted that he be dropped. The entire academic world would have been against us on principle and we might have been forced into the position in which we would have had to make charges and given him the opportunity to reply. I am confident that Lowell Reed's advice, based on his great knowledge of academic thinking and procedure, was sound and that we took the proper course in referring the matter to him.[31]

In a second letter to the same trustee the following week, Barton recalled a conversation they had had in which he expressed the opinion that, quite apart from the question of guilt or innocence on the charge of lying under oath, Lattimore should be dismissed because of the manner in which he let the university become involved in his public fight. Ironically, his misgivings about the Johns Hopkins University receiving any notoriety led him in the end to favor Lattimore's retention.

> I can only say to you that I changed my mind after talking with Lowell Reed and became convinced that the interests

> of the university will best be served by the procedure which he recommended. This was hard to swallow, but I am still convinced that it was better than continued unpleasant publicity and the effort to avoid a hearing if we had dismissed Lattimore and if he demanded a hearing and had been supported by the faculty in such a demand. . . .
>
> The publicity incident to Lattimore's relations with the Johns Hopkins University, including the fiction as well as the facts, has been extremely harmful to the university and annoying to all of us; I believe that we have followed the course best calculated to end it.[32]

Barton's views were shared by most trustees. As they saw it, they did not have a great deal of choice. They agreed that what they did was the most unobtrusive way to end the debate. On the whole they were fairly well pleased with the handling of the Lattimore case and with the outcome. They were particularly pleased that they would not have to find a solution to what to do about Lattimore or concern themselves with him anymore. Happily, the problem had been assumed by President Reed and his administration, and was out of their hands. They were grateful for this. They were pleased that Lattimore would be moving to the History Department, which they understood to be headed by "about one of the most conservative and distinguished members of the faculty." The fact that the chairman was a conservative was particularly reassuring.

In an exchange of letters with his fellow trustee Francis White who had not long before been posted as ambassador to Mexico, John Nelson gave his assessment of the September board meeting and expressed the opinion that although it was against their "best hopes and wishes" the trustees concluded that it would be a mistake to fire Lattimore: "[T]his is all that could be done at the present time." Nelson agreed with Barton's observation that most trustees had become convinced that if they took any action against Lattimore one sure consequence would be a new round of unwanted publicity, with Lattimore ending up as a "martyr." He had fought Senators McCarthy and McCarran; he would surely fight the board.

Nelson also expressed the belief that in hindsight White was right in his efforts to dismiss Lattimore immediately after the McCarran committee hearings, and the majority of the trustees and the administration were wrong in opposing the plan. He placed the blame for the reluctance to take decisive action with former President Bronk. As he saw it, "Bronk was never on our team," and he hoped that will be given full consideration in selecting the next president.

I feel that if [Isaiah] Bowman [who preceded Bronk as president] had been on the job, he would have handled the situation in accordance with our general views, but after all, these university presidents have their strength and weakness in different directions and it is so difficult to get someone who has all the characteristics necessary to qualify as president of the university.

Nelson was optimistic that Lattimore would soon be gone. He believed that because he had few friends on the faculty, Lattimore would be socially isolated and "that the faculty will finally eliminate him." In a postscript he raised the possibility, about which he expressed his own doubts, that Lattimore would be insulted by and not accept a lesser position in the History Department and would quit in anger.[33]

Ambassador White was in agreement with Nelson's general assessment of the situation.

I think the matter of Lattimore has been handled as well as, and in fact the only way, it could be handled under the present circumstances. I was, of course, bitterly disappointed that we did not get rid of him when we could as I proposed, but in the light of present circumstances, I see nothing else that could have been done.[34]

In the end, only one trustee, Jacob France, resigned over the decision not to terminate Lattimore. Claiming his decision was "based entirely on a careful, earnest and diligent study I have made of the record and opinion of the McCarran committee," he was adamantly opposed to Lattimore's politics and character, and to giving him a forum to teach. He believed that Lattimore was not the type of person who should be on the faculty of Johns Hopkins.

The students of the Johns Hopkins University are leaders of the future. They should be trained to love their country—love and respect our form of government and those whose duties it is to administer our laws and to come to the defense of our form of government when it is threatened by people who would destroy it. They know, or should know, the history of each and every professor. The conduct, activities and writings

> of Owen Lattimore are not such as to set a good example for students of the university.[35]

Board President Barton's wariness about unnecessary publicity was behind his decision to wait two months before announcing the resignation of his colleague. As he wrote to President Reed:

> I have not mentioned the matter to anyone other than you and I do not think that any of us should talk about it until the board meets in January.
>
> We seem to have been spared further publicity in so far as Lattimore himself is concerned, and we do not wish to stir it up from the other side.[36]

The reporting of the board's decision in the press was perfunctory, limited, and somewhat inaccurate. This matter-of-fact coverage was in marked contrast to the sensationalism in the past. Even before he was formally invited to return, news stories reported Lattimore as being "back on the job"[37] and "again lecturing at Johns Hopkins." In one account carried on the wire services, a university spokesman is quoted as saying that Lattimore's return to active status "was automatic."[38]

Those convinced that Lattimore was malevolent, someone against whom the country needed protection, were not unexpectedly angered by the board's decision.

> Dear Dr. Reed,
>
> I see by the news journals that Johns Hopkins has reinstated that foxy character, Owen Lattimore.
>
> Thus does the Biblical Dog return to its vomit.
>
> Candidly yours[39]

The rancor was directed at the university authorities more than at Lattimore. The administration and trustees were again pictured as weak, unpatriotic, and uncaring and Lattimore was seen as an evil sorcerer with a hold over them. (Moral entrepreneurs commonly attribute great power to those with whom they are in collision.) The outcry, however, lacked the fervor the university had come to expect, and by itself did not cause misgivings.

Lattimore's Return—and Its Conditions

A week after the board's decision on Lattimore, President Reed wrote him asking about his plans with regard to returning to Baltimore. He noted that the two should meet "at as early a date as possible . . . for a discussion of your situation."[40]

Lattimore immediately answered, saying that he would be arriving in Baltimore after he had visited a new grandchild in New Haven, Connecticut.

> Unless I hear from you here in Copenhagen, at the above address, or in New Haven . . . that an earlier appointment is desirable I shall plan to reach Baltimore on Monday, October 3, and will hope to see you soon thereafter.

He added that he realized the lack of a clear statement by Johns Hopkins after the charges against him had collapsed "must be proving increasingly embarrassing" to Reed.[41] His letter was friendly; at the same time, Lattimore's spirit clearly had not been subdued. He seemed unaware of how thin the thread was that held him to the university.

In reply, President Reed reiterated how "anxious" he was to talk with Lattimore "at the earliest possible moment." He invited Lattimore to his home for dinner and "an opportunity for discussion" the evening of his return or, if that were impossible, to come to his office at 8:30 the following morning. Since he was so eager to explain matters to Lattimore and set the conditions of his return before Lattimore made other contacts and drew other conclusions, he agreed to hold both times open until Lattimore decided which time would be more convenient.[42] Lattimore accepted the dinner invitation.[43]

In a memorandum for the record, President Reed wrote that at the beginning of his interview with Lattimore he quoted the action of the board and told Lattimore that before Reed proceeded to act under his authorization he needed to be assured that Lattimore truly desired to return to academic work. As Reed recalled, when Lattimore was informed that he would be appointed as a lecturer in the History Department he objected, stating that when he was given the title of Director of the Page School it was stated that this was equivalent to the rank of professor. President Reed denied knowing anything of such an arrangement, and asserted that he would not support it. He was firm in insisting that Lattimore return to the university as a lecturer at the same salary he was being paid before his leave of absence.

According to President Reed, much of the discussion focused on the "emotional character" of Lattimore's efforts to clear his name. President Reed emphasized the necessity of Lattimore in presently "getting out of such an atmosphere and into the atmosphere of academic work." He warned Lattimore that some of the requests he would receive to speak and write would not be "thoroughly genuine in their academic quality"; they would come for "reasons of notoriety." Only Lattimore could "sort the true from the false." In effect he would have to be his own censor.

President Reed reported that he declined Lattimore's offer to have the university administration review each invitation that came across his desk. It would be up to Lattimore to pass on such academic questions; he was expected "to use good judgment and show good taste in matters of this sort." Lattimore was reminded that he could always seek advice from colleagues. Lattimore expressed to President Reed his wish to remove himself from the limelight; he simply wanted to return to academic work. He would accept the compromise.

When Lattimore finally agreed that he "desired" to return to the university as a lecturer in the History Department, President Reed suggested that the two of them meet with his new department chairman "in order that I might make the action with regard to [Lattimore's] return definite." The three met the next morning to review the understanding that had been reached between President Reed and Lattimore.[44]

It was clear that Lattimore was less anxious about the problems surrounding his return to the university than were President Reed and other administrative officers and some trustees. His son's career and family and a head cold that had plagued his wife on her return from Europe were of greater concern. In a convivial letter to his son after his arrival in Baltimore he casually and almost ironically described his conversation with the president.

> Dear Dave,
>
> Well, we made it, and here we are at home. We had a brief but satisfying glimpse of New Babby, which would have been more satisfying if Eleanor had not had a dreadful cold, which prevented her from getting too close. In fact Eleanor spent one whole day in bed, over at the Reynolds. We've never seen Emmy more beautiful. The new hairdo is ravishing. She looks so well that I'm sure when she goes back to the hospital they'll find nothing serious to worry about. Mike and Maria were as engaging as ever. Mike has the world in focus and knows what's what. He told us that you were in Ithaca to find a nice new house, and he told E over the phone to stay in bed and not get up until the doctor told her to.

Last night I had dinner *à deux* with Pres. Reed. Briefly, he wants to restore me to duty; lecturer; History Dept., and would love it if I would stick my head in a bucket and never give any public lectures. Scared to death of local irreconcilables and "unfavorable publicity." I pointed out there is such a thing as being so bemused with parochial "public relations" that you lose sight of the real issues of the Hopkins' good repute in the Nation and the world. Well, we'll see how things work out.

INTERRUPTION

At this point a call from Reed. Went in for interview with him and Painter, of Hist. Dept. Upshot: I am now back on duty. Lecturer (but with tenure; not subject to yearly appointment) in History Dept. One lecture course this term: China in History (subject of my new book for Oxford Univ. Press). First lecture a week from tomorrow.

So that's us. Now about you.

We'd like to come up and help you with house hunting; or if you have already hunted a house, with moving, or whatever. In view of work here, I *might* not be able to come, though I'd like to. Eleanor could come anyway, any time. But before either or both of us see you, there's an idea that you might want to think over, as a subject of discussion. From a long distance, in Europe, we've been trying to think of your problems. Our thinking may be way off the beam, because of sketchy data. On the other hand we may have thought of things that you just haven't been able to get around to, because you've had your nose right up against the grindstone.

What we've been thinking is that for several years now you have been living under pretty severe pressures. Not immediate pressures, that force instant crises and prompt, major decisions, but pressures that hover in the background—sketchy income, small children, crowded quarters, part time work, intermittent study, conditions under which it is impossible to schedule an orderly working day, foresee what can be done in a month, or budget a year's work and accomplishment. Such pressures can be pervasive and insidiously exhausting. It seems to us that after your very difficult summer you must be bone tired, and perhaps more hard pressed than you realize by your growing family responsibilities and problems. This coming year is also bound to be a tough one for Emmy, even without the added difficulty of your being overworked and over tired and always torn between wanting to help her and

> wanting to get on with your work and needing some time to yourself.[45]

Lattimore's attitude here supports those who on more than one occasion argued that his commitment to Johns Hopkins was less than Johns Hopkins' commitment to him. His failure to show what others believed was adequate institutional loyalty had become for administrative officers and as time passed for more and more of his colleagues the focus of criticism. University authorities seemed determined to have him become a better campus citizen. Given Lattimore's background, this was unlikely. As he and the public had never been permitted to forget, he had not been trained in a university. He was to some degree an outsider.

Lattimore was more a public intellectual, writing for an educated public on public issues, than an academic specialist. He was a well-published author who also had an academic appointment. This gave him a different perspective than that of most academic men. It was precisely because he was involved in public discourse that he had been targeted in the first place. Most academics know that professional activities or even teaching, for that matter, do not as a general rule get faculty in trouble. Public controversy does, and that is, as most academics know, something that should be avoided. However, by the nature of their work, keeping out of the limelight is difficult for public intellectuals.

What to Lattimore was an appropriate response fed the perception that he was determinedly obtuse regarding the injury that had been inflicted on Johns Hopkins. It was said that under the circumstances most professors would have shown more institutional loyalty, would have worked harder to reduce the university's cost, or at least shown a modicum of regret. Lattimore appeared almost casual about his obligations and this was incomprehensible to many.

The Aftermath

Lattimore's return to Johns Hopkins brought letters and comment. Compared to other events in the previous five years that attracted public interest, this time the total number of both was quite a bit smaller, as was the ratio of the unfavorable to the favorable.

Some alumni were disappointed, and gifts were lost:

> I have tried to contribute each year to the Hospital Roll Call, but feel that I cannot continue as long as the university

returns a traitor as a teacher, namely, *Owen Lattimore*. I had hoped that he would not again be put on the faculty but such is not the case. It is true that he was cleared by a Judge Youngdahl, but he too is of the same color and no credit to our country.

The university is making a very great mistake in rehiring Mr. Lattimore.[46]

The resistance to Lattimore's resuming his academic duties largely focused on the fact that undergraduates would be exposed to him:

> I understand that *Owen Lattimore* is now reinstated as an active professor—which means *teacher* of young people—in your university. Yet, in a widely circulated book, *McCarthy and His Enemies,* such serious implications are printed against *Mr. Lattimore* that it would seem that they *must* be answered if not true. Yet, I have not heard your answer, or Mr. Lattimore's. Have I missed something?[47]

> Dear Sir:
>
> Regret not knowing your name but that does not stop many of us from regretting you have seen fit to reinstate Owen Lattimore on your staff. Surely you do not believe a man of his principles and character should have any position where he can mold character. Believe me I am not in the minority deploring this reinstatement. Get rid of him.[48]

Individuals who approved of the board's decision also related their views to the administration:

> Only recently I read, in an out of the way corner of my newspaper, about Owen Lattimore's return to your campus, vindicated after his long ordeal. I also learned what I had not known; that he was kept on the Hopkins payroll and professor roll throughout the ordeal.
>
> Accordingly I am proud and happy to hail you and your university for its steadfast faith. I am just a bit troubled because this event has not brought more public acclaim to you and him. Perhaps it has, but I missed it in the news. Public acclaim or no, it is heart-warming and faith-renewing. Here then sir is a toast to you and your great university. Long life and success![49]

> Your diplomatic handling of the Lattimore case is praiseworthy.
>
> As a New Zealand university graduate, I feel the stand you took, by not debasing a fellow colleague and intellectual, is ethically sound and most commendable.
>
> The Pacific area has looked aghast upon the McCarran-McCarthy rantings.
>
> Information regarding the above was garnered from the editorial column of last evening's paper—as per attached.[50]

From a public relations standpoint, the board's action proved undoubtedly correct. Lattimore's arrival on campus was uneventful; an editorial in a campus publication described it as having happened "quietly and without commotion."

> The Far Eastern expert and his case became in the recent turbulent years a necessary symbol of the strong and righteous sentiment against the McCarthy redwash techniques. But McCarthy is politically dead, at least on a national level, and the anti-symbol is no longer a necessity. It is too much to hope that the McCarthy ideals of bluster and bluff and intimidation are dead along with their most recent United States champion, but at any rate they are slumbering. Unfortunately, they will without doubt rise again, but when they do there will be other anti-symbols to combat them and eventually rouse a sluggish public to its ethical senses.
>
> For Mr. Lattimore, the windowed existence is over—or it should be. The man is primarily a lecturer and a student of the Far East, and he should now be allowed to make his contribution to the Hopkins and society in those comparatively unemotional fields.[51]

Not surprisingly, the board's action was nearly universally praised on campuses across the country. The attention in the press was mostly favorable. Outside of Baltimore the news stories reporting it were factual and relatively brief. An editorial in the *St. Louis Post-Dispatch* commending the faculty and administration, but not the board of trustees of the university, was reprinted in newspapers around the country and overseas.

> A UNIVERSITY STOOD FIRM
>
> Had the faculty and administration of the Johns Hopkins University scared easily, they might have been stampeded into hasty and irrevocable action in the case of Owen Latti-

> more. When first Senator McCarthy, and then Senator McCarran, and then the Truman administration's Department of Justice, and then the Eisenhower administration's Department of Justice, undertook to brand Professor Lattimore a Communist agent and perjurer, a certain corporate fortitude was required for Lattimore's university to withstand the pressure to fire him.
>
> Johns Hopkins did withstand the pressure. After he had been legally indicted, the university placed Lattimore on leave with pay until his case could be legally disposed of. It never prejudged his case, never equated an accusation with a conviction, never bowed to the storm of popular hysteria.
>
> The storm has moderated now. . . . The United States government has secured the dismissal of its case against him. And Johns Hopkins can take pride in a record which closes with the quiet announcement that Professor Lattimore has resumed his duties as a lecturer at the university.[52]

President Reed received as much attention as Lattimore—most of it favorable. Like President Bronk before him, he was more likely to respond to those who praised him than to those who did not.

> I appreciated very much the note that you sent me during the latter part of the summer relative to Owen Lattimore. I didn't reply at the time because there was little that I could say until I had had an opportunity to negotiate directly with him. As you undoubtedly know, he is back in active service in the university as lecturer in the Department of History. We are all pleased to have the matter successfully settled, and I hope that Owen is now established in such a way that he can successfully pursue his academic career.[53]

In the fall of 1955 it appeared that Owen Lattimore and the Johns Hopkins University had weathered the storm. Lattimore would be teaching a single course for which the readings were mostly in French and German; the following semester he would be offering something with "less definite requirements" that could be more attractive to undergraduates.[54]

Continuing Criticism

The administration and board of trustees at Johns Hopkins held out the hope that the worst was over; it was taken for granted that the charges that had been made against Lattimore by Senators McCarthy and McCarran and repeated in the press would eventually be forgotten. As President Reed saw it, the events of 1950–55 that haunted Lattimore and Johns Hopkins would be more quickly forgotten the more quickly he removed himself from the public eye. There was an expectation on the part of the Hopkins administration that whatever Lattimore did he remain unobserved and unnoticed. This was not to be.

Lattimore was asked to make several public appearances. He was an engaging and knowledgeable speaker; he was an expert on an important subject that many wanted to learn more about; and he was a public figure, a celebrity. As a consequence of these opportunities, he received more than his share of publicity, more attention than is generally accorded to academics and certainly more attention than the authorities at Johns Hopkins believed was necessary and proper.

For example, in December Lattimore was asked by a chapter of the American Civil Liberties Union to give a talk in Hartford, Connecticut, on fear and foreign policy. Both the sponsor and the topic were somewhat controversial. Ten days before the lecture the insurance company that had volunteered the use of a large auditorium, after receiving threats that veterans' groups and others would picket the event, withdrew its offer.[55]

The meeting was moved to a church parish house and attracted an audience of 600 and a handful of protesters who distributed anti-Communist literature. In his remarks, Lattimore was critical of American foreign policy in Asia, especially on the question of Formosa. Not unexpectedly, all of the events were fully reported in the press.[56]

Almost everything Lattimore did came to the attention of the university administration. When Lattimore turned up without an invitation at a seminar on international relations given by two colleagues, a faculty member who had on other occasions been hostile to him reported this to the provost. This seeming breach of academic etiquette, describing how "Lattimore took an active part in the discussions," was put in a confidential memorandum for the record.[57] The information was also verified by a telephone call: "Lattimore took an exceedingly active part in the discussions . . . [and] appeared unannounced and uninvited."

> There has been no meeting of the seminar since that session reported in my earlier memorandum, due to the examinations and holidays. Under the circumstances Moos and

> Tucker propose to make the next session the last for the academic year. Instead of continuing formal meetings of the group, they propose to assign members to the job of writing papers, which will involve individual consultations with Moos and Tucker.[58]

A full description of the incident was forwarded to President Reed for his confidential file.

President Reed found the attention Lattimore had been receiving "so great and so contrary to the spirit" of their agreement that he called Lattimore and the chairman of the History Department in for another discussion.

The president emphasized to Lattimore that he felt the "recent publicity was not in keeping" with what they had agreed to earlier. He reminded Lattimore about "the importance of his behavior" in light of the "highly emotional character of the problem within which he was involved." He explained what appeared in the media resulted in complaints from the public, the trustees, and even some faculty. He pointed out that Lattimore's activities were negatively affecting the careers of other faculty. Compared with the complaints Lattimore had generated in the past, this assessment was alarmist and exaggerated.

According to his written account, President Reed "emphasized the fact that this situation could not continue and that the responsibility for correcting the difficulty rested with him [Lattimore] and with him alone."

Lattimore talked about specific meetings he had addressed and topics he had discussed, and asked the president whether these were appropriate. The president replied that

> the president of the university did not pass judgment on the invitations that the professor accepted nor on the subject matter of their talks, and I told him that it was just as inappropriate for me to do this in his case as it would be in the case of any other professor. I reemphasized in connection with this phase of our discussion that the purpose of my talk was to make sure that he had full knowledge of all of these forces so that he might exercise good judgment with regard to his behavior. . . .
>
> As the discussion came to a close I again repeated that the present situation was intolerable and that the responsibility rested squarely on him.[59]

Lattimore was clearly caught in a dilemma. He sought concrete advice that the president refused to give, claiming that he did not want to infringe upon Lattimore's academic freedom.

History Department Chairman Sidney Painter agreed with President Reed that it was a mistake for Lattimore to continue accepting invitations to give public lectures. He actually felt that it had been a mistake for Lattimore to have given any in the first place. He confessed that he was bothered by the fact that Lattimore had ignored the president's advice, and believed that Lattimore should have consulted his colleagues before plunging into public controversy. He personally was "troubled and a little hurt." He advised Lattimore that it would be a "decent thing" to cancel the remainder of his scheduled talks.[60] On this issue, faculty felt that Lattimore had used poor judgment and overstepped his bounds. The support from many quarters was at best lukewarm.

Two weeks later Lattimore requested an appointment with President Reed at which time he gave him his schedule of outside lectures for the winter and spring, and asked for his judgment as to whether he should cancel any or all. The president repeated that he could not take the responsibility for making any decision as to what Lattimore could or could not do. It was inappropriate:

> In our previous discussion I had emphasized the fact that he must act in a responsible manner in this difficult situation and that it would be entirely improper for the president of the university to place the university in the position where it censored either the places where a member of the faculty lectured or the subject matter of the lectures. He expressed his appreciation of this point of view and reemphasized the fact that he understood how serious the situation was and that he would do everything that he could to avoid publicity.[61]

Lattimore's status at Johns Hopkins was not what it had been.

Invitation to India

In July of 1956, Lattimore wrote to President Reed and the chairman of the History Department telling of an invitation he had received from the Indian School of International Studies in New Delhi to assist it in establishing a program in Far East and Central Asia studies, and requesting an unpaid leave of absence in order to pursue this opportunity. In the letter to President Reed he described the lectures he had given in Israel and Rome in the summer and spoke of a conference on the writing of Far Eastern history he had attended in London and one on Chinese history in Paris he would be attending after he completed some library research in Finland.[62] One might think that the Johns Hopkins administration would look favorably on granting him a leave that would take him off campus and out of the country. However, it did not.

In a brief response, President Reed said that he would defer taking action on Lattimore's request until they had met in the fall to discuss the matter.[63] Lattimore in turn thanked President Reed and noted that if he could not begin making arrangements until after the proposed meeting, it might be necessary for him to postpone the starting date of the leave.[64]

In the fall, after Lattimore described in an interview the work he hoped to undertake in India, President Reed decided against granting him the leave. The president pointed out that the board of trustees had given him the responsibility of determining Lattimore's relationship with the university, and he repeated that he needed to "become convinced that he [Lattimore] desired an academic program carried on within this university and without the degree of publicity that he had sought in the past." He reminded Lattimore that he had only been reinstated for a year and that that was not enough time "to carry on an academic career" given all of the time away from campus over the years. He disagreed with Lattimore's contention that his outside activities benefited the university; they were only of value to an institution for someone who "had established an academic place for himself within the university," which, to his mind, Lattimore "had never done." As Reed saw it, this was in part due to the fact that he had been given an extraordinary number of leaves since his appointment at Johns Hopkins.[65]

Lattimore asked for an official letter denying the leave, which President Reed wrote.[66]

A Different Administration, the Same Problems

Milton S. Eisenhower's assumption of the Johns Hopkins presidency did little to change Lattimore's relationship to the administration or improve his chances of being granted a leave of absence. Unlike his predecessors, Eisenhower was not a noted scientist or scholar. He had earned a reputation as a proficient academic-bureaucrat; he brought the managerial revolution in higher education to Johns Hopkins. His managing of the controversy surrounding Lattimore reflected his skills.

With the appointment of a new president there was a renewed effort to bring about Lattimore's dismissal from Johns Hopkins. The new flow of postcards and letters protesting Lattimore's continuation on the faculty were much like those received by Presidents Bronk and Reed.

> Dear Dr. Eisenhower,
>
> Now that you have become president of this great college we hope you will do your best to get rid of Youngdahl's pal, Lattimore, and others of this ilk. Pinkos (to be polite) like Lattimore are a disgrace to any college to say nothing of the treasonable implications. We will be waiting patiently to read of Owen Lattimore's "resignation" soon.
>
> Sincerely,
> Adams (Protestant Faith) Family[67]

> Dear Doctor Eisenhower:
>
> It has just come to my attention that Owen Lattimore is now back teaching a course on "The History of China" at your university.
>
> From my study of the hearings of the Judiciary Committee of the United States Senate covering Lattimore's testimony about the Institute of Pacific Relations, he seems hardly qualified—especially since he played such a vigorous part in trying to destroy Chiang Kai-shek's Nationalist government on the mainland of China by helping the Reds there. Furthermore, he perjured himself several times before this committee.
>
> I would be interested in hearing from you regarding this.
>
> Yours very truly[68]

The complaints, however, were handled quite differently by the new administration. They were now receiving an acknowledgment and brief explanation from an assistant to the president.

> Your note concerning Mr. Owen Lattimore, who is a lecturer in the History Department at the Johns Hopkins Uni-

> versity, has come to my desk, and in the absence of the president, I should like to reply to your inquiry.
>
> You say Mr. Lattimore perjured himself before a senate committee. I think the facts are these: Following Mr. Lattimore's appearance before the committee, he was indicted on several counts of perjury. However, after a long series of court proceedings, the Circuit Court of Appeals dismissed several of the counts, and soon thereafter the Attorney General announced the discontinuance of proceedings against him.
>
> At the time of the indictments, the university put Mr. Lattimore on leave of absence until the matter could be settled by the courts. When the proceedings were dismissed, he returned to his duties.
>
> Since you have addressed your inquiry to Doctor Eisenhower, you should know that these decisions were taken before he assumed the presidency of the university; I was assured that they were taken after the most thorough and serious deliberation and consultation by the university faculty, administration and trustees.
>
> Very truly yours[69]

President Eisenhower was putting some distance between his administration and Lattimore's presence on campus. He was making certain that it was understood that he was not responsible for personnel decisions years before his appointment. Indeed, he attempted to convey the impression that as far as he was concerned the matter of Lattimore's own appointment was so insignificant in the total picture of the management of the university, questions and problems about it may not have even been brought to his attention. This was a responsibility delegated to others. Under his administration, Owen Lattimore did not merit personal attention.

The Lattimore case was now being handled by functionaries in a formal way. It had become routinized in a growing bureaucratic apparatus. Not only would the public see the nascent bureaucratic face of the university, but so would Lattimore.

In his first interview with President Eisenhower, he again unsuccessfully sought direction about accepting particular speaking engagements. President Eisenhower merely repeated President Reed's earlier statement that the administration could not be placed in a position of approving or disapproving a faculty member's public talks. It only expected faculty "to show good judgment and good taste." He also advised Lattimore to discuss such questions with his colleagues, and reminded him that he had a special responsibility to concentrate on academic matters and avoid publicity.

Lattimore also renewed his request for a leave in order to spend a year in India. The University of Delhi had renewed its offer. He wanted to assist it in establishing a division of Asian Studies, which he believed would be useful academic work. He told of another invitation to the University of Paris, possibly for a summer term.

In responding negatively to Lattimore's request, President Eisenhower repeated President Reed's reasons for originally doing so, emphasizing that the question of a leave would seem to suggest that Johns Hopkins was "of secondary importance in Mr. Lattimore's plans."

A New Issue and New Tensions

In the face of Lattimore's insistence that a year in India would enhance his contribution to Johns Hopkins, President Eisenhower postponed a final decision until after he had an opportunity to consult other administrative officers.[70] He then wrote Lattimore denying his request, stating that he had yet to prove his desire and intention to devote himself to serious scholarly work. He would have to demonstrate persuasively a commitment to the advancement of scholarship. President Eisenhower wondered whether Lattimore's activities in India would enhance his scholarly reputation.[71] He reported his decision to the board of trustees, and it was duly supported.[72]

Lattimore was less concerned about not being given leave than about the insinuation by the president that his scholarship was inadequate—that it was journalism rather than the work of an academic—and that his appointment at Johns Hopkins was in jeopardy. He promptly asked President Eisenhower for a meeting "in order to clear up some points that must be the result of misunderstanding."[73]

At the same time, a number of other faculty communicated with the president, objecting to his suggestion that Lattimore's scholarship was in some way inadequate. One colleague attested to Lattimore's broad knowledge in anthropology, geography, history, and linguistics.

> During the last few years we have discussed work on which he was currently engaged. But from these discussions and from

> his publications I have strongly the impression that he has been engaged in scholarly investigations and in keeping up with the work of other scholars, and I know that he has been thinking about broad problems of historical interpretation—for example, in regard to relations between East and West in Ancient and Medieval times and in general about the movement of frontiers. I have also found very interesting for comparison with the West his studies of monasticism, feudalism, and nationalism in Asia. I personally derive stimulus for my own thought on problems of economic history from having him a member of the Department.[74]

A geographer sent more praise and a sheaf of published testimonials to the president.

> Dear Dr. Eisenhower,
>
> Recently I heard that Owen Lattimore's record as a scholar has been questioned. I am very much concerned over this. I have known Lattimore for many years and, since I came to this university, have conducted with him a joint seminar each year. As a former Far Eastern resident and student of the Orient I have had much experience of Lattimore's scholarship, which I hold in very high esteem. However, much wider testimony on the matter than mine is available. A few years ago, during the political attacks on Lattimore, the enclosed pamphlet was prepared which I thought you might be interested in seeing, since it contains the views of some of the world's leading authorities in the relevant fields of scholarship.[75]

The chairman of the History Department provided a listing and some copies of Lattimore's recent publications.

> Dear President Eisenhower:
>
> In connection with our various discussions, I thought this list of Mr. Lattimore's recent publications and copies of some of them might be of interest to you.[76]

C. Vann Woodward's assessment was also very much at odds with President Eisenhower's:

> I have examined Mr. Lattimore's publications during the past two years and sought what light I could upon their merits

> from people qualified to criticize them. I also attended a lecture he gave at Oxford University in 1955 and have had him speak to my own graduate students upon the theme of frontiers that he developed in a lecture at Rome. His American Philosophical Society monograph and his book on *Nationalism and Revolution in Mongolia* (1955) are specialized and will be of interest mainly to a limited circle of scholars. They could in no way be characterized as journalistic or popular, and they appear to represent the kind of work that deserves our encouragement. These publications would seem to reflect credit upon the university and to add to their author's scholarly standing. My conclusion is that Mr. Lattimore's activities since his return from leave are evidence of his intention to work in harmony with our tradition.[77]

The president and Lattimore met to eliminate the ambiguity that had resulted from the former's letter, and Lattimore expressed his appreciation for what he believed was an opportunity to clarify matters.

> Dear President Eisenhower:
>
> I have been wanting to write to thank you for the time and care you devoted to our several interviews, but have been delayed by a seizure of trouble with my back which has made it impossible to sit up to a typewriter.
>
> Most of all, I appreciate your making it clear that I, and others who had read your letter to me of 22 January, had misread your meaning and made the mistake that you might be questioning on the one hand my academic tenure and on the other hand my standing as a scholar. It was very pleasant to be assured that you were not in fact questioning my standing in either of these two respects.
>
> Yours sincerely[78]

To make sure his position was unmistakable, President Eisenhower responded:

> Dear Mr. Lattimore:
>
> The content of your letter of March 22 impels me to write this note to make it completely clear that I made two principal points in my conversations with you.

One was that it began to become apparent to me that some of your colleagues, and perhaps yourself, had tended to misinterpret one remark in my letter of January 22. I explained that it had been my intention in that letter not to question your ability to be a scholar, but to express the view that you had yet to demonstrate convincingly your intention to pursue a scholarly career in keeping with the traditions of Hopkins.

The other point had to do with my firm understanding that you and Doctor Reed had agreed that your return to the university and your continued career here were conditional upon your demonstrating your intention to pursue a scholarly career. I fully support Doctor Reed's position in this regard.

I've written this simply in a further effort to make certain that my position is understood.

Sincerely[79]

The president's suggestion in the third paragraph that Lattimore's appointment was contingent on his activities, scholarly and other, reverberated across campus. This was not Lattimore's understanding, nor, apparently, that of the majority of faculty. He did not see himself on trial, as having continually to prove himself. He was a faculty member with a tenured appointment, which meant that he had already proven himself. His appointment was permanent, continuous. It could be lost only for nonperformance, incompetence, or moral turpitude. President Eisenhower's attempt to imply that Lattimore was less than a serious scholar in order to refocus the debate was unsuccessful. It was only a temporary digression.

The construction that President Eisenhower put on tenure was inconsistent with the way it was conventionally defined by faculty. His letter, not surprisingly, brought a review of the facts and instruction from the chairman of the History Department:

Dear President Eisenhower:

Mr. Lattimore brought me your recent letter in a state of considerable indignation. I think I have persuaded him to let the matter drop, but this doesn't alter the fact that the situation is still one that can do great harm to the university. It is necessary to face the fact that your interpretation of Mr. Lattimore's position differs from that of the vast majority of the faculty. As you told me you had not looked the matter up, I shall briefly review the facts as I know them.

The board of trustees long ago gave Mr. Lattimore "indefinite tenure" as Director of the Page School. He was still in this position when he was attacked by Senator McCarthy. Then when Mr. Lattimore was indicted, he was very properly placed on leave. While he was on leave, the Page School was abolished. But the Academic Council in voting to abolish the school resolved that Mr. Lattimore should be a lecturer with the same tenure he enjoyed as Director of the Page School. In short the faculty felt that Mr. Lattimore was on leave until his case was disposed of and if he were not convicted would automatically be restored to duty with his previous rights of tenure. When the charges against him were dismissed, there was a good deal of criticism of the delay in restoring him to duty.

In short, while the trustees gave President Reed the choice of restoring Mr. Lattimore to duty or not doing so, as a particular matter I cannot see that he had much choice. If he had not restored Mr. Lattimore to duty, there would have been a major row, a number of members of the faculty would have resigned, and the American Association of University Professors would have been appealed to. It would have done the university irreparable harm.

Now in the case of many, perhaps most, of the members of the faculty this question has nothing to do with affection for or sympathy with Mr. Lattimore. It is the principle of tenure that is the issue. The trustees gave Mr. Lattimore indefinite tenure. He has not been proved to have done anything to justify his dismissal.

In short, while I believe most of my colleagues would agree that President Reed's advice to Mr. Lattimore was sound and that Mr. Lattimore should follow it, few if any would agree that his tenure of his position was conditional in any sense which set him off from other members of the faculty on indefinite tenure.

On this question of tenure, I stand with my colleagues. I believe that the trustees acted unwisely if not improperly in giving Mr. Lattimore tenure without a recommendation to that effect from the Academic Council, but by doing so they created a tenurial right which we are bound to defend. And any suggestion that this right is threatened could now as earlier have very serious effects on faculty morale.

Yours sincerely

The chairman's letter received only an acknowledgment by telephone from the president's office;[80] Lattimore was not mollified. It was necessary for the chairman to write to the president again, making the consequences of his singular interpretation explicit.

Dear President Eisenhower:

I hate to bother you with the matter again, but I was over optimistic when I said that Mr. Lattimore was ready to drop his worries. He insists that your last letter casts doubt on his tenure and that if the doubt is not cleared, he must take the matter to the American Association of University Professors. While I cannot believe that they would pay any attention to so vague a grievance, one can never be certain.

It is not my place to advise you on what you should do under the circumstances. Mr. Lattimore would be satisfied with a note saying that his tenure is the same as that of his colleagues with indefinite tenure. But I can see why you may hesitate to write such a letter.

Yours sincerely[81]

This time President Eisenhower was induced to clarify what he had meant in his earlier letter.

Dear Mr. Lattimore:

Professor Painter has written me that you feel I have, in some way, posed a threat to your tenure in the university.

The only basis I can imagine for this feeling is my failure to respond affirmatively to your letter to me of March 22, 1957, which contained this statement: "I appreciate your making it clear that I, and others who had read your letter to me of 22 January, had misread your meaning and made the mistake of thinking that you might be questioning on the one hand my academic tenure and on the other hand my standing as a scholar. It was very pleasant to be assured that you were not in fact questioning my standing in either of these two respects."

Since, in the conference which you, Professor Painter, Mr. Macaulay and I had in my office, I made no comment whatsoever with respect to tenure, but confined my remarks to your scholarship and to the understanding you and Doctor Reed had when you returned to the university. I wrote you on March 28, 1957, simply to set the record straight.

I have said nothing that could be construed as an effort to change your status. Please be assured that, should circumstances ever impel me to raise questions regarding your position in the university, or that of any other member of the faculty, I would do so openly, through recourse to establish academic procedures, and not by indirection.

Yours sincerely[82]

This response, although seemingly conciliatory, did not alleviate the doubt. President Eisenhower really had not abandoned his inference that Lattimore's appointment was "conditional upon . . . demonstrating." On the other hand, he did indicate that he would not act unilaterally to dismiss Lattimore. More importantly, he was now certainly aware of faculty sentiment, and the risks inherent in pushing Lattimore too far. His contention that he did not threaten Lattimore's tenure since he did not use the term was disingenuous. The letter was enough, however, to defuse the critical situation he had created.

Deepening Estrangement

Lattimore found the university administration's inflexibility most disconcerting. Here is how Eleanor Lattimore described these events to some friends:

> Owen should be the one to write you about his long and complicated hassle with the university, which was brought on by his request for leave to go to India, and which has caused us a lot of anger, frustration and depression. But he still can't write it because of the downest down of all. His sacroiliac suddenly went off the track again, or whatever it is they do, and he is flat on his back on a hard board, with a good deal of pain and in no physical condition to write letters. Our doctor-turned-psychiatrist next door would say that the back attack was *caused* by the anger, frustration and depression, but we don't really think it was. . . .
>
> Ike Jr.'s [President Eisenhower's] letter was distressing not only because it made India impossible but because it revealed such a complete misunderstanding of Owen and his position here and a really insulting attitude toward him. We had known of course that it was entirely possible that Ike didn't know anything about Owen except what he'd read in the papers during the McCarran hearings—which could give anyone a distorted picture—and what he may have heard from the

> few assiduous enemies he [Owen] has around Baltimore. But we had hoped he might have been exposed also to at least some of the truth and was the kind of person who would be disposed to believe it rather than the sensational papers.
>
> But the letter made it obvious that he had somehow acquired the wrong story, and Owen wasn't willing to leave his letter in the record without some attempt to clear it up. This seemed to involve endless consultations with colleagues, letters to Ike from several professors saying that O[wen] *had* demonstrated whatever he was supposed to have demonstrated, etc. The later interviews were pretty frustrating and inconclusive, though they did seem to clear up a few points such as Owen's academic qualifications and the fact that his tenure here wasn't dependent on his "demonstrating" anything.
>
> Of course we were tempted to say "to hell with you" and go off mad, but that wouldn't have hurt anybody but ourselves, since we don't really have a better place to go to—yet. When we find a better one or eye one that can be made to appear better, we're all set to hop off to it, and no little pension will hold us![83]

At the end of the year Lattimore received the invitation he had been expecting from Fernand Braudel to lecture in the late spring and early summer at the University of Paris (*École des Hautes Études*). The History Department recommended to the president that he be given leave with pay, since the invitation was a personal honor with only a modest stipend that would not cover his expenses.[84] A leave, but without pay, was granted by the administration. Provost Macaulay reminded the chairman of the History Department that

> for the months of April and May, 1958, which are part of the regular academic year. . . . Mr. Lattimore will be expected to make arrangements with the Treasurer's Office to pay his share of retirement and group insurance premiums.[85]

Lattimore no longer had direct access to the university president. Now matters were handled by memorandum, routed through the chairman of the History Department. Administratively, Johns Hopkins was becoming more complex. The staff specialists in the administrative offices handled questions and problems more impersonally. Along with the formal channels and proliferation of staff, there was an elaboration of rules and university policy. Rules and regulations, at least in the case of Lattimore, were more deliberately enforced. Without the status of an insider, Lattimore's ties were gone, as were the opportunities for privileges once taken for granted. Lattimore, who once had an administrative title and personal relationships with the president and his staff, was made particularly aware of this. The formal responses to his inquiries he received from an assistant to the president in the late 1950s were in sharp contrast to the handwritten notes and gifts for his son from President Bowman of the 1930s.

Lattimore was made to feel on the fringes in other ways. There were across-the-board salary increases from which he was excluded. He had aroused suspicion and he had made some enemies. It would take some faculty longer than others to forget the problems he had caused the university. Not everyone was pleased to see him on campus, and he was made well aware of this. His activities off campus also displeased many; they were embarrassed that a controversial figure associated with the university was expressing controversial ideas.

Lattimore criticized the [Dwight D.] Eisenhower administration's policy toward Formosa. He accused the government of withholding important information about China from the American people. He still repeated that Chiang Kai-shek had been "overwhelmingly rejected" by the Chinese people even before Mao Tsetung's Communist government came to power. The Communist government was stable; it was unrealistic to hope that there would be a popular uprising against it. Thus, it was foolish to believe that Chiang would ever return to the mainland. America's Formosa policy was to keep the island from the Communists so it could serve as a military base. It would not be against American interests to abandon Chiang.

He also observed that the Communist government in China was rapidly becoming one of the important countries in the world (although he did not publicly press the case that the United States should recognize Red China or vote to admit it to the United Nations). He observed that America's policy of containment of China made enemies of others, and pointed out that native Formosans might be unhappy with the way the Nationalist forces had taken over their island. He expressed doubts that Communist China was controlled by the Soviet Union, but was sure that American foreign policy was "steadily cementing" such an alliance.[86]

These were not popular ideas; they contradicted conventional wisdom, and they did not appease the moral entrepreneurs. Lattimore remained a target. It was easier to attack Lattimore than to change the government of China. A 1961 visit to Outer Mongolia by Lattimore set off a new, limited, but particularly acrimonious, assault on Lattimore and the university, reminiscent of the storms of a decade earlier. The press made much of the matter. News items routinely included the information that Outer Mongolia was a "Soviet-controlled satellite," that Lattimore taught at Johns Hopkins, that in the past he had supported Mao Tse-tung's government rather than the Nationalists, and that in the early 1950s a senate subcommittee had cast suspicion on his loyalty.

In a speech on the senate floor, Thomas J. Dodd, a Democrat from Connecticut, asked that his colleagues make a formal inquiry into the reasons for Lattimore's extended visit. He too pointed out that Lattimore taught at Johns Hopkins and had been described in a report as a "conscious, articulate instrument of the Soviet conspiracy." He called Lattimore "the dominant personality" in the Institute of Pacific Relations, an organization "considered by the American Communist party and by Soviet officials as an instrument of Communist policy, propaganda and military intelligence."

> Human memory is weak, and the facts of Owen Lattimore's central role in the Institute of Pacific Relations are now faded or forgotten. Indeed, from a number of editorials that have appeared in recent months, I have the impression there is an organized campaign under way to obliterate the record of the past and rewrite history in a manner acceptable to all fellow travelers and to those who believed or still believe that the Chinese Communists are "agrarian reformers. . . ."
>
> Owen Lattimore, in addition to being an apologist for the Chinese Communists and one of the original proponents of the "agrarian reformer" thesis, also pretends to expertness [*sic*] on Outer Mongolia. The Outer Mongolian government, according to monitored radio reports, has taken Lattimore to its bosom during the course of his present visit. . . . Lattimore told an Outer Mongolian audience that it is high time that their country was admitted to the United Nations.[87]

When Lattimore returned from his summer trip, he recommended that the U.S. government recognize the Mongolian People's Republic: "I don't see how it could possibly do any harm. The Mongolian attitude is the more contacts with the outside, the better."[88] Not everyone felt the same way, and some made the administration and board of trustees aware of this fact. They demanded to know why Lattimore went to Ulan Bator, who sent him there, what he was teaching students, and "why is he being retained?"[89]

For these reasons his situation at Johns Hopkins had not become entirely comfortable, and was showing no signs of improving. It was clear that Lattimore had absolutely no chance of regaining the confidence of the Johns Hopkins administration. In recommending Lattimore to be advisor to Chiang Kai-shek in 1941, President Isaiah Bowman had written to the White House:

> So far as Lattimore's qualifications are concerned, I can think of no better choice. He is more thoroughly informed about China than any other American that I know. He speaks the language fluently. He has a pleasant personality with sufficient independence of spirit and thought so that he can differ with people and yet remain aimiable [*sic*]. Everything that I know about him in either the foreground or the background is in his favor. . . .
>
> All of the members of my committee are enthusiastic over Lattimore's presentations. They are well informed, documented, cogent and clearly presented. I would recommend him heartily and without reserve.[90]

Lattimore's world had obviously changed, and more change would clearly be welcomed. Yet, given the climate of the Cold War, other American universities would be even more inhospitable.

At the first opportunity Lattimore decided to leave Johns Hopkins. In fall 1962, he agreed to become director of the Research Institute and head of the Department of Chinese Studies at the University of Leeds in Yorkshire, England. The University of Leeds was establishing a new department focusing on contemporary China, and the program would have a strong emphasis on teaching Chinese language, both of which appealed to Lattimore. President Eisenhower was authorized by the board of trustees to act favorably on Lattimore's application for early retirement, and he resigned from Johns Hopkins effective at the end of the following summer.[91]

In the end, the formalism of bureaucracy, as a procedural device, appears to have completed what Senators McCarthy and McCarran and other moral entrepreneurs could not by themselves do. It induced Lattimore to resign from Johns Hopkins.

7

Implications: On University Governance

The purpose of this book is not simply to tell what happened to Owen Lattimore at the Johns Hopkins University during the Cold War years, although the personal drama was quite extraordinary. Clearly, the events that unfolded at the university after Lattimore's loyalty was questioned in 1950 have significance that extends well beyond this single case. They illuminate the conditions wherein the Cold War was mediated by institutions. They show the obvious: how an institution of higher learning is administered is quite germane to the fate of faculty.

It is often remarked, and sometimes lamented, that we live in an age of biography. But the Lattimore story is more than a simple profile of one man. It is not a mere chronicle or specific history. It is more than a cautionary tale of the eventual triumph of bureaucratic tactics, of sparring by administrators, over academic principles that earlier had been accepted by administrators and the professoriat. C. Wright Mills has reminded us that the substance of social analysis are "problems of biography, of history and of their intersections within social structures."[1] These are the coordinate points of the proper study of the human condition. The Lattimore case is thus useful in informing us of larger social events—the meaning of the Cold War for academic life.

That the Hopkins board of trustees voted to keep Lattimore in spite of the fact that the sentiment of a substantial number of its members was to sever the institution's ties [read: fire] with him is particularly noteworthy. As most trustees saw it, he had become a millstone who had cost the university both goodwill and money. Whatever the facts, during his testimony before the McCarran committee, Lattimore was an indignant and truculent witness. He was uncooperative and sarcastic. He did not strike the right attitude.

He was not cautious; his testimony was not measured; he was not "academic" enough. As is made most clear by Chapter 3, the severity and rancor of the repeated attacks on Lattimore and the university were formidable. A significant number of the postcards and letters received by university authorities reveal a profound hatred—ignorant, irrational, and resolute. The board was divided. Many of its members who took the greatest interest in campus affairs believed that it would be best for the university if Lattimore were terminated, and their views were fairly well known. Over time, problems mounted. One embarrassment followed another. The public posture of the university was inaction and equivocation. As the case dragged on, some board members eagerly pressed their colleagues and the university administration to take immediate action. Lattimore was a nonstandard appointment who was seen as easily expendable. Many found his strident defense of himself offensive; he was a nuisance who would not voluntarily resign. They were convinced that the situation would not improve until Lattimore was gone. Such moves were thwarted, always by the administration, consonant with faculty sentiment. University authorities feared the reaction of the faculty and further unfavorable publicity.

The Lattimore case came to represent the resistance of the academic world to attacks on education and educators. To many of the professoriat, Lattimore was nothing more than the victim of an unexplicable national hysteria. Whether believed deserved or not, his troubles were clearly more public than any other academic harassed by the moral entrepreneurs. The controversy generated by his testimony and the litigation that followed gave him notoriety across the country. The details of who Lattimore was or what he had or had not done to bring himself under suspicion might have been murky to some, but that he was a significant figure in the story of the Cold War was known and understood. Indeed, in the often cited Lazarsfeld and Thielens (Fund for the Republic) national survey of the attitudes and anxieties of "social scientists in a time of crisis," one of the questions used to measure faculty members' willingness to take an active stand on academic freedom was: "Suppose you were faculty advisor to a student organization here on this campus that proposed inviting Owen Lattimore, Far Eastern expert (now under indictment in Washington), to speak at a public meeting here. Do you think Lattimore ought to be allowed to speak here or not?" (It is of passing interest that 80 percent of the nearly 2,500 respondents agreed that Lattimore should be allowed to speak and that 40 percent of those who favored the speech said that they would protest vigorously if their campus president were to ban it.[2])

Johns Hopkins came to symbolize a school that did not casually abandon faculty in spite of the fact that in the end Lattimore could have been treated better. This was unusual, although there were, of course, other schools that protected faculty—Antioch College, University of Connecticut, Illinois Institute of Technology, Massachusetts Institute of Technology, University of Rochester, Sarah Lawrence College.[3] (None of these other incidents came close to being as widely publicized as the Lattimore case.) The November 19, 1954, minutes of the executive committee of the board of trustees of Fisk University demonstrate this well:

> In view of the present status of the case, the president suggested that the committee discuss the action to be taken with respect to Dr. Lorch which matter had been referred to it by the board.
>
> The recent citation for contempt of congress prompted one suggestion that Dr. Lorch be suspended from his teaching duties until the issue was resolved. Chairman McLean proposed that instead of suspension there might be leave of absence with pay until the end of the contract period in June. Mr. Baldwin inquired regarding residential status in the event of such action and was informed that his housing on the campus was coterminous with his teaching contract.
>
> Mr. Bennett asked how other colleges had met this kind of situation. Chairman McLean noted that Johns Hopkins had continued Owen Lattimore on leave of absence with pay since indictment for perjury.[4]

However, the Lattimore case was only a symbol for faculty, not a model for administrators and trustees on other campuses to emulate in seeking a solution to what to do about faculty who had become an embarrassment. Few other institutions followed as brave a policy as Johns Hopkins. The ideology that academic freedom was in great peril may have resonated from campus to campus and bolstered the defenders of Lattimore and Johns Hopkins, but it surely did not become a rallying point for academic authorities around the country determined to hold their ground in the defense of faculty. On the contrary. The lesson of what happened at Johns Hopkins, of how destructive moral entrepreneurs could become and how deep their grievances were, was not lost on other academic administrators and trustees, or anyone else who read the newspaper. The message was quite clear. It would be almost impossible not to conclude that defending faculty was sometimes quite costly. It is obvious from the history of the Cold War years on campus that the actions taken by the authorities at Johns Hopkins did not work to strengthen the resolve of other administrations.[5]

After being besieged by moral entrepreneurs, most academics—on the Left or otherwise—were unable to find refuge on the campuses where they taught. Like congressional investigators, academic administrators conducted formal inquiries and sought punishment for those who they believed constituted a danger. Campus presidents and their staffs decided the fate of faculty—almost always immediate suspension, a hearing, the loss of a job, probation, or a warning. Few incidents were ignored. It hardly mattered whether the accused was a Communist, had been a Communist, was somewhat to the Left, had been somewhat to the Left, or was none of these. Suspicion and denunciations made faculty vulnerable. Academic administrators made the political activities and beliefs of faculty their business. The governance of institutions of higher learning loomed large in the Cold War on campus. Nothing was more important, not only to faculty who were victims of campus inquisitions, but also to faculty and the general public attempting to interpret the political tensions of the day. Accordingly, the matter of the governance of colleges and universities is now considered.

Attention is first directed to the question of where power resides in institutions of higher learning. It is believed by many that governing boards are fully in charge and that administrative officers follow their direction. The Lattimore case shows that this conception is for the most part untrue, that, as far as understanding academic life is concerned, trustees are naïve, do not commonly exercise power, and merely reiterate what academic administrators tell them. Administrators and not governing boards were largely, but certainly not always, responsible for how the Cold War was played out on campus.[6] The second section of this chapter considers what theories of organization can add to an understanding of events at Johns Hopkins during the 1950s. Next the idea is developed that institutions of higher learning are not structured so as to make administrators responsible to faculty. This, of course, is true of any bureaucracy. Bureaucracies are hierarchical; they are not democracies. Individuals need only be responsive to or valued by or look in the direction of those above them, not those below them. The high-handed behavior of most academic administrators during the Cold War was wholely consistent with this bureaucratic model. The Cold War years exploded the notion that relations between administrators and faculty are collegial, notwithstanding the ideology of shared governance and faculty's vaunted opinion of their own importance. The final section makes it clear, however, that a tradition of faculty rights and academic freedom—can serve to protect faculty at critical times.

Governing Boards and Academic Governance

The control of institutions of higher learning by lay boards is a uniquely American phenomenon. In Europe, from which so many aspects of American higher education have been borrowed, faculty largely govern themselves, although there is sometimes direct involvement from the state. Some believe it was the introduction of lay boards that has led to the diversity, competition, growth, and robustness of American higher education, and that governing boards act as a buffer between, on the one hand, faculty and students and, on the other, those with power in society. Boards serve to reassure the public that an institution is in respectable hands. Others are less sure that the arrangement or the outcome has been that beneficial. For example, Hofstadter has argued that lay government "has hampered the development of organization, initiative, and self-confidence among American college professors, and it has contributed, along with many other forces in American life, to lowering their status in the community."[7] Faculty are seen and see themselves as subservient, as employees, as hired hands. Whatever the view about its usefulness, it is believed by many, if not most, that a governing board (or at least the group of its most involved members) in meaningful ways sets the tone and direction of a college or university. This general agreement notwithstanding, the conclusion seems dubious.

To be sure, the formal charter gives a board considerable power. It has legal authority over educational policies and professors, individually and collectively. It is supposed to make policy. It is supposed to frame the decisions that guide an institution's present and future, while delegating the details of management to the administration. It has ultimate control, the final word. Its fiscal responsibility and oversight would certainly seem to assure this, as would the fact that it selects the institution's president.

That governing boards of American institutions of higher learning have considerable power has long been accepted and unquestioned. In his classic essay describing the early nineteenth century collegiate system, Francis Wayland begins and ends by setting forth the board's broad charge.

> They hold the property of the institution, appoint and remove all officers of instruction and government, fix and alter their salaries, enact all laws, and see that these laws are carried into effect, or at least they assume the responsibility of performing all these duties. This corporation is created in the first instance by the legislative act which grants the charter to the college, and they have the power, in most cases, of filling their own vacancies. The office is commonly for life. For the discharge of its duties these corporators are responsible to no one. . . . They make no report of their proceedings, for there is no power to which they are amenable. They are wholly independent of all authority.[8]
>
> They are the appointed guardians of education. In them is vested the whole power of ordering, directing and governing the institutions of higher learning. They hold all the funds appropriated either by private or public munificence to the purpose of elevating the standard of knowledge in the youth of our country. They appoint and remove officers, fix the rate and manner of their compensation, ordain the studies to be pursued, and on them it is devolved to see that the designs of the public or the founder are carried into effect.[9]

This succinctly lays out the range of responsibilities of governing boards as they have been commonly understood.

However, there is more to the picture, and by itself Wayland's formulation misrepresents how policy is made and carried out in institutions of higher learning, at least in universities if not as a rule in all secular colleges. Taking into account all the facts at hand, it is more accurate to conclude that presidents and their staffs for the most part control the outcome of the decision making in institutions of higher learning, not governing boards. Governing boards do something less than govern; presidents do a great deal more than administer or simply preside.

Wayland's model was the small, denominational liberal arts college with a traditional and narrow focus. Since the turn of the century there has been a new ideal: complex institutions devoted to a variety of activities. Fields of study have multiplied, and all have graduate or professional programs. Budgets are both larger and more detailed. The increased complexity has led to the elaboration of administrative functions and to many more academic administrators. The growth of academic administration in the twentieth century has meant not only greater numbers of them but also their greater authority. Academic administrators have made themselves and have become a consequential force on campus.

As businessmen, bankers, and lawyers replaced clergy on governing boards in the twentieth century, the definition of governing boards changed. Their function came to be seen as resembling boards of directors of businesses or industries. Many board members of academic institutions had experience on boards of banks, businesses, and public utilities. They knew how to be directors and had a model for how it should be done. College and university presidents were now looked upon less as paragons of virtue and piety and disciplinarians, but as business executives—as chief executive officers—who were given wide discretion to make their institutions function effectively. All the while, the role of governing boards has greatly diminished. The transformation of American higher education has been extensive. It is obvious that not too many decades after Wayland's analysis, certainly by the Cold War years, governing boards were largely irrelevant to the governance of universities. This is not to overlook the fact that authority resides in the board, to whom administrators must answer. The precipitous dismissal of an errant president by a board from time to time would seem to make this most apparent. Quite simply, there has been a managerial revolution in the larger, sectarian institutions with presidents, vice presidents, directors, deans, and their subalterns playing a greater part in policy formulation. At first academic administrators began to manage by default. By the mid-twentieth century it was by design. Since this conclusion is contrary to what is widely held, it deserves more elaboration.

It has long been taken for granted by those who study or write about academia that the governing boards of institutions of higher learning are, as Hubert Park Beck put it, "more than mere figureheads and actually do decide basic matters of university policy." Although many would agree with Beck, on reflection, it is obvious that he has overstated the case. Admittedly, an institution's president and his administrative appointees work at the pleasure of the board. Indeed, the fact of lay boards created the need for officials—college and university presidents and abundant staffs—to whom responsibilities could be entrusted. Yet the assumption that a campus president is nothing more than an agent of the governing board does not follow. Nor is it true that when academic administrators make a decision, they are in reality acting conditionally, not authoritatively.

On the surface, there is nothing that does not feed the image that governing boards are every bit in control. The dominance of governing boards in academic affairs has for so long been a received doctrine that it has never really been examined. In general, even the most acute observers of academic life have not questioned it. Members of governing boards do not deny it. They would certainly like to believe that they are in control. Those regarded as having the greatest knowledge about governing boards, such as Beck, have not challenged the assumption: "the university president and his hierarchy of subordinates regularly carry on in close conformity to what is believed to be wishes of the governing board."[10]

There is no body of evidence from any study of governing boards that would refute what has been taken for granted for so many years, namely, that they in fact govern institutions of higher learning, that they "are more than mere figureheads." At the same time, there is no body of evidence to support it. It is merely received wisdom, and, as additional discussion should make clear, not sociologically sound.

To be sure, since a governing board selects an institution's president, there is as a matter of course a consensus of views between the two more often than not. In Veblen's words, "the board will create an academic head in its own image. . . . The upshot of it all . . . it delegates these powers to one of [its] own kind. . . . "[11] Under the circumstances, the question of whether a board or a president initiates decisions and primarily exercises power will seldom even occur. In most instances, which one dominates is not an important question.

More attention has been given to the trustee-faculty, relationship than to the trustee-administrative relationship. Moreover, the study of governing boards of institutions of higher learning has been limited to the analysis of the social characteristics of their members. What occupations do individual members follow? A study of college A found that most were businessmen; is this true for university B? What is the sex or age composition of the board at school C? Why is it that there are not more women on governing boards? How do individuals find their way onto governing boards? Although interesting, the answers to these questions tell us little about how governing boards actually function.

The examination of how the Lattimore case was handled at the Johns Hopkins University suggests that the conclusion that governing boards are invariably at the center of important decisions in institutions of higher learning is both too simple and inaccurate. Although governing boards are granted legal powers, how this power is exercised needs to be considered. How a governing board uses power is certainly affected by more than the biographies of its members.

The Lattimore case makes a larger truth apparent: that more often than not, governing boards are instruments of academic culture and of administrators and, to the degree that faculty influence administrators, indirectly, of faculty. They are not only the simple product of their members' social characteristics. Boards do not necessarily always act on the class interests of their members. They listen to campus presidents as well as to politicians and the press and to public opinion and alumni as well as to other influential citizens and friends. Presidents Bronk and Reed were respected scientists. They had been given considerable latitude by the board, and their opinions and recommendations were taken quite seriously even by those trustees who thought otherwise.

Boards are by no means populists, but the range of opinion that they receive and act on is not as narrow as one would expect given their own social homogeneity. Most board members are strangers to academic life. They are only accidentally interested in higher education. They are generally chosen to be board members because they have money or connections with money or power, not because of a keen interest in higher education and its problems. Serving on a board enhances their prestige. It does not necessarily move them to begin to see the world from the point of view of the professoriat. Most trustees are followers in academic affairs, not leaders. Few become activists.

Some board members might feel that they lack the expertise to overturn summarily the advice of an academic administrator. Some might be only marginally involved in campus affairs, appearing irregularly for board meetings and on ceremonial occasions. Most are quite busy with their own lives and careers. For the most part, their membership on a board is not a principal interest, although, to be sure, many do seem to take their responsibilities quite seriously. Under the circumstances, they could be expected to welcome or accept direction, some or perhaps even a great deal. It could hardly be otherwise. The evidence from this study suggests that most will defer to what those who manage the day-to-day affairs of a college or university recommend. They are largely ignorant about too many of the details of academic life for it to be different. How could they penetrate large issues, let alone manage day-by-day affairs?

Principles of tenure, academic freedom, and faculty autonomy are quite arcane to lay people. The subtleties were not really understood by the most involved board members at Johns Hopkins.

Even after Presidents Bronk or Reed or Provost Macaulay explained procedures, there were questions and confusion. And, as Appendix K makes quite clear, trustees appear only marginally interested in academic matters, hardly surprising for lawyers, businessmen, and men of affairs—not teachers or scholars.

Much of the board members' knowledge of academic life may come from dim memories of their undergraduate years. They may know how faculty go about teaching, but not about research. Most know next to nothing about the nuances of academic life. Most know little about the details of curricula. The differences between sociology, social work, and socialism might not always be clear. Should the properly educated college graduate be required to complete two science courses? Should psychology be counted as a science? What is the pedagogically ideal student/faculty ratio for teaching introductory science courses? Since more underclassmen will be enrolling in biology courses, should the size of that department be increased at the expense of foreign language faculty? It is unreasonable to expect members of a lay board to have a real understanding of such complex questions. Indeed, one could conclude from a single session of a faculty senate meeting that full comprehension of such issues is often beyond many who spend their professional lives on campus.

This means, of course, that academic administrators have considerable say in what decisions a board takes. The board may control budgets, priorities, and planning, but the administration controls the flow of information. This fact lessens a board's effective control, as do custom and indifference. A board could not even complete an agenda for a regular meeting without the assistance of administrative officers. There may not be enough money for both a fine arts center and a new athletic facility. The board might have to choose between the two. It must rely on a campus president in setting priorities. A board could not begin to discern how one choice over the other might affect overall campus life without turning to the campus administration. Most presidents have advanced degrees and have been faculty members. They have presumably mastered some of the complexities of academic affairs, enough to get ahead; most lay board members have not. This experience gives the office of the president a certain authority vis à vis a board. One dimension of a common classification of social power is expert power, the controlling of necessary knowledge or information.[12] With the single exception of the investment of endowment, trustees could not know more about academic life than campus presidents and their staffs. They are not expected to know more. In the Lattimore case, the board had numerous questions, but very few answers.

Of course, there are many examples to the contrary. There are administrators that are less than fully competent, who are too vague or too unreliable. There are also governing boards that have been known heavy-handedly to block an appointment, see that a faculty member is dismissed, or in some other way meddle in minutiae. There are still discussed instances—1) the loyalty oath controversy in the early years of the Cold War, 2) the Angela Davis case some twenty years later, 3) revoking their delegation of the power to make tenure appointments after an administrative officer approved tenure for Herbert Marcuse, and 4) the attempt to deny academic credit for a course offered by Eldridge Cleaver—in which the Board of Regents of the University of California has done so. These displays of raw power in California (Texas is another state where numerous such examples can be found) run contrary to the general thesis being put forth. Perhaps this is why they are so well remembered. Generally, it is a campus president that keeps the organization moving. Power can be defined as the ability to get things done. Ipso facto, presidents are given and are expected to exercise power.

How boards make decisions and what they make decisions about are empirical questions that deserve a great deal more attention than they have heretofore been given. The minutes of the board of trustees of the Johns Hopkins University for the period it was under the most intense pressure for not moving more forcefully against Lattimore indicate that in most matters, certainly academic matters, it was a follower rather than a leader and that academic matters were of secondary interest (see Appendix K). The weight of the facts about what happened under admittedly a single set of conditions at the Johns Hopkins University might not be enough to convince everyone fully that boards may be basically followers, not leaders. Nonetheless what has been reviewed is suggestive enough to raise the question; the facts in this case imply that academic administrators may be more independent than is generally acknowledged. If criticized for an unpopular stand, academic administrators can hide behind the board. They can make faculty believe that they work under the control of an imperious board, while the truth is that a board generally pursues policy recommended by the administration. This is common bureaucratic legerdemain. Academic administrators are no more or no less duplicitous than any bureaucrat. They can convince a board to put its imprimatur on what it has been led to believe is a proper and autonomous course of action. They can manipulate the institution's bureaucracy to serve their ends. They can misinform a board and withhold important facts. Much of what faculty and students do, wish, and believe is channeled to the board through the president. He or she can make a board believe that one outcome will be less costly, more painful, or more socially responsible than another. The possibilities to dissemble are endless. Even if they wanted to, it would be difficult for trustees to be involved in very much daily management.

A board is more the captive of academic administrators than the other way around. It must rely on them. A board is committed to the president it has selected. He or she has to work quite hard to lose this trust. Significantly more often than not, boards support administrations that have a vote of no confidence from some campus constituency (students, faculty, the council of deans). Stupidity, plagiarism, extraordinary excesses, dangerous vanity, and a fascinating variety of misdemeanors and felonies are overlooked by boards in their blind faith in those on whom they have laid hands. It is too facile to contend that this kind of support is merely a payoff to a toady for years of loyalty and effective dirty work. Boards truly trust and are inclined to back campus presidents.

One purpose of the lay governing board is to shield the campus from interference from the larger community. In the Lattimore care, the board of trustees at Johns Hopkins did this relatively well, albeit reluctantly. While indicating ambivalence about Lattimore, it publicly defended the university and its policies. It addressed—not always with a great deal of conviction—some of the charges of the moral entrepreneurs. It tried to come to an understanding with benefactors. Efforts were made to mollify alumni. The social standing of a majority of the trustees put them in an ideal position to do so. Board Chairman Barton, for example, was also chancellor of the Episcopal Diocese of Maryland and a senior partner in a prominent Baltimore law firm. His successor, Charles S. Garland, had won the Wimbledon doubles championship, was a captain of a Davis Cup team, had been president of the Baltimore Association of Commerce, president of the Investment Bankers Association of America, governor of the New York Stock Exchange, and served as a director of a bank, a railroad, and other businesses including Merck and Company of which he was chairman. The board itself resisted the temptation to dismiss Lattimore. It could be expected that trustees which had become identified with the university, and derived prestige and disesteem from its fortunes, would defend it. In defending the university, they were defending themselves.

The administrations of Presidents Bronk and Reed understood faculty sentiment and articulated faculty interests. The voice of the faculty was heard directly through committees and the governance structure. The administration, and ultimately the board, chose to heed faculty advice—both formal and informal. To be sure, the respect shown faculty was unusual, and so was the outcome. The final result appears to have been less costly to the integrity of the university than if the board had not listened to the administration. More than anything else, administrators and board members needed patience, a quality that during the Cold War was not always evident in their counterparts around the country. They were clearly displeased by the flow of events, but they resisted changing course because of threats. The evident ambivalence and timidity on the part of each administration perhaps indicates more a commitment to the principle of academic freedom than to Lattimore the man. The light the university cast was feeble, but it was visible in the prevailing dark.

It has long been believed that not being taken seriously about issues which truly count encourages inconsequential discussion and inefficient deliberation among faculty. The faculty at Johns Hopkins were evidently listened to, and as a consequence there was a minimum of solemn public hand wringing, endless ritualistic meetings, and frenetic meddling. Dramatics are not the same as faculty governance. Faculty appointed by the administration to serve on committees knew that they would be considering more than trivia, and that their deliberations mattered. Interested faculty needed only to communicate an understanding of the issues and their views; a sympathetic administration did the rest.

Drawing conclusions from his own and Ellen W. Schrecker's research on the impact of McCarthyism on academic life, David R. Holmes writes that "it is seriously misleading to suggest that administrators 'created' the problem [of the Cold War on campus]. . . ." Speaking for himself, Holmes adds: "Weak or misguided presidents did not, in my view, cause the Cold War to appear on campus. This is far too narrow an interpretation."[13] The view may in fact be narrow, but events at Johns Hopkins would suggest precisely that. Those academic administrators elsewhere who did not defend faculty or who acquiesced to clamor and threats did in fact invite the Cold War on campus. If Lattimore did not have to be fired, few others had to be fired, fewer, indeed, than were fired.

Understanding the University's Response

The authorities at Johns Hopkins spent much of the decade of the 1950s buffeted by condemnation prompted by the Lattimore case. In responding, they were often uncertain and even confused.

Sometimes the muddle was inexplicable. They evidenced little authority in dealing with a disgruntled public whose attention was kept riveted on the university by moral entrepreneurs. They were caught in organizational role conflict. On the one hand, they were tied to defending academic freedom and the principle of tenure. It is somewhat of an irony that many did not much believe in the value of either precept. Some were unsure of what they even meant. Yet, they were stuck. On the other hand, there were pressures from moral entrepreneurs, the media, donors, and alumni to fire Lattimore. Their response was largely to do nothing, a common practice of organizations when confronted with a critical situation.

There is little indication that the university's response to the bind it found itself in was rational or deliberate. If it had been, it would have found a solution instead of having a solution find it. As it turned out, the problem variously got shuffled around, lost, and reborn. It never was fully comprehended, nor was a policy arrived at which would neutralize it. Outcomes that may have looked like the results of conscious decisions were not. Irrational and unique circumstances also affect the course of events.

A presupposition of the rational decision model of institutional choice is that, at a minimum, the administration and board of Johns Hopkins would have determined what was in the institution's best interest and on the basis of their assessment would have attempted to resolve the problem. A presupposition of the conflict resolution model is that the outcome would have been the product of a series of trade-offs among different interest groups. Neither of these theories is very useful in explaining what happened at Johns Hopkins, because both are predicated on institutional stability and continuity, two conditions that were to some degree lacking at Johns Hopkins.

The most obvious fact contributing to the lack of continuity was the turnover in presidents. Beyond that, however, the involvement of a lay board in the decision-making process created a haziness about leadership that this arrangement invariably creates in American institutions of higher learning. It is expected that the trustees' own professional interests take precedence over institutional interests which may require study, reflection, and more than passing understanding, as was the case at Johns Hopkins. At a number of critical points there were trustees who were profoundly worried and perplexed about Lattimore or how his presence on campus might affect the fate of the university. But when the flow of letters decreased, when the noise generated by the moral entrepreneurs was tolerable and the pressure abated, when the pressure changed direction and there was a call for a stout defense of Lattimore or some principle, or when the president would take the lead in defining the university's position, the concern would quickly dissipate. There were more trustees who really did not care than those who cared occasionally. For the most part, the Lattimore case was an intermittent, partial issue for a limited time (which, like Lattimore, eventually went away). Those in authority endured and outlasted the problem.

At the same time, some trustees were as concerned that everyone understand the scope of their authority (that they had a right to fire Lattimore) as about the outcome of their deliberations (whether Lattimore would actually be fired). In other words, they cared as much about the certification or validation of their status, about the symbols of government, as about the content of the actions of the board. They were not particularly focused on ends, on deciding what to do about Lattimore and doing it. This stance did not help move the board towards finding a solution.

As for stability, in addition to the changes in the physical plant and the extended budget crisis experienced by Johns Hopkins in the early 1950s, university officials made the unsettled impasse resulting from the Lattimore case more unsettled by deciding to close the Page School. Denials notwithstanding, this gave the impression that university authorities were prematurely punishing Lattimore or that they were attempting to drive or nudge him to resign. This resulted in a backlash of sympathy. It energized some of Lattimore's allies, convincing them that they needed to take the offensive, that they should press the university. It, in effect, created a situation that invited faculty to become more involved in Lattimore's defense. It resulted in interested faculty having more influence in determining his fate. As a consequence, the board had less.

Because university authorities initially tried to ignore it, the Lattimore case was exacerbated. When they took decided steps against Lattimore—when they did not ignore him—they created more problems for themselves. It was only after Lattimore was ignored in the late 1950s that he made the break for which they had wished for so long. Their timing was not the best.

Academic Administrators and the Cold War

In 1919 before the governing board at Harvard University met to consider whether or not to fire the socialist Harold J. Laski, President A. Lawrence Lowell defiantly asserted "if the Overseers ask for

Laski's resignation, they will get mine."[14] In this earlier era, Laski, like Lattimore and many of the professoriat who were victims of the Cold War, had become the center of bitter political controversy. He had publicly supported the right of the Boston police to organize and join the American Federation of Labor (AFL), and had blamed the police commissioner for forcing a strike and creating the civil disorder that followed. Led by the press and scores of alumni, there was a great outcry for Laski's dismissal. Laski was not fired, and the Cold War on campus would have been much reduced if more college and university presidents had followed Lowell's example or explained and defended faculty views and rights to their boards. Too many were uncharacteristically mute. Even at Johns Hopkins the authorities said little.

Nothing could show more clearly than the Lattimore case that it is possible for institutions of higher learning to stand by faculty and principles of academic freedom and tenure under the most adverse circumstances. Given the general political climate, the charges and the impressive list of adversaries, beginning with Senator McCarthy, Lattimore could not have been more vulnerable. He was a popular target. Anyone with a complaint, pencil, and postcard was free to express his or her grievance. The five-year duration for which it took the case to be resolved also was a factor that worked against a favorable outcome for him. For these reasons, the Lattimore case is exemplary.

Not only were the pressures to placate those demanding Lattimore's dismissal both intense and extensive, but the Cold War years were perhaps the bleakest period in the history of American higher education. Xenophobia and the stifling of dissent increased the risks for all academics. For over a decade there was a systematic onslaught on the integrity and independence of the professoriat. On most campuses, faculty could not depend on academic administrators to help them defend themselves; quite the contrary. In many instances, academic administrators became adversaries to faculty. In words and deeds they did little more than echo the public consensus. In this sense, the situation at Johns Hopkins was nearly unique.

The dominant ideology of the Cold War was that communism was an evil with which it was dangerous to compromise. Those who questioned this premise, those who believed that contact and negotiations between the Soviets and Americans could ease international tensions, were suspect, and were often labeled as Communists. There was a considerable body of opinion that liberalism or nonconformity was a step on the road to communism, that an attack on liberalism or nonconformity was an attack on communism. Definitions of terms were elastic. Liberals were indiscriminately labeled as Communists; radicals as saboteurs. Those who were different, who did not respond with ritualistic conformity, were believed to lack loyalty to traditional economic institutions and to the Nation. Civil and academic authorities agreed that Communists—proven or suspected—should not be allowed to teach college students. When there was a charge of communism, faculty were required to respond, and to convince a campus president that it was false. In effect, some faculty had to take and pass a series of political tests. Academic administrators expected nothing less. Professors were expected to avoid public controversy and were held accountable for everything they said on or off campus. They were expected to sign loyalty oaths and to cooperate with congressional investigating committees; this often meant implicating others. Academic administrators often imposed greater restrictions on faculty than the state imposed on its citizens. Faculty from around the country were being hounded and harassed by moral entrepreneurs. Most academic administrators saw to it that all charges, no matter how far-fetched or mean-spirited, were given careful attention. Besides the many faculty who lost their jobs, there were many others whose careers were threatened. Because no one really expected academic administrators to stand behind faculty, faculty knew that they were vulnerable.

Campus presidents were apparently not overly bothered that they might be viewed as something other than advocates of fair play and faculty rights. Other concerns—the clamor from the public, self-interest, opportunism—were clearly transcendent. Securing their own positions was very much on their minds. Notwithstanding their training and background, they ignored academic values; their behavior was determined by structure and status. They were managers of institutions that marketed conformity and security. The public need not feel insecure, only faculty.

As a result there were campus investigations. Some faculty were put on probation. Some had their tenure revoked. There were suspensions before and after formal hearings. Those who did not agree to undergo or who failed a political test were almost always fired. Those whose political past was not completely above suspicion were often fired. Those who academic administrators felt were an embarrassment to the institution were sometimes fired. Faculty who received only a fraction of the notoriety of Lattimore were cashiered before charges against them could even be verified. In brief, a number of academics were forced to recant their political beliefs, some lost their jobs, and many more nearly did.[15] The effect on campuses was chilling.

In the face of pressure or in anticipation of unfavorable publicity, most of the time academic administrators caved in, appeased critics, and sacrificed faculty. Rather than challenging the political Right, they anticipated and accommodated. They were attempting to be fixers when they should have been builders. With prudence, they moved carefully and professionally. It was not always clear, however, what their goal was. They did not seem to recognize that prudence was a tactic (a means), not a strategy (an end). Despite a putative commitment to academic freedom, the majority of the colleges and universities caught in the anti-Communist furor succumbed to it. Few administrators stood fast in support of faculty under fire. Only rarely did one show courage when it was necessary. Most often heroics were not expected, at most only adherence to academic norms. The lack of zeal for protecting faculty was compensated in zeal for finding justification to terminate them. Administrators were more likely to be arbitrary than sympathetic. When faculty committees at the University of Michigan, Rutgers University, and the University of Washington concluded there was no reason to punish faculty whose politics were too far to the Left, the campus presidents precipitously overturned the recommendations and fired them, arguing that the committees did not understand the dangers of communism and subversion and had not acted responsibly.[16]

In the face of pressures during the Cold War years it is commonly heard that private universities of high prestige such as Johns Hopkins were in a position to resist, whereas less visible public institutions could not; they had to respond to politicians who directly controlled their budget. Many academic administrators in state colleges and universities certainly felt a great need to bow and scrape to those who voted on their funding, but it is unclear how much they were compelled to do so. Private institutions were no more financially independent than public institutions. Moreover, academic administrators in numerous colleges and universities of some reputation—private and public—also believed it was dangerous for them to retain political undesirables on their faculty. They seemed to have the same concerns about retaliation by those—private donors and public officials—who provided funds. To argue that because more private institutions stood fast, it was easier for them to thwart McCarthyism is circular (what logicians call the fallacy of *petitio principii*).

In rushing to judgment in condemning faculty, academic administrators appeared to abandon common sense. They were contributors to a long-held American practice of dismissing faculty without cause. They occasionally adopted the methods and mentality of the moral entrepreneurs. In doing so, they compromised the independence of the institution. They also sometimes disregarded decency. Most important, they showed quite conclusively that with few notable exceptions academic administrators were not honest brokers between faculty and the larger community. Who an individual was or what his political beliefs might have been was not as important as the fact that academic administrators had a great deal of power and faculty had very little. Academic administrators control institutions of higher learning.[17] It is a dangerous myth to consider a campus president as primus inter pares. Although most academic administrators are educators by training and experience, and some even by identification, they are not always educators by behavior. Among other things, all too often their concerns about public relations precludes this.

As the Lattimore case makes clear, the situation around the country could have been quite different. It is unlikely that any institution had more pressure to dismiss a faculty member than did Johns Hopkins. The fact that it did not yield suggests that generally academic administrators might have behaved differently, and at little personal risk. Did they have to take it upon themselves to enforce a political orthodoxy? Did they have to demand that faculty avoid public controversy? Did they have to hold faculty responsible for everything they said on or off campus? Did they have to cooperate with the forces of repression? To be sure, they felt it was expedient to do so. They might have resisted the moral entrepreneurs. They might have firmly articulated academic values. They might have restated the value of intellectual independence. In most cases the dismissal of faculty seemed shameful and unnecessary. What happened at Johns Hopkins raises the question of whether academic administrators had truly viable choices.

It should be clear by now that for the most part American institutions of higher learning are not structured in a way that encourages administrators to support faculty. Administrators are not responsible to faculty. To succeed, they need only convince the board that there is peace and order on campus and that they are fiscally prudent. This engenders cautious, low-risk responses. It seldom calls for high-minded, principled action. This is in large part why with regularity academic administrators abandoned faculty during the Cold War years. They were responding to the reward structure of institutions of higher learning, and this set them on a course which tied them even more to actions not in the interest of faculty. They became more a product of their situation. Capitulation in the face of any threat became the norm.

Thus, the structural conditions in American institutions of higher learning affected the behavior of administrators as much as anything else. It is hard to imagine academic administrators having behaved differently. Since each status carries characteristic images of the sort of people who should occupy it, and this fact encourages any incumbent to turn into that kind of a person, administrators behaved as generally expected. In short, an organization makes the person. It was not a failure of character that led to the Cold War on campus. The rare administrator who protected faculty was able to do so largely because he was normatively or structurally responsible to faculty. It is clear that the Johns Hopkins administration was normatively responsible to faculty. An administration that is not an extension of faculty is not accountable to it, regardless of the rhetoric of shared decision making and putative democratic norms.

Shared Governance and Other Traditions

In some cases, and to some extent, a continuing appointment (tenure) protected faculty from being arbitrarily and unjustly fired during the Cold War.[18] The fact that Lattimore's lectureship had always been defined as indefinite rather than term gave the board pause. To be sure, he was protected less by the belief that the principle of tenure was inviolable (the tenet that faculty could and should be terminated only for adequate cause: incompetence, moral turpitude, or financial exigency) than by the desire of the board of trustees to avoid hearings and dissension should he be asked to resign or be fired outright. Consistent with the business model, many trustees apparently felt that the board had the discretion to dismiss any faculty member that it wished. Few doubted that Lattimore's usefulness as an expert on the Far East to Johns Hopkins had been much reduced, and that for that reason he should be let go for the good of the university. What was at issue, what was foremost in the minds of trustees, was that his judgment was bad, his politics were suspect, and he had been resolutely ill-mannered to some powerful senators. Indeed, in light of his unprofessorial behavior many expressed surprise that for the good of the university he did not voluntarily resign.

The tradition and culture of the Johns Hopkins University were salient in guiding the board's and administration's handling of the Lattimore case. The respect shown the views and advice of faculty was consistent with that for which the university had always stood; from the time of its founding, university officials had taken for granted that faculty were not merely employees, but were the keystone of any institution of higher learning. Since its inception, it has been repeatedly enunciated at Johns Hopkins that the university, in the Germanic fashion, could not become prominent without finding and recruiting distinctive individuals and allowing them to do their work unhindered.[19] If the university were to succeed, faculty could not be ancillary to matters that touched their lives. This implies not only maximum freedom, but also holding faculty and what they stand for in high regard.

It was broadly understood by the Johns Hopkins administration that it would simply not do to ignore faculty opinion. That was not the custom at the university. The member of the board who made the initial overture to Daniel Coit Gilman to become the founding president of the university noted in his letter that the bequest for the university was not bound by " 'shackles of state, or political influence,' or denominational ties or sectional bias."[20] Academic considerations would be in the ascendancy. From the beginning, independence and respect for faculty were valued by all constituencies at Johns Hopkins. Before he accepted the presidency, Gilman was told in a letter that the board desired "the absence of . . . political spirit on the part of the president of the university."

On taking the presidency, Gilman wrote:

> The institution we are about to organize would not be worthy the name of a university, if it were to be devoted to any other purpose than the discovery and promulgation of the truth; and it would be ignoble in the extreme if the resources which have been given by the founder without restrictions should be limited to the maintenance of ecclesiastical differences or perverted to the promotion of political strife.
>
> As the spirit of the university should be that of intellectual freedom in the pursuit of truth and of the broadest charity toward those from whom we differ in opinion it is certain that sectarian and partisan preferences should have no control in the selection of teachers, and should not be apparent in their official work.[21]

Gilman obviously did not see faculty as underlings who could be dictated to and who could be expected to do unquestioning what they were told. He believed, for example, that the president of Johns Hopkins should "have the right to appeal any decision of the faculty to the board"; that there should be an office of the dean, who would be a representative of the faculty and would function as a vice president and faculty secretary; that to help govern the university there should be an Academic Council with faculty representatives.[22] He was a proponent of faculty power,[23] an idea deeply implanted at Johns Hopkins. He saw the university president as a representative of the faculty to the trustees and of the trustees to the faculty. At the same time, he envisioned a very circumscribed role for trustees: "trustees should not, except in great emergencies, or in cases of serious controversy, interfere with or overrule the action of the faculty, when exercised in the matters which fall within its sphere. In all ordinary cases the trustees should register and confirm the conclusions which the faculty have worked out."

> While the president should be expected to make suggestions and proposals for the advancement of the college, it should be within the province of the faculty to counsel him in his action pertaining to educational matters. . . . If he has a just idea of his office, he will shrink from assuming any great responsibility, unless it be in an emergency, without the sanction of his advisors. Although he should have a voice in the selection of teachers, his choice should never be final; in making a nomination he should take counsel, if not of all the faculty, at least of those who are most conversant with the duties of the station in question. . . . [24]

Clearly, a commitment to shared responsibility in the management of institutions of higher learning only obtains in a small number of schools around the country, although Gilman believed it was a necessary arrangement where faculty did more than simply teach. He envisioned "the freedom of 'the university' and not the restrictions of 'the college.' "

At about the time Johns Hopkins enrolled it first student, the trustees reacted to an instance of outside pressure by resolving: "the board does not interfere with the scholastic arrangement of the university." At the fifth Commemoration Day, Gilman noted that there had been no complaints about limitations on freedom of action: Johns Hopkins' bequest had not placed restrictions on the trustees, the trustees had not placed restrictions on the faculty, and the faculty had not placed restrictions on students.[25] Forbearance had been an early and permanent mark of the university. It was not merely rhetoric, but something that had taken root. There have been few lapses.

It is of singular interest that Walter Hines Page, one of the first fellows at the university and later the editor of the *Atlantic Monthly* and ambassador to Great Britain under President Wilson, after whom the school headed by Lattimore was named, shared this commitment to faculty autonomy and self-government. In a famous test of academic freedom at Trinity College (later renamed Duke University) a half century before the Lattimore case, Page intervened on behalf of a beleaguered faculty member, John S. Bassett, a professor of history, who himself had received a Ph.D. from Johns Hopkins. Bassett had published an article in the October 1903 issue of the *South Atlantic Quarterly* in which he asserted that during the five previous years there had been a general increase of prejudice against Negroes across the country, particularly in the South. This could be seen in, among other things, new voting restrictions, the passage of Jim Crow legislation, and more and more lynchings. It was due, Bassett argued, to feelings of racial superiority on the part of whites: "It is doubtful if the average southern white farmer would admit that the highest Negro in America is superior to the southern hired man who is white."

Bassett pointed out that it was a serious mistake to place Negroes automatically into an extreme social group, and that "[Booker T.] Washington . . . [was] the greatest man, save General [Robert E.] Lee, born in the South in a hundred years."[26] He was critical of politicians for appealing to social antipathy in order to win elections. He thought it possible that the future would bring both more overt conflict between the races and greater equality.

Not surprisingly, the article generated uncompromising outrage, and Bassett was attacked daily, week after week. The newspapers were particularly harsh in their judgment and commentary. He was accused of slander and libel, ridiculed, and his character, intelligence, and sanity were questioned. There was an outcry that Bassett be removed from the faculty of Trinity, and a campaign to boycott the college received widespread support.

To alleviate the pressure on the school and its president, Bassett submitted his resignation, but before the trustees could act on his offer, Page wrote to the college's benefactor Benjamin N. Duke.

> As to the correctness or incorrectness of the opinion he expressed in his article that has given offense, that is a question of no importance. But it is of the highest importance that a

> professor from Trinity College should be allowed to hold and to express any rational opinion he may have about any subject whatever; for this, of course, involves the question of freedom of speech. I take it for granted that Dr. Bassett is not going to suffer any practical harm. If he does not, that will be a splendid vindication of the free atmosphere of the institution. Professors in southern institutions have many times lost their places and been driven from home for offenses less than this. When this, therefore, brings no such result, it is a splendid tribute to the college, and to its atmosphere.

In a second letter, Page repeated his appeal: "I hope that he [Bassett] will not be permitted to resign—will not be driven out on the cry of 'nigger.' Trinity must stand, as you stand, for free thought & free speech. It will give the college a worldwide good reputation for courage if it withstands this cry & keeps Bassett. God help us all to a little courage—don't you say so?" Just before the trustees met to consider the matter, Page wrote for the third time.

> It is the best chance that ever came or that ever could come for Trinity to show that it is the home of free thought and of free speech. I think you ought to thank God for such a chance—as I have no doubt you do.
>
> The fight is squarely drawn. It is a fight for free speech—for the freedom of Trinity College. I know how you feel about it, & I know you will win.—I wish I had a hand in it myself. I'd give a year's growth for a chance to stand up & say what I think & how I feel.
>
> When you win this fight, you may forever afterwards be sure that *Trinity College will be free—and everybody will know that it is free*. Liberal people all over the United States will rejoice and congratulate the college. Every really great & free institution in the whole country will rejoice; and Trinity will stand higher than it could be made to stand by many years of good quiet work. It is a *great* chance—a chance to show the whole world that there is at least one institution in the South & in North Carolina that is free. It will be the best thing that could happen for the State & for the South.
>
> What if fools criticize it? What if even some good men criticize it? What if half the boys were withdrawn? Nothing better could happen. What is a great college for? Isn't its main purpose to be a place for absolute freedom of thought & speech? For every boy that may be withdrawn, the college will

> get a dozen a few years hence, when men come to their senses. For every man who takes offense, a hundred better men will be pleased & will rally to you.[27]

Bassett was endorsed by the faculty, president, and trustees, and kept his job. With the victory, Page did not lose interest in the principles of free speech and academic freedom he had championed. He concluded a magazine article describing the political currents that set off the storm at Trinity with the same themes he had used with Benjamin Duke.

> By this emphatic action Trinity College did an enormous service to academic life everywhere and gave an impetus to southern liberality of opinion that cannot be overestimated. It has made friends for itself and admirers in every enlightened community in the whole country, and its future development will be watched with pride.[28]

In spite of the parallels of this incident with Lattimore's experience, there is no evidence that any member of the board of trustees at Johns Hopkins thought of Bassett or Page's liberal spirit during the 1950s and that this bit of history informed and affected anyone's decision. Still, it merits attention as nothing could better show the deep and long-standing sentiment at Johns Hopkins for an unswerving regard for faculty rights, and the appreciation that faculty are something more than mere employees who as a matter of course place their careers at risk by running afoul of moral entrepreneurs. There is little doubt that the source of the values held by those who chose to stand by Bassett was the same as that held by those who chose to stand by Lattimore.

One still hears criticism of the academic community for not resisting McCarthyism. To be sure, there were too many well-known instances when academic authorities too readily capitulated, and such condemnation is obviously well deserved. The Lattimore case not only shows how the administration and board at one particular institution stood its ground, but also that there were pockets of resolve and that it was possible to protect faculty under fire. The Cold War did not make an inquisition (a Cold War on campus) inevitable, although the authority and normative structures of the American college and university made it likely.

Some argue that differences in traditions of shared governance among institutions, variations in the power of presidents vis à vis governing boards, and the special vulnerability of public institutions made it very difficult for academic administrators universally to defend faculty. On its face, this seems plausible. We do not know, however, if more academic administrators could have defended faculty as this was generally not an option considered or taken. Academic administrators readily buckled to the threats and demands of the moral entrepreneurs—politicians, alumni, editors, and special interest groups. To contend that standing firm was not possible is not convincing. To be persuasive, one would need to point to some failed attempts to repulse assaults on faculty. To contend either that American higher education completely caved in to McCarthyism or that it was impossible not to do so is to misrepresent facts and possibilities.

Bureaucratic Settings and Professional Norms

The prospects that academics will be able to reduce the effects of administrative decisions on their working and nonworking lives are not promising. The reasons for this are structural: the professoriat are employees in bureaucracies.

As understood by sociologists, a bureaucracy is a rational, efficient organization. Its most salient characteristics are hierarchial authority, an unambiguous division of labor based on specialized competence in which statuses are clearly delineated, systematic rules, and impersonality. Institutions of higher learning have many features of bureaucratic organizations. They are first of all complex organizations. Although the administrative hierarchy is not typically highly elaborated, authoritarian, or rigid, authority is graded and functions are precisely delegated. Institutions of higher learning are at least semibureaucracies. Faculty are involved in some dual control. Although sometimes diffuse, authority does filter down from above. It is more centralized than collective. Authority resides in formal offices overseen by administrators, and there is some subordination. Officially, institutions of higher learning are hierarchically organized.

As a rule, faculty have little direct power over the running of institutions of higher learning. At the same time, their activities form the basis for organizational rules and administrative decisions. Academic administrators control resource allocation which directly influences what can be done and how it can be done. They have the power to hire, fire, promote, assign, reward and discipline. Faculty play only a passive role in fiscal matters, personnel problems, and the determination of educational and research objectives. It is academic administrators who have the power to allocate human and fiscal resources. Freidson describes the authority of academic administrators.

> [T]hey decide not merely what individual faculty members will be paid and what the standard work load will be but also what faculty positions will be filled, which is to say, what courses can be taught competently, what disciplines will be staffed, what programs will exist, and what the curriculum itself can be. The faculty has the discretionary right to determine how those resources, once granted, will be put to use but not the right to determine how those resources are to be allocated in the first place. . . . [T]he power to allocate resources that remains in the hands of the administration places limits on the work the faculty is able to do and the manner in which it is able to do it.[29]

In a word, faculty have minimal control over the economy of the organizations that employ them. As Reece McGee put it:

> Real power in academic institutions is the power over budget, for budget decisions determine who is to be hired and who is not and what he will be paid, what programs will be encouraged or shut off from futher support, and what lines of endeavor will be rewarded.[30]

Academic administrators, and not faculty, serve as policymakers in an ultimate, truly managerial sense. Faculty may set out choices, but it is the administration that chooses. Faculty propose, but administrators dispose. To be sure, in their own teaching and research faculty are free to use their discretion. According to the National Labor Relations Act those with the authority "to hire, transfer, suspend, lay off, recall, promote, discharge, assign, reward, or discipline" are employers,[31] and by this definition academic administrators would certainly qualify as such. Those whom they could hire, transfer, and the like—that is, faculty—would by elimination be their employees.

Academics may not control the terms of their work, but they are free to control its content and the technical instruction of their recruits. In routine matters, they are free from meticulous supervision and direction. There is some diffusion of formal control. Faculty are, for example, responsible for the recruitment, training, and selection of new faculty. It can thus be said that interwoven in institutions of higher learning are both bureaucratic and equalitarian elements. But the former dominate.

According to the commonly accepted definition of the term, college and university faculty are professionals. One characteristic of a profession is that those who follow it exercise control over their work and its outcome. They also decide on the methods of control they use. Ideally, professionals determine what to do, how to do it, and the aim or goal of their activities. They have had prolonged and specialized training, mastery over a body of knowledge, and are committed to using this knowledge in accordance with standards set by other professionals, not the organization in which they are employed. Self-government and autonomy are professional norms. In other words, the professions are those occupations that control their own work. They develop standards of performance and rules of conduct. They evaluate their colleagues on the basis of how closely they adhere to these standards.

Although they have professional status, academics are not free agents. They must carry out their work in a bureaucratic setting. As employees of institutions of higher learning, the professoriat are without important freedoms, most particularly some involving control over the terms and conditions of work. Vulnerable to administrative direction, they lose autonomy. The controls of employment and employees in a semibureaucracy routinize academic work. Faculty must abide by rules and policies not necessarily of their making. Professional norms and bureaucratic norms are sometimes incompatible. Quite simply, employment in a complex organization reduces professional autonomy. Bureaucratic organizations are often at odds with the work requirements, norms, and values of professionals. Colleges and universities sometimes get in the way of academic work, teaching and research.

The apparent incompatibility between professional and bureaucratic norms make faculty quite vulnerable. It is not simply that the work situation of faculty creates tension. The fact is that faculty are employees in organizations and that this condition impinges on professorial autonomy. At times, the autonomy of the professoriat can be greatly curtailed. The need of colleges and universities to coordinate many complex tasks make full professional autonomy impossible. At the same time, academic administrators are not trained or competent to delegate, supervise, or evaluate the work of the professoriat—art historians and zoologists, statisticians and philosophers. Yet, administrators are given authority by governing boards to delegate, supervise, and evaluate.

The fact that academics are professionals may preclude the possibility that institutions of higher learning will become plain and simple bureaucracies. However, organizational realities and pressures pretty well preclude the possibility that any academic institution can evolve into a company of equals. When professional and bureaucratic values clash, as they did in the Lattimore case, there invariably will be victims. The fact that Lattimore even had to defend himself at Johns Hopkins made him one.

Appendix A: Inquiry into Lattimore's Loyalty: Chronology of Main Events, 1950–55

March 1950:	Senator Joseph R. McCarthy charges that Owen Lattimore is the "top Soviet [Russian] espionage agent" in the United States.
April 1950:	Lattimore defends himself before the Tydings committee.
July 1950:	Tydings committee report calls Senator McCarthy charges "a fraud and a hoax."
July 1951:	Lattimore questioned in executive session by McCarran committee.
February–March 1952:	Lattimore questioned for twelve days by McCarran committee about his political beliefs and associations.
July 1952:	McCarran committee report recommends indictment of Lattimore for perjury.
December 1952:	Grand jury returns seven-count indictment. The Johns Hopkins University places Lattimore on leave.
May 1953:	Federal Judge Luther W. Youngdahl dismisses main count and three minor counts, leaving three minor counts. Government appeals Youngdahl's decision.
July 1954:	Appeals court sustains Judge Youngdahl, 8–1, on main count; sustains him on one minor count; reinstates two minor counts.
October 1954:	Government reindicts Lattimore on two new charges, to replace the old main count, after moving that Judge Youngdahl disqualify himself for prejudice.

January 1955: New indictment dismissed.

June 1955: Government drops case against Lattimore.

*Appendix B: Owen Lattimore's Comments on Senator McCarthy before the Tydings Committee**

But that office, the position of United States senator, likewise, carries with it a responsibility which this man Joseph McCarthy has flagrantly violated. As a citizen who holds no official position, it is my right and duty to list these violations which are illustrated by the senator's conduct in my own case.

He has violated it by impairing the effectiveness of the United States government in its relations with its friends and allies, and by making the government of the United States an object of suspicion in the eyes of the anti-Communist world, and undoubtedly the laughing stock of the Communist governments.

He has violated it by instituting a reign of terror among officials and employees in the United States government, no one of whom can be sure of safety from attack by the machine gun of irresponsible publicity in Joseph McCarthy's hands.

He has without authorization used secret documents obtained from official government files.

He has vilified citizens of the United States and accused them of high crimes, without giving them an opportunity to defend themselves.

He has refused to submit alleged documentary evidence to a duly constituted committee of the senate.

---

*Congress, Senate Subcommittee of the Committee on Foreign Relations, *State Department Employee Loyalty Investigation: Hearings before a Subcommittee of the Committee on Foreign Relations,* 81st Cong., 2d sess., 8 March 1950–28 May 1950, 418, 420, 439, 441.

He has invited disrespect to himself and his high office by refusing to live up to his word. Twice on the floor of the senate he stated that any charges that he made under the cloak of immunity, he would repeat in another place so that their falseness could be tested in a court of the United States. He said that if he should fail to do this he would resign. He has been called to repeat his charges so that they could be tested in a court action. He has failed to do so. And he has not resigned.

. . . I wonder a bit how a man so young as Joseph McCarthy, whose acquaintance with national and international affairs is so recent, can have become such a great expert on the difficult and complex problem of China and the Far East. My wonder on this score increased when I read his speech on the senate floor. Some of his material is from Chinese and Russian sources. Or perhaps I should say that some of his exotic material on Mongolia appears to trace back to some Russian source of distinctly low caliber.

I did not know that the senator was a linguist. But really, the material that the senator read is so badly translated and so inaccurate that I am sure that I should not like to place the blame for it on the learned senator. Indeed, I fear that the sound and fury come from the lips of McCarthy, but that there is an Edgar Bergen in the woodpile. And I fear that *this* Edgar Bergen is neither kindly nor disinterested.

Senator McCarthy, without, I am sure, knowing what he is about, has been and is the instrument or the dupe of a bitter and implacable and fanatical group of people who will not tolerate any discussion on China which is not based upon absolute, total and complete support of the Nationalist government in Formosa. They do not hesitate at—they even insist on—policies that potential allies of ours in India, Indonesia, Pakistan and other countries will call ruthless imperialism. Their conclusion—that is, that the United States should put all of its eggs in the Nationalist government's basket—may be right or wrong. I think it's wrong.

But I am *sure* that the methods of that faction of these people who are McCarthy's Edgar Bergen, are wrong—as wrong as wrong can be. Their methods are to intimidate persons like me and even officials of the United States government from expressing views that are contrary to their own. Their weapon of intimidation is McCarthy's machine gun: namely, accusation of disloyalty and traitorous conduct. I get a certain amount of wry amusement out of the fact that some of these people are acknowledged ex-Communists. Perhaps that status gives them a special right to criticize those of us who do not happen to be Communists, ex- or otherwise. Certainly, it provides them with ideal training and unique skill for the kind of campaign of vilification and distortion that the so-called China Lobby is conducting through the instrumentality of the senator from Wisconsin.

I say to you, gentlemen, that the sure way to destroy freedom of speech and the free expression of ideas and views is to attach to that freedom the penalty of abuse and vilification. If the people of this country can differ with the so-called China Lobby or with Senator McCarthy only at the risk of the abuse to which I have been subjected, freedom will not long survive. If officials of our government cannot consult people of diverse views without exposing themselves to the kind of attack that Senator McCarthy has visited upon officers of the State Department, our governmental policy will necessarily be sterile. It is only from a diversity of views freely expressed and strongly advocated that sound policy is distilled. He who contributes to the destruction of this process is either a fool or an enemy of his country. Let Senator McCarthy take note of this.

*Appendix C: Testimony of General Barmine, Head of the Russian Department of the Voice of America and a Former Officer in the Russian Army**

Mr. Barmine. When the question of using military men of the intelligence apparatus came to discussion, several names were mentioned of foreign nationalities. . . .

Mr. Morris. Who were the Americans?

Mr. Barmine. Owen Lattimore and Joseph Barnes.

Mr. Morris. They were mentioned as "our people" by Berzin who could be assigned to this project you were complaining about where you did not have the personnel to staff.

Mr. Barmine. We played with this idea. . . .

Senator Eastland. He spoke of Mr. Lattimore and Mr. Barnes as two agents of Soviet military intelligence.

Mr. Barmine. He spoke of them as "our men."

Senator Ferguson. Meaning Russian men?

---

*Congress, Senate Internal Security Subcommittee of the Committee on the Judiciary, *Institute of Pacific Relations: Hearings before the Subcommittee of the Committee on the Judiciary,* 82d Cong., 2d sess., 26 February 1952–3 March 1952, 193–211.

Mr. Barmine. It was my understanding meaning military intelligence.

Senator O'Conor. Had you ever heard of Owen Lattimore and Joseph Barnes before that?

Mr. Barmine. No.

Senator O'Conor. Did you later hear of them?

Mr. Barmine. They were the first American names that ever came to me.

Mr. Morris. These names came up not only once but they came up more than once?

Mr. Barmine. Yes. . . .

Mr. Chairman. During a subsequent conversation did they tell you what organization these men were working with?

Mr. Barmine. When it came to the second time, as I remember, that was the first time the Institute of Pacific Relations was mentioned. The question was that there were more important things and they would be more suitable with the plans in connection with the Institute of Pacific Relations, the building up of the branches of the Institute of Pacific Relations, and the military using it for a cover shop for military intelligence work in the Pacific area. . . .

Mr. Barmine. . . . He said that we had some important planning developments in connection with the Institute of Pacific Relations and the men would be valuable more in connection with this, so let us forget about them.

Senator Ferguson. What men would be valuable in that institute?

Mr. Barmine. Lattimore and Barnes, Americans. . . . The idea was, as was explained, that the Institute of Pacific Relations being an organization [which] can carry research work, [which] can open branches around the Pacific in the countries where we were not yet recognized—the Soviet Union at this time has no embassy all around the Pacific areas—with this difficulty about contacts, the idea which I was given was that that is the idea, undercover work when you can have legal reasons and innocent reasons to travel to do specifically military research and reconnoitering work and gathering of information materials, because military intelligence is comprised of the gathering of printed material, classified and unclassified, of every kind. You have reason to keep the foreign members of the military network on the job, you can send them from one area to another, you can have for them a legitimate reason to have their offices to gather information, to get in contact with people who know something about geography, topography, and many other things.

So the explanation I was given was that the Intelligence Division considered this a very valuable outlet, a very valuable cover organization, they have an important plan for it, because it would be extremely convenient. . . . [A]t this time this was considered important for Russia, which was developing to use this and to build within this organization the convenient apparatus which could have this very innocent and respectable cover.

Mr. Morris. May I bring that out so it is clearly understood? In other words when you discussed the Institute of Pacific Relations with General Krivitsky he told you that that particular Soviet operation, the cover shop in the institute, was doing very well and you would be amazed at what important contacts they were making in connection with their work?

Mr. Barmine. Yes. . . .

Mr. Morris. Mr. Barmine, did he also confirm your impression of Barnes and Lattimore, your recollection of Barnes and Lattimore, that is?

Mr. Barmine. He knew about them.

Senator O'Conor. He has not told us specifically what General Krivitsky told him about Barnes and Lattimore.

Mr. Barmine. That they are working within the Institute of Pacific Relations and they are still, what he said, "they are still our men."

Senator Jenner. When the chief of the military intelligence says, "he is one of our men," would that leave the impression in your mind that he was a top Communist in America?

Mr. Barmine. Not necessarily. That assumes it; that doesn't preclude it. . . .

Senator Eastland. Did you tell any agency of the United States government what you knew about Lattimore and Barnes?

Mr. Barmine. When I was asked by the FBI agent who came to me I told him exactly the same thing as I told you. I was asked about it several times . . . and it was several years ago already and then they came repeatedly. So I couldn't tell you exactly the date.

Senator Ferguson. But the FBI did have that evidence that you have told here this morning about Mr. Barnes and Mr. Lattimore; is that right?

Mr. Barmine. Well, if you call it evidence—

Senator Ferguson. Well, your statements that you gave here.

Mr. Barmine. Yes.

*Appendix D: Testimony of Harvey M. Matusow, Staff Member of the Ohio Un-American Activities Commission, and Former Communist Party Member**

Mr. Morris. Mr. Matusow, did you work at a Communist party book shop while in the Communist party?

Mr. Matusow. Yes; I worked at three different book shops.

Senator Eastland. Now, did you carry books by Owen Lattimore?

Mr. Matusow. We did, sir.

Senator Eastland. Why?

Mr. Matusow. In 1948, as I think this document will show, the Communist party literature set-up had not caught up with the fast-moving events in China; that is, the war in China and the setting up of the Chinese Communist government. The only material they had published by the Communist Party, either International Publishers or New Century Publishers, [was] a pamphlet by Mao Tse-tung, the *Turning Point in China,* and *China's New Democracy.* Two pamphlets, nothing else. Well, the party had to get the line disseminated. People were asking "what is the line on China?" And

*Congress, Senate Internal Security Subcommittee of the Committee on the Judiciary, *Institute of Pacific Relations: Hearings before a Subcommittee of the Committee on the Judiciary,* 82d Cong., 2d sess., 13 March 1952, 3823–47.

we had instructions in the bookshop that came down from the New York State educational department of the Communist party, to refer the members of the party to the following books. . . .

Mr. Matusow. . . . *Solution in Asia,* by Owen Lattimore, was used in the Communist book shop at the Jefferson School and the workers' book shop. It was required or recommended reading for students at the school. . . . Those books I just outlined were basically the books that the party stated carried out [the] party line on China.

Senator Ferguson. Did you understand those were the only kind of books that were sold in those book shops, that if it was not party literature it was not sold?

Mr. Matusow. That is correct.

Senator Ferguson. Do you mean to tell me that only Communists bought in these bookshops, or were they open to the world?

Mr. Matusow. They were open to the public.

Senator Ferguson. The name "Communist" did not appear in any way with it?

Mr. Matusow. That is correct.

Senator Eastland. He has gone further than that, though. He said that the books that he mentioned, that Communist party members were advised that those books represented the Communist party China policy. Is that correct?

Mr. Matusow. That is correct, sir.

Senator Eastland. That was Lattimore's book.

Senator Ferguson. But I am getting a general idea, rather than just Lattimore's book, that if I came in to that bookshop to buy a book, I wouldn't know anything about it being a party-line book.

Mr. Matusow. That is correct, sir.

Senator Ferguson. But suppose I come in as a Communist. Did you ever have anybody come in the bookshop and say, "I am a Communist and I want such a book?"

Mr. Matusow. Yes, in my position in the bookshop, I knew by sight probably 10,000 party members in New York. I had seen them at various mass meetings or they knew me to be a Communist. We will put it that way. On that basis, many people would come in to me and say, "we are holding a club educational at this meeting," at so and so club tonight, and "we have to prepare for the subject of China." They might not have had this outline or had the outline and wanted to expand on it. "What book is recommended to supplement the outline or recommended reading for the club?" That happened on many occasions. On the question of China, I was told to recommend . . . *Solution in Asia* by Lattimore.

Mr. Morris. On the China group?

Mr. Matusow. That is right.

Senator O'Conor. Could I ask one question: You stated that you were instructed to recommend. By whom, just what method was followed to give you the authority or the word that that was to be the book or books recommended?

Mr. Matusow. That came down from the New York State educational department of the Communist party, through the state literature director who was a member of that commission.

*Appendix E: Senator McCarthy's Principal Evidence against Lattimore** [*with some clarification in brackets*]

1. Lattimore was a member of Russian military intelligence, and during his connection with the Institute of Pacific Relations that organization was "cover shop for Soviet military intelligence work in the Pacific area." [Charge made, not substantiated.]

2. Jack Stachel, a leading American Communist, told Louis Budenz to "consider Owen Lattimore as a Communist." [Budenz's charge not corroborated.]

3. According to instructions issued to Budenz by party leaders, Lattimore was a "party member under Communist party discipline." [Budenz's charge not substantiated.]

4. David N. Rowe, professor of political science at Yale University and a lieutenant colonel in military intelligence, testified: "As of today among Far Eastern specialists in the United States, Lattimore is probably the principal agent of Stalinism." [Rowe's assessment credible to some, not others.]

5. In 1943, Lattimore passed to the American politburo an important change of the party line on China. [Charge not substantiated.]

6. Highly secret Communist party documents sent to Moscow bore the identification symbols "L" and "XL," Lattimore's party identification symbols. [From Budenz's charge; not substantiated.]

*Senator Joe McCarthy, *McCarthyism: The Fight for America, Documented Answers to Questions Asked by Friend and Foe* (New York: Devin-Adair Company, 1952), 52–66.

7. Lattimore was a member of a Communist cell in the Institute of Pacific Relations. [No evidence of cell.]

8. Lattimore was "given an assignment by the politburo" to recruit Communist writers to sell the American people the Communist party line on China. [Charge made, not substantiated.]

9. Lattimore used the Soviet diplomatic pouch to send material to Moscow.

10. Lattimore received correspondence from Richard Sorge, head of a famous Communist spy ring in Asia.

11. Lattimore was a member of the editorial board of *Amerasia* from 1938 to 1941. Government agents later found secret government papers in the magazine's office.

12. A few days before the arrest of two figures in the *Amerasia* case, the two were seen in Lattimore's home "declassifying documents," though neither Lattimore nor the two others had authority to do so. [Documents said to be galley proofs.]

13. Lattimore's wife lectured at the Tom Mooney Labor School in San Francisco, a recognized Communist party training center.

14. Lattimore bought a half share in a Vermont farm adjacent to property owned by alleged Communist leaders. He later sold it to Ordway Southard, an acknowledged Communist from Alabama, and took a mortgage for the entire price without any down payment.

15. On a tour of China, Lattimore addressed a mass meeting at the Communist military stronghold at Yenan.

16. While head of the Pacific division of the Office of War Information, Lattimore engineered the employment of Communist Chinese. [Distortion of facts.]

17. Lattimore advised the head of the Institute of Pacific Relations in July, 1938, by letter, to support the official Chinese Communist position in China, and to back the international policy of Russia in general.

18. Before going to China in 1941, Lattimore spent two hours with the Russian Ambassador in Washington. At that time Russia was still allied with Germany in a nonaggression pact.

19. Shortly before the Japanese attack on Pearl Harbor, while the Secretary of State was trying to negotiate a way to preserve the peace with Japan, Lattimore sent an urgent cable to the White House from China at cross purposes with the State Department's plan. At that time, Communist policy was to support Chiang Kai-shek in his fight against Japan.

20. In 1949, Lattimore, at the request of Secretary of State Dean Acheson, wrote a secret document for the guidance of Philip Jessup. In the document he advised: (a) that the United States withdraw all support from Korea, (b) that no support be given to anti-Communist forces in Formosa, (c) that the United States should refuse to support any league of Asiatic countries against communism, (d) that the United States should agree to the admission of Red China into the United Nations, (e) that the United States should pull its forces out of Japan. [Distortion of facts.]

21. At a State Department conference in 1949, attended by, among others, Governor Harold Stassen, General George C. Marshall and John D. Rockefeller, III, Lattimore "consistently argued for the adoption of a ten-point program on Asia which followed the official Communist line." [Distortion of facts.]

22. On his visit to China with Henry Wallace in 1944, Lattimore was toasted by a high Soviet official as one "on whom rests great responsibility for China's future."

23. On July 17, 1949, in an article in the New York *Sunday Compass,* Lattimore advocated that the United States "let South Korea fall" but not "let it look as though we pushed it."

24. Lattimore's books have been praised by Communist publications. [And also criticized.]

25. Lattimore's book, *Solution in Asia,* was required reading at the Jefferson School of Social Science, a school run by the Communist party in New York City. [Testimony to senate committee.]

26. The Communist cause "benefited greatly by Lattimore's book reviews for the *New York Times* and the *New York Herald Tribune,* in which he consistently endorsed and praised such books on China as those of Edgar Snow, Israel Epstein, Guenther Stein and Laurence Rosinger." These books "gave the Communist line on China, including the idea that the Chinese Communists represented the party of land reform, free and improved education, better sanitary conditions and agrarian reform."

Appendix F: Time, *1950: Investigations: "A Fool or a Knave"**

It was Owen Lattimore's turn to answer Wisconsin's blustering Joseph McCarthy and the senate's big caucus room was packed to capacity. A short, mild-looking man with a scraggly sandy mustache, Professor (Johns Hopkins) Lattimore settled himself down at the microphones at one end of a T-shaped table, plumped down a fat, 42-page statement in front of him, adjusted his spectacles. Then he fixed a cold eye on his accuser, who smiled indulgently on him from the ranks of distinguished visitors behind the committee table.

Witness Lattimore had come to answer what he called McCarthy's "base and contemptible" charges that he was a top Soviet agent. But it was a little difficult, he declared, to decide just what he now stood accused of. The first time he had been named by McCarthy he had been let off as a simple "pro-Communist." Then he had become "the top Russian espionage agent," as suddenly he had been demoted again to a "bad policy risk."

Twisted Quotes. What was the evidence that he was a Russian spy? Lattimore demanded. McCarthy had talked darkly of an ex-Communist who would swear that Lattimore had been under party discipline. "I do not know the name of this alleged witness," said Lattimore. But leaning forward earnestly, he made a sweeping denial that he was or ever had been a Communist, a Communist fellow traveler or a Communist dupe.

The rest of McCarthy's accusations, said Lattimore, were based on "perverse and twisted" quotations from his books, on phrases lifted out of context, on old, discredited rumors and gossip from highly suspect sources.

---

*"Investigations: 'A Fool or a Knave,' " *Time,* 17 April 1950, National Affairs section.

Said Lattimore: "I get a certain amount of wry amusement out of the fact that some of these people are acknowledged ex-Communists. Perhaps that status gives them a special right to criticize those of us who do not happen to be Communists, ex- or otherwise."

Maybe Wrong. Lattimore spoke with the smooth assurance of the experienced lecturer and he had the crowd with him. A few days before, he had made public his August 1949 memorandum to the State Department on U.S. policy in Asia. At the hearing, he testified that the whole question raised by McCarthy actually got down to an argument over the best course for the U.S. to follow in the Far East. After re-stating his opposition to Chiang Kai-shek and the Chinese Nationalists, he urged one of two courses: 1) encourage Chinese nationalism even though it be Communist nationalism in the hope of making a Tito out of Mao or preferably 2) "encourage in every possible way conditions that will make possible the survival of a so-called third force, a democratic group within China."

"Now, gentlemen," said Lattimore, "my analysis of this may be partly or wholly wrong. But if anybody says that it is disloyal or un-American, he is a fool or a knave." At the end of his statement Lattimore paused for a moment, looked squarely at his accuser, added: "Let Senator McCarthy take note of this."

"Up to This Moment . . . " Just before the subcommittee's cross-examination ended, Chairman Millard Tydings broke in. Three Democrats and one Republican on the committee, Tydings said had looked at a summary of Lattimore's FBI file prepared by Director J. Edgar Hoover "and it was their unanimous opinion that there was nothing in the file to show you had ever been a Communist or connected in any way with espionage. . . . The FBI file puts you completely, up to this moment at least, in the clear."

McCarthy had promised to stand or fall on his case against Owen Lattimore, and he clearly had little left to stand on. But one crutch was hesitantly proffered him. The fifth member of the committee, Iowa's Republican Bourke Hickenlooper, next day looked at the FBI summary and said he could not give any blanket absolution without a look at the full files, although he was "not making any final conclusions either way."

Hickenlooper's was just about the only encouragement that Joe McCarthy got all week long. Even before Lattimore took the stand, Republican Henry Cabot Lodge told the senate that McCarthy had proved none of his charges. Then Republican Seth Richardson, who heads the Civil Service Commission's Loyalty Review Board, and Republican Conrad Snow, who heads State's own security board, testified that the whole loyalty program had not turned up a single example of espionage.

At week's end, McCarthy made one last desperate attempt to regain the offensive. Appearing at a meeting of the Marine Corps League in New Jersey to get the league's award for Americanism, ex-Marine McCarthy boldly announced that he was prepared to repeat his charges in public, as Lattimore had demanded, and dared anyone to sue him for libel. But what he produced was a far cry from his original talk of communism and espionage; it was simply a weasel-worded statement that Owen Lattimore,

Ambassador-at-large Philip Jessup and the State Department's John Service sometimes agreed with policies that paralleled the Kremlin line.

Having thus produced a dull thud, unstoppable Joe McCarthy set forth again. Protected once more by senate immunity, he turned over to committee investigators the name of a man who, he said, would swear that Owen Lattimore was or had been a member of the Communist party.

Appendix G: Time, *1952: Investigations: "Absent-Minded Professor?"*++

The hue and cry over Owen Lattimore, the professor and publicist who played an influential role* in the shaping of U.S. Far Eastern policy, is part of a greater clamor of alarm: What U.S. mistakes led to the Communist conquest of China and the assault in Korea? Who is responsible for the mistakes?

Last week, as Lattimore testified in his own behalf before a panel of inquiring senators, the U.S. learned a good deal more about the professor and a little bit more about the how and why of mistakes in the Far East.

WITNESSES AGAINST. The public examination of Lattimore's record goes back to 1950. After Wisconsin's Senator Joe McCarthy charged that Lattimore was a "top Soviet espionage agent," the senate Tydings committee held hearings and gave the professor a ringing clearance. But not everyone was convinced that the last word had been said. Since last July, a Senate Subcommittee on Internal Security, headed by Nevada's Pat McCarran, had been going over the ground again. Main points in testimony:

Only one witness, ex-Communist Louis Budenz, definitely called Lattimore a Communist.

++"Investigations: Absent-Minded Professor?," *Time,* 10 March 1952, 22.

*Among Lattimore's governmental assignments: President Franklin Roosevelt's personal emissary to Chiang Kai-shek (1941–42), head of the OWI Pacific operations (1942–44), traveler with Vice President Henry Wallace in Soviet Siberia and China (1944), co-writer of the Pauley Mission Report on Japan (1946), participant in State's conference on China policy (1949).

Another witness, former Red Army intelligence officer Alexander Barmine, said that his Russian superiors referred to Lattimore as one of "our men."

Documents were produced from the files of the Institute of Pacific Relations to show pro-Communist influence on *Pacific Affairs,* I.P.R. magazine edited by Lattimore (1934–41).

Presidential aspirant Harold Stassen, ex-diplomat Eugene Dooman, Professors William McGovern, Kenneth Colegrove and Karl Wittfogel variously testified that Lattimore, Far East specialist and Director of the Walter Hines Page School of International Relations at Johns Hopkins, followed a line favorable to the Communists, and that his ideas had powerful backing in the State Department.

THE DEFENSE. To rebut this testimony, Lattimore came last week before the McCarran subcommittee with a 50-page statement that bristled with some of the angriest denunciation ever directed by a witness to a congressional inquiry. Lattimore's statement (released to the press before he took the stand) categorically denied that he had ever been a Communist or pro-Communist. It minimized his influence on U.S. policymaking and said that actually he stood for containment of communism, Point Four and peace. It berated the McCarran inquiry as "stacked" against him, accused it of launching "a reign of terror" against U.S. diplomats. Not since the late Harold Ickes had any polemicist turned on more derisive invective.

Lattimore called McCarthy the "Wisconsin whimperer . . . a graduate witchburner." He raked Budenz as perjured and immoral, Stassen as "irresponsible," the Nationalist Chinese as "driftwood on the beaches of Formosa." He even flailed away at people who had not appeared before the committee; for California's Senator William Knowland, who believes the Nationalists should get more U.S. support, Lattimore picked up a Communist-favored sneer, "The Senator from Formosa."

When the professor started to read his statement before the senators, he found the going rough. At every sentence he was interrupted by indignant questions. Gruff Pat McCarran said the professor's tactics of "intemperate and provocative expressions" were also Communist tactics.

Maryland's Herbert R. O'Conor asked: "What steps were taken by you to prevent Communists from having a voice in the Institute of Pacific Relations?" Lattimore answered: "I was not responsible for employment." Pressed further, the professor, long cited as an American authority on Soviet Asia, said he was really an innocent on ideologies: "I was not an expert on communism. . . ." Had any mistakes been made in U.S. China policy? Sidestepped Lattimore: "I make a distinction between mistakes and lack of success."

CROSS-EXAMINATION. It took three days for Lattimore to finish reading his statement. Then, in a more subdued atmosphere, his cross-examination began. Again the professor fell back on his self-claimed naivete about communism and Communists.

Some 20 contributors to *Pacific Affairs* had been previously identified before the subcommittee as Communists or pro-Communists. Lattimore swore, "I don't believe I ever knew or was told" they were Communists. The senators then confronted the professor with I.P.R. documents, and he began to retreat a little.

Before the Tydings committee Lattimore had said he did not know Frederick Vanderbilt Field, an active I.P.R. official,** as a Communist until "1940–41," when Lattimore's term as *Pacific Affairs* editor was ending. A letter from the I.P.R. file persuaded him to change his mind. He must have known Field's ideology as early as 1939. "My memory was in error by about two years," he admitted. One I.P.R. memo, from Field to Lattimore, read like an order: discussing a certain article, it cautioned editor Lattimore that "the analysis is a straight Marxist one and . . . should not be altered."

"ANSWER YES OR NO." Subcommittee counsel Robert Morris produced an I.P.R. report of a meeting in Moscow (1936) at which Lattimore conferred with top representatives of the I.P.R.'s Russian council. The Russians, geographer V. E. Motylev and Comintern veteran G. N. Voitinsky, discussed *Pacific Affairs.* Motylev asked for a "more definite line" in articles. According to the I.P.R. report: "[Lattimore] said he would like to meet the Soviet suggestion as far as possible. . . . If the Soviet group would start on such a line, he would be able to make [other councils] cooperate more fully. . . ."

Michigan's Senator Homer Ferguson: "That line was the Communist party line, wasn't it?"

Lattimore: "In my opinion, no."

Ferguson: "What line was it . . . if it wasn't the Communist party line?"

Lattimore: "The line of the Soviet Council of the I.P.R. . . . Nothing Communist about it . . . "

Chairman McCarran (banging gavel): "Answer yes or no."

Lattimore: "I believe the Russians have at various times followed lines . . . that had nothing Communist about them. . . ."

Lattimore had told the Tydings committee that he didn't have a desk in the state department; he had also told an executive session of the McCarran inquiry that he never took care of the mail of Lauchlin Currie, then an assistant to President Franklin Roosevelt. Under cross-examination, he confessed to being absent-minded. He did, after all, remember having a room in Currie's offices in the old State Department building; he used it frequently. Furthermore, it was true that during Currie's absence, he read Currie's mail.

This week the senators continued their probe of the professor's faulty memory. They were not proving Lattimore a Communist; but they were exposing what looked like a powerful Communist web of propaganda and persuasion, around him, the I.P.R. and, ultimately, around U.S. policymaking.

**Last Week Field was freed from federal prison at Ashland, Ky. He had been sentenced last July for contempt of court, i.e., for refusing to answer questions concerning Communist bail funds.

Appendix H: Examples of Letters Critical of Lattimore

Dear President Bronk:

As one who is familiar with your educational institution, and is friendly with many of your alumni and faculty members, I want to protest against the continuation of Owen Lattimore as a member of your staff, irrespective of any and all considerations at this time.

I have spent considerable time in the fight against communism in Washington and elsewhere. I attended all the sessions of the Un-American Affairs [*sic*] Committee at which both Chambers and Hiss testified. I attended four sessions of the first Hiss trial and ten of the second trial. I know personally many of the attorneys and the judges who participated in the legal proceedings.

The same persons who warned me against Hiss have also warned me against Lattimore. The same persons who defended Hiss have been defending Lattimore. I watched Lattimore testify before the McCarran committee. I have never seen a more arrogant and contumacious witness.

Your institution is losing prestige and support every minute by your failure—I am speaking of the entire administration rather than of you personally—to suspend Lattimore immediately without pay. I do not see how you can expect to continue to receive support from persons whose manner of life has been so constantly under attack by Lattimore and his friends. The dispute is not over the question of academic freedom; the dispute is definitely confined to those who think that there should be an inalienable right to attack communism at home as well as abroad. There is no hysteria except among the fanatic Communists and fellow travelers who wish to expand their fields for propaganda instead of contracting them to the vanishing point in respect for the verdict of the voters two months ago.*

*Henry E. Mills to Detlev Bronk, 31 December 1952, the Johns Hopkins University Archives, Office of the President Records, File #902.

Dear Dr. Bronk:

I have not had the privilege of knowing you, although I have heard some of your alumni, who are friends of mine, speak about you.

For several years, hardly a week has passed without some new and startling disclosures about the unfortunate activities of Owen Lattimore, and I, like a great many other citizens, have been wondering how it was possible for a man with his character and record, to still continue his activity as a professor at the Johns Hopkins University. To be sure, as an American citizen he has a perfect right to whatever political ideas he may choose to extol, and to say what he pleases, but there is no question about it that his influence in the various official and unofficial positions which he has held, over a period of years, has been most unfortunate, not to say disastrous for our country. And holding the views which he does, he certainly is not to be trusted as a guide and instructor for our young people, at Johns Hopkins or any other place. I am sure that this is a correct statement of public opinion prevailing with regard to Dr. (?) Lattimore at this time.

It is all the more difficult for people to understand that you are retaining a man of such questionable character and reputation, even now, after he has been indicted for perjury and there is every likelihood that he may land in the penitentiary, before very long.

Unfortunately, the American people have had to put up with a lot of scandal in and around our government, during the last few years, but they have made it unmistakably clear last month that they want a change. The men in our government and particularly also on the staffs of our universities, should only be men of the highest character and integrity, to whom we, and especially our youth may look up to with confidence and admiration. That could hardly be said of Owen Lattimore and I feel strongly that you owe it to the people, in deference to public opinion, to ask for his resignation, at the earliest possible moment. We need moral leadership. Let us follow the example of our new president and get rid of anything and anybody that does not come up to our new and higher standards.**

**Henry Renfert to Detlev Bronk, 23 December 1952, the Johns Hopkins University Archives, Office of the President Records, File #902.

Appendix I: Examples Showing How News of the Korean War Affected Content of Letters

1. The sorry plight we are in today and the indubitable inferences from the proofs against this man Lattimore are sufficient to arouse the scorn and even the hatred of all Americans now trapped in the morass of Asia by reason of the treasonable machination of men either ignorant of the defiling ideology of Asiatic communism or else malicious with intent to further its designs here and in Asia—as indeed has been done. Is it not time you took some action in the case of Owen Lattimore before you may be identified with him to bring more discredit on your institution?*

2. Surely you do not believe in the promotion of communism here or in the backing of any man who may be shown by formidable proofs to have contributed to the frightful and sanguinary war we wage today against this brutal, godless and lying terror, this new barbarism now sweeping Asia, and largely put where it is through the traitorous machinations of any man assuming to be employed and endorsed by an American university such as yours.

According to the McCarran committee this man Lattimore is today partly responsible for the slaughter of our sons in Korea and the terrible burden weighing down every man, woman and child in America, as the mass terror and deceit of Moscow lays us open here to defeat and dishonor.

If any man contributed to this end, and you have the full means to know the facts, and that man has the effrontery and you the indecency to keep him on your staff and pay him money to teach, then you are as guilty as he is, and just as treasonable.

---

*Clarence P. Milligan to President, received 25 March 1952, the Johns Hopkins University Archives, Office of the President Records, File #902.

Your own self respect would or should force you to get rid of a man like Lattimore and to do it NOW, or be classed with men of that type against whom the strongest proofs have been offered under the seal of the United States.

Surely you do not intend to lie down and sleep over a situation such as this, and thus hold yourself in the contempt of every decent American.[†]

3. If you do not know of it and cannot see the baleful influence it casts on your college, then you have not yet begun to be an educated man of the sensitivity befitting one of your high place.

As an American citizen close to whom has come death of some dear to me to rectify the treason of this man Lattimore and his ilk that let loose the new barbarism and godless brutality of communism on us in Asia, as an American citizen, I think I am entitled to some excuse from you for your dereliction and gross negligence to put it mildly in keeping this fellow in your employ.

Every time this dastardly story of perfidy is repeated your college is linked with this fellow. If you have any pride you should take heed of it and act accordingly.[‡]

4. You as an educational factor assuming to control and teach American youths, of which over 100,000 have been casualties in Korea as we Americans struggle and fall under taxation, I repeat, a man like you should be compelled to follow this Lattimore sell out and this story of a man still with the effrontery to take our money and stay on your staff, and KNOW what brought us to this brink by making you sit down and read *While You Slept,* by John T. Flynn, and also to listen to this man every night on a nationwide radio, as he exposes institutions of your type and the rascals who led us where we are today.

I ask you to get this book of Flynn's and to read it, and if you can still stand the stench of this THING, you are as bad as any man who sold us out to this new barbarism now clutching our throats and bidding fair to take over the Christian world.[§]

5. If you will read or if too lazy, get some smart student there to read for you the account of John T. Flynn's proofs as to the communism or procommunistic activities the very criminal course of this man Lattimore now traced in the blood of our children in Korea and the taxes on our backs, you will I believe, if you have a spark of decent loyalty or sympathy in your

---

[†]Clarence P. Milligan to President, 29 March 1952, the Johns Hopkins University Archives, [Office of the President Records, File #902].
[‡]Clarence P. Milligan to President, 31 March 1952, the Johns Hopkins University Archives, Office of the President Records, File #902.
[§]Clarence P. Milligan to President, 31 March 1952, the Johns Hopkins University Archives, Office of the President Records, File #902.

make up, get rid of this man before you and your institution are publicly branded as a coadjutor with treason against the United States.[‖]

6. The charges which Senator McCarthy makes in this questionnaire about Lattimore, and the frightful situation brought on by pro-Communists here in America to hasten the fall of National China and involve the United States in a war in the Orient, which we may well lose, and which is costing us untold distress, loss of our gallant youth and back breaking taxes, all this should move you to take some action—and to take it now.[#]

[‖]Clarence P. Milligan to President, 5 April 1952, the Johns Hopkins University Archives, Office of the President Records, File #902.
[#]Clarence P. Milligan to President, 26 April 1952, the Johns Hopkins University Archives, Office of the President Records, File #902.

*Appendix J: Excerpt from a Speech by Senator Pat McCarran Tying Owen Lattimore to the Communist Conspiracy**

In the brief time which remains to me, let me just tell you, in broad and general outline, a few of the things the Senate Internal Security Subcommittee has uncovered. Remember, my whole purpose is to arouse you to full recognition of the fact of the existence of the Communist world conspiracy, and the further fact of its real and present danger to the United States of America as a force operating from within. Remember also that everything I shall say is documented by sworn testimony, testimony under oath.

These are simple facts. The leaders of the Communist world conspiracy recognized twenty-five or more years ago the key position of China in Asia, and the necessity of capturing China for communism if the Communist world program was to come eventually to fruition. They thereupon began a campaign pointed toward the eventual communization of China as the key to the communization of all Asia. At the same time, they recognized that the United States was potentially an insurmountable obstacle to the attainment of Communist objectives in China and in Asia; and that if these Communist objectives were to be gained, the United States of America would have to be immobilized during the process. Recognizing that this immobilization, in all probability, could not be achieved through military action, the leaders of the Communist world conspiracy so long ago as 1927

*Senator Pat McCarran, "Eliminating Subversives from Government," Speech presented at the Metal and Nonmetallic Mineral Mining Convention and Exposition, the American Mining Congress, Denver, Colorado, 22–25 September 1952, p. 3–5, Nevada Historical Society.

had a well developed strategy of influencing the thinking of America, especially the thinking of officials and scholars, with regard to Asia; and for gaining control of public opinion, official opinion, and scholarly opinion, in this country, with regard to Asia, to an extent which would serve Communist purposes when the crisis in China became acute. They had this strategy developed more than twenty-five years ago; and they were already, even then beginning to work out the tactical means for carrying the strategy into effect.

These means were many and various; they included the infiltration of a scholarly and research organization known as the Institute of Pacific Relations; they included Communist penetration into the ranks of American scholars and students of Asia; they included the careful "indoctrination" of government officials, the slow building of influence within the State Department and elsewhere in our government. The time came when a substantial majority of all current texts and research works on China bore the influence of the Communist propaganda line. The time came when clever men, thoroughly indoctrinated with the Communist line respecting Asia, perhaps even believing that line, held important positions in the State Department and in other agencies of government, and were prepared and ready to go even higher when the way was opened for them. The time came when the fate of China, and the ultimate fate of all Asia, hung in the balance, where it could be tipped by the action or inaction of the United States; when strong support by us of the Chinese Nationalist government would mean defeat for the Chinese Communists and a severe setback, if not eventual frustration, for all the Communist aims in Asia.

The time came when a man named Owen Lattimore, a man of [a] carefully buil[t] reputation as a scholar and teacher, a man widely accepted at his own valuation of himself as an expert on Asia, a man with many friends in high places, laid on the desk of the president of the United States, memoranda favoring reversal of the policy which we were then following, of supporting the Chinese Nationalist government and opposing the Chinese Communists; memoranda urging that the top officials of the State Department dealing with Asia be replaced; memoranda urging that the United States halt aid to the Nationalist government of China as part of an effort to bring about a coalition between the Chinese Nationalist government and the Chinese Communists; memoranda which favored what amounted to total reversal not only of our then existing course of action in Asia, but of our whole traditional attitude with regard to China; memoranda which amounted to a recommendation that we abandon an ally at the moment of his greatest peril, and actually turn the weight of our influence against him.

The time came, my friends, when the course of action recommended in those memoranda, laid on the desk of the president of the United States by Owen Lattimore, became the official policy of the United States of America. The top officials of the State Department dealing with Asian affairs were removed or replaced. Mr. Grew was out. Mr. Ballantine was out. Mr. Dooman was out. Mr. Dean Acheson was in. Mr. John Carter Vincent was in. Others moved up. The time came when the essence of the Lattimore memoranda turned up in two documents written by John Carter Vincent, one a memorandum which was transmitted to the War Department and which came back from that department changed in form, but not in content or purport. These two documents, with a brief letter of transmittal, signed by the president, then became the mandate under which General Marshall undertook his ill-fated mission to China.

The time came when Chiang Kai-shek, denied the aid he had a right to expect from us, was forced off the mainland of China by Communist armies built up and strengthened for the campaign during the truce which we had demanded. The iron curtain clanged down at the shores of the Chinese mainland. We lost face throughout Asia in immeasurable degree. The world Communist conspiracy gained eight hundred million subjects, and an open door to the rest of Asia. The stage was set for Korea.

*Appendix K: Digest of the Minutes of the Board of Trustees and the Board of Trustees Executive Committee, the Johns Hopkins University, 1952–55**

"Business as Usual"

The following capsulizes the written record, totaling over four hundred pages, of matters considered by the full board of trustees and its executive committee during the years when the Lattimore case was in the forefront on the campus of Johns Hopkins, from when he appeared before the McCarran committee in 1952 until the perjury counts against him were dismissed by the courts and he returned to his academic duties in 1955. The analysis was undertaken in an effort to learn more about how the board went about its business during this period. In brief, a comparison of these minutes with materials from other years indicates that the board did not operate any differently during these four years than in earlier or later times; its activities and concerns were fairly constant. The Lattimore case did not take an inordinate amount of its time. Whatever matter it considered, it was provided with a great deal of information by the university administration that affected its decision. The board's handling of the Lattimore case was no exception.

Between 1952 and 1955, the board of trustees convened seventeen times, while the executive committee of the board had thirty-nine meetings.

---

*Minutes of the Board of Trustees (14 January 1952 through 24 October 1955) and the Board of Trustees Executive Committee (4 February 1952 through 28 November 1955) the Johns Hopkins University, made available by Ross Jones, Vice President and Secretary, the Johns Hopkins University.

The meetings followed a regular schedule, except five—one giving total attention to the Lattimore case and another largely concerned with it—which were called to consider out of the ordinary developments. The meetings were sometimes preceded by a luncheon, and, less often, followed by a reception. A tour of a new or remodeled facility also was not uncommon before or after a meeting. The board or executive committee rarely met in July, August, or September.

The meetings of the board of trustees lasted from as little as an hour and a half to as long as three hours. Most ran about two and a half hours. The shortest executive committee meeting was one half hour and the longest was two hours and fifteen minutes. Most were under an hour and a half. From time to time, social and other commitments on the part of board members made it necessary for it to curtail meetings. At the same time, there was more than the occasional meeting and minimal responsibilities expected of trustees on some of the more active standing committees of the board, for example, the Committee on Finance, the Committee on Budget, the Committee on Buildings and Grounds. Nonetheless, it is evident that only a few spent much time on campus or engaged in university-related business. The familiarity of most with the details of academic life was slight. The minutiae of campus life were not of interest to most trustees.

> Mr. White suggested that minor items requiring action should be eliminated from the agenda of the full board and that these three [or four] meetings each year should be devoted to questions of major university policy and consequently of general interest to members of the board who are not members of the executive committee. There was agreement on this point also. (March 2, 1953)

The number in attendance at the board of trustee meetings ranged from between twelve and twenty-seven (which represented nearly the full board) members, with an average of nineteen present. The attendance at the executive committee meetings ranged from five to twelve members, numbering eight or nine at half of the meetings. Some trustees had quite good records of attendance. The university administration was represented with an average of four individuals, not including the president who was counted with the trustees, at all meetings. Administrative officers were there in sufficient numbers so that the administrative point of view could be well represented, although there is no way of determining from the written record how, if at all, the administration went about presenting its perspective. (There, of course, is also no way of knowing how accurately these minutes represent the events they report or what went on among trustees when they were not in the boardroom.) At the special meeting of the executive committee when the decision was taken to place Lattimore on a paid leave of absence after he was indicted, seven trustees and five administrative officers were present.

Until Detlev Bronk resigned the presidency of the university at the end of the 1952–53 academic year to become president of the Rockefeller

Institute for Medical Research, he presided over almost all board and executive committee meetings. During Lowell Reed's interim presidency, the meetings were directed by an elected officer of the board.

Most information that came before the board was in the form of committee reports and readily received the approval of the larger body.

> Dr. Reed referred to the minutes of the October 4, 1954, meeting of the executive committee which stated that:
>
> The University Memorials Committee had reviewed the policy of naming buildings on the Homewood campus for the donor or for a scholar or a scientist. The University Memorials Committee recommended that the new engineering building be named Ames Hall in honor of the late Joseph S. Ames, who was an eminent scientist. The executive committee had recommended to the board of trustees that the new engineering building be named Ames Hall as recommended by the University Memorials Committee.
>
> It was unanimously voted that the new engineering building be named Ames Hall. (October 25, 1954)

Resolutions were routinely unanimously adopted. On some occasions no formal vote was taken. The board and the executive committee in effect operated by consensus. There was general agreement on both means and ends. The atmosphere of the meetings seemed to be quite relaxed, even when the discussion centered on the most serious questions. The one issue that seemed to generate the most disagreement, especially in 1952, among trustees was how to deal with Lattimore. Even here there was not great disharmony, only a lack of accord on how to minimize the negative effects—most particularly, the threat of lost financial support—of his remaining on the faculty of the university. Individual trustees did not appear to be out to pursue personal agendas. There seemed to be a tacit understanding of what the needs of the university were and how these could be readily achieved.

The president regularly reported on research grant applications and funding, on appointments and reappointments, on donors and donations, on degrees he had awarded and on other routine actions he had taken since the last meeting, and such detail was approved by the trustees as a matter of course. If there was dissent about any routine decision it was not noted in the official record. Hardly any question was discussed that created ideological controversy. Even potentially controversial topics such as discussions of the: "University's position in regard to government research contracts and the danger of becoming too dependent on overhead from such contracts to meet operating expenses" (12 January 1953) did not disturb the apparent tranquillity. The minutes indicate that as a rule there was a rapid transition from one topic to the next. Differences of opinion among board members or between board members and administrative officers seemed to be minimal. Little slowed the smooth and swift progress of a meeting.

The topics on which the board members received the most detailed information were those that involved the expenditure or borrowing of money. The board gave the largest proportion of its attention to financial matters and building projects. Discussions about the budget consumed the most time, and this was the subject of many of the longest meetings. The budget deficit and the financing of new buildings were regular agenda items. The state of the endowment was also of special interest to the board, as was the building program. How the endowment was invested, how the revenues it generated were being used, and how it could be increased were periodically reviewed. The board scrutinized loan agreements and bids for large construction projects. There was even a special meeting to discuss the contract for a new building. Trustees were instructed on how to make fund-raising effective, and on its progress. The board took note of larger gifts, and often heard accounts about the university's fund-raising activities. The board took care in examining appropriations, most notably those that were substantial or unusual. It acted on the acquisition and disposal of property, for example, land, buildings, a boat. It worked on arrangements for lending works of art. When new academic programs were proposed, it was most concerned about how they might be financed and what economic burdens they would add to the institution. It was most interested in the welfare of the Medical School and growing research institutes. Efforts at public relations were frequently praised, and ideas were put forth on how to improve them. The board worked hard to put the best face on things.

> Mr. Barton stated that this special meeting had been called by him, after consulting with Dr. Reed and with Mr. Charles S. Garland, vice president of the board of trustees, for the purpose of having the trustees express their views as to the future position of the university as to Mr. Owen Lattimore. He said that this matter had not been mentioned in the notice for publicity reasons and that the matters mentioned specifically were—a possible report by the committee to make recommendations as to the new president of the university and the status of the dormitory for the Medical Institutions. (9 September 1955)

The financing of construction of facilities for faculty and students required the most expert knowledge on the part of the board members. Specifics about mortgages and bonds were taken up time and again. Apparently, there was considerable expertise among board members on such matters, although the board made use of an investment counsel for security advice and a real estate firm to complete transactions relating to buildings and property.

> For the Committee on Finance, Mr. Garland noted that minutes of the Committee on Finance and its subcommittees are regularly circulated to all members of the board. He then added that:

> As of March 31, 1955 endowment investments had a book value of $47,600,000 and a market value of $68,900,000, with common stocks representing about 57% of total market value.
> The committee has authorized sales to reduce common stocks to 56% of total market value if the Dow Jones Industrial Average reaches 435 as the first steps in a program for additional reductions if the market continues its upward trend.
> The committee has also authorized a program to invest up to $3,500,000 in U.S. Government-guaranteed mortgages. (23 May 1955)

Specifics about the awarding of contracts were repeatedly a topic for discussion before the entire board. The board was active in planning increasing parking facilities and the renovation of buildings.

> Mr. Macaulay reported that after receipt of bids it was discovered that the cost of renovating the old Alumni Memorial Hall would exceed the estimates in the amount of $52,000. This situation, Mr. Macaulay reported, had been discussed by the trustees Committee on Buildings and Grounds, and the committee had unanimously agreed that there should be no drastic curtailment of the program for renovating the old dormitory. At a subsequent meeting, which included the Committee on Buildings and Grounds and the Administrative Council, it was agreed that an effort should be made to eliminate as many as possible of the capital improvement and extraordinary maintenance projects previously approved by the trustees in the 1954–55 budget, and to apply any savings resulting from such eliminations to the increased costs of restoring the dormitory. After review by Mr. Taylor and Mr. Macaulay, it was determined that $31,529 could be saved by eliminating certain improvements already provided for. It was voted to approve the joint recommendation of the Committee on Buildings and Grounds and the Administrative Council that an additional $52,000 be approved for 1954–55 for the renovation of Alumni Memorial Hall and that $31,529 of appropriations for other plant projects for 1954–55 be canceled. (21 June 1954)

The board deliberated the demolition of dilapidated buildings, reviewed and examined architectural plans, negotiated with the City of Baltimore about an exchange of property and about enhancing the flow of traffic, scheduled an inventory of property, and examined insurance policies. No fiscal question was ignored. In executive session, the board agreed that in developing the budget, the president and the budget officer should complete a line item review, and that other steps be taken "toward the drawing of as tight a budget as possible." In brief, the board was as involved in banking and real estate as in setting the course for an academic institution. Whether from custom or indifference, on academic matters it relied on the judgment of the president and his staff and did not interfere nor as a matter of course employ direct authority. It did not appear to advise the university administration on day-to-day problems. The president wielded the greatest power in such matters. The board seldom took decisions that affected single departments and seldom mentioned the undergraduate curriculum and students. Their intellectual growth was less important than the fact that they appeared contented.

> Dr. Bronk reported a high morale in the student body and a generally favorable reaction to the new plans, with little or no criticism of the amount of the increase in tuition rates. (14 January 1952)

The board was apprised of the development of professional and graduate programs.

More reactive than active, the board generally did not consider an issue unless it were a problem. It was most interested in Lattimore when he was making headlines in 1952; it was most interested in budgetary matters when the university was running a large deficit in 1954, and it spent an entire meeting reviewing this matter and considering options on how to reduce it. When there were no pressing issues, it discussed the naming of buildings and quadrangles, the relationship of the university with the federal government, the design of the mace, recruiting members for and reorganizing the board so that it could become more effective, expanding the administrative apparatus of the university, the selection of recipients for honorary degrees, and the election or appointment of board and administrative officers.

Board members were displeased by the notoriety Lattimore brought to the Johns Hopkins University. They felt that the university was being damaged by Lattimore's relationship with it. The distraction contributed nothing to the university and was a drain on resources. Pressure from the moral entrepreneurs made them uncomfortable and defensive. Mindful that Lattimore's truculence had greatly contributed to his and their problems, they were less moved by the fact that Lattimore's stand was courageous than by the fact that it was unpopular. If he had only been more cooperative. But he had not been and thus had become another uncertainty to which it was necessary to respond. Over the four-year period, the board spent significantly more time discussing, revising, and re-revising the pension plan than it did discussing Lattimore. The minutes did not indicate concern on the part of any trustee that Lattimore's presence on campus might have an adverse effect on students or the teaching program. Nor did the question of whether or not he was a Communist seem to arise. The board was satisfied that the administration gather facts about Lattimore and study them so that it would be prepared to take action in the event that it felt compelled to do so.

Notes

Introduction

1. Joseph Keeley, *The China Lobby Man: The Story of Alfred Kohlberg* (New Rochelle, N.Y.: Arlington House, 1969), 101–2. According to the *Oxford English Dictionary,* the term was first used in the *New York Post* on April 5, 1950.

2. William F. Buckley, Jr., "How Things Really Are in China," *Buffalo News,* 20 November 1990, sec. B, p. 3.

3. Tom Wicker, "Heresy and Disloyalty," *New York Times,* 25 July 1989, sec. A, p. 23.

4. William F. Buckley, Jr., "The Cold War's a Myth, Mr. Wicker?" *Buffalo News,* 19 July 1989, sec. B, p. 3.

5. Ellen W. Schrecker, *No Ivory Tower: McCarthyism and the Universities* (New York: Oxford University Press, 1986).

6. Ibid., 11.

7. David R. Holmes, *Stalking the Academic Communist: Intellectual Freedom and the Firing of Alex Novikoff* (Hanover, N.H.: University Press of New England, 1989).

8. Charles H. McCormick, *This Nest of Vipers: McCarthyism and Higher Education in the Mundel Affair, 1951–52* (Urbana and Chicago: University of Illinois Press, 1989).

9. Lionel S. Lewis, *Cold War on Campus: A Study of the Politics of Organizational Control* (New Brunswick, N.J.: Transaction Books, 1988).

10. Ibid., 268.

11. Dalton Trumbo, *Additional Dialogue: Letters of Dalton Trumbo, 1942–1962,* ed. Helen Manfull (New York: M. Evans, 1970), 569–70.

12. Even Lattimore's life and views have been the subject of book-length accounts. See John T. Flynn, *The Lattimore Story* (New York: Devin-Adair Company, 1953) and James Cotton, *Asian Frontier Nationalism: Owen Lattimore and the American Policy Debate* (Manchester, England: Manchester University Press, 1989). A fairly balanced and accurate description of Lattimore's entanglement with the federal government can be found in Stanley I. Kutler, *The American Inquisition: Justice and Injustice in the Cold War* (New York: Hill and Wang, 1982), 183–214. A nearly definitive account relying heavily on government documents of the debate surrounding Lattimore has been recently published: Robert P. Newman, *Owen Lattimore and the "Loss" of China* (Berkeley: University of California Press, 1992).

Chapter One

1. Owen Lattimore, "Rebuilding Our Policy in Asia," *Atlantic Monthly* (January 1950): 21–23.

2. Ibid., 23.

3. Owen Lattimore, "Asia Reconquers Asia," *United Nations World* 4 (March 1950): 21–24.

4. Ibid., 22.

5. Ibid., 23.

6. President Franklin D. Roosevelt to Generalissimo Chiang Kai-shek, 23 June 1941, FBI Headquarters File 100-24628-Owen Lattimore, Espionage (R)-5864a.

7. Richard Watts, Jr., "China Stirred by Assignment of Lattimore," *New York Tribune,* 24 August 1941.

8. Ray Richards, "Prof. Owen Lattimore's Job under Probe by House Subcommittee," *Baltimore News-Post,* 7 June 1946.

9. Alfred Kohlberg, "Owen Lattimore: 'Expert's Expert': The Monocle, the Commissar, the Old Homestead, and Snafu," *China Monthly* 6 (October 1945):10–13, 26.

10. Ibid., 12.

11. Ibid., 11.

12. Ibid., 26.

13. Owen Lattimore, "Reply to Mr. Kohlberg," *China Monthly* 6 (December 1945):15–17.

14. Ibid., 17.

15. Max Eastman and J. B. Powell, "The Fate of the World Is at Stake in China," *Reader's Digest* (23 June 1945): 13–22.

16. Ibid., 15.

17. Ibid., 22.

18. *Congressional Record,* 79th Cong., 1st sess., 28 November 1945, 91, pt. 8:11110.

19. "Owen Lattimore Is on Legion List," *Baltimore Sun,* 6 May 1947, sec. [1], p. 36.

20. Alfred Kohlberg, "China via Stilwell Road," *China Monthly* 9 (October 1948):283–87.

21. Ibid., 286.

22. "Memorandum for the Director, Re: Owen Lattimore," FBI Headquarters File 100-24628-Owen Lattimore, Espionage (R)-103.

23. As quoted in "Excerpts from Text of Majority Report on Charges by Senator McCarthy," *New York Times,* 18 July 1950, sec. [1], p. 16.

24. As quoted in William S. White, "Freda Utley Calls Lattimore No Red Spy, but a 'Judas Cow,' " *New York Times,* 2 May 1950, sec.[1], pp. 1, 9.

25. As quoted in William S. White, "McCarthy Accuses Point Four Official," *New York Times,* 14 March 1950, sec.[1], pp. 1, 4.

26. As quoted in William S. White, "Lattimore Denies He Was Ever a Red; Tydings Clears Him," *New York Times,* 7 April 1950, sec.[1], pp. 1, 6.

27. As quoted in Congress, Senate Committee on Foreign Relations, *State Department Employee Loyalty Investigation: Report of the Committee on Foreign Relations,* 81st Cong., 2d sess., 20 July 1950, 67.

28. As quoted in William S. White, "Truman Calls 3 Senators Saboteurs; Asks G.O.P. Name Foreign Affairs Aide; McCarthy Insists He Has Evidence," *New York Times,* 31 March 1950, sec. [1], pp. 1, 2.

29. "The Texts of Ambassador Jessup's Statement and of the Senator McCarthy Letters," *New York Times,* 21 March 1950, sec. [1], p. 24.

30. As quoted in Congress, Senate Subcommittee of the Committee on Foreign Relations, *State Department Employee Loyalty Investigation : Hearings before a Subcommittee of the Committee on Foreign Relations,* 81st Cong., 2d sess., 8 March 1950–28 May 1950, 440.

31. As quoted in Owen Lattimore, *Ordeal by Slander* (Boston: Little, Brown, and Company, 1950), 34.

32. “Owen Lattimore's Memorandum on United States Policy in the Far East,” drafted for State Department Advisory Committee, August 1949. Reprinted in the *Baltimore Sun,* 4 April 1950.

33. As quoted in White, “Truman Calls 3 Senators Saboteurs; Asks G.O.P. Name Foreign Affairs Aide; McCarthy Insists He Has Evidence.”

34. As quoted in Congress, Senate Committee on Foreign Relations, *State Department Employee Loyalty Investigation: Report of the Committee on Foreign Relations,* 827.

35. Richard Rovere, *Senator Joe McCarthy* (New York: Meridian, 1959), 5. Rovere adds: “[I]n their conduct of the Nation's affairs, Harry S. Truman and Dwight D. Eisenhower, from early 1950 through late 1954, could never act without weighing the effect of their plans upon McCarthy and the forces he led, and in consequence there were times when, because of this man, they could not act at all.”

36. “Text of Professor Lattimore's Statement Denying He Is a Communist and Denouncing Senator McCarthy,” *New York Times,* 2 April 1950, sec. [1], p. 4.

37. As quoted in Congress, Senate Committee on Foreign Relations, *State Department Employee Loyalty Investigation: Report of the Committee on Foreign Relations,* 67.

38. Congress, Senate Subcommittee of the Committee on Foreign Relations, *State Department Employee Loyalty Investigation: Hearings before a Subcommittee of the Committee on Foreign Relations,* 280.

39. Ibid., 768.

40. Ibid., 418.

41. Ibid., 419.

42. Ibid., 435–36.

43. Ibid., 484.

44. Thurman Arnold to George K. Gardner, 19 April 1950, Thurman Arnold Collection, American Heritage Center, University of Wyoming.

45. As quoted in William S. White, “Red Charges by McCarthy Ruled False,” *New York Times,* 18 July 1950, sec. [1], pp. 1, 17.

46. Congress, Senate Committee on Foreign Relations, *State Department Employee Loyalty Investigation: Report of the Committee on Foreign Relations,* 72–73.

47. As quoted in “Excerpts from Text of Majority Report on Charges by Senator McCarthy: Text of McCarthy Reply,” *New York Times,* 18 July 1950, sec.[1], p. 16.

48. As quoted in "Tydings Criticized on Lattimore Case," *New York Times,* 14 August 1950, sec.[1], p. 18.

49. As quoted in "McCarthy Urges Acheson Be Fired," *New York Times,* 16 May 1950, sec.[1], p. 14.

50. "McCarthy Hits Sale of Lattimore House," *New York Times,* 28 July 1950, sec.[1], p. 22.

51. Lattimore, *Ordeal by Slander,* 222.

52. Congress, Senate Internal Security Subcommittee of the Committee on the Judiciary, *Institute of Pacific Relations: Hearings before the Subcommittee of the Committee on the Judiciary,* 82d Cong., 2d sess., 26 February 1952–3 March 1952, 2915.

53. Ibid., 193–211.

54. Ibid., 522–23.

55. Ibid., 3984.

56. Ibid., 304, 657, 1323, 3315.

57. Ibid., 1013.

58. 26 February, 27 February, 28 February, 29 February, 1 March, 3 March, 4 March, 5 March, 6 March, 10 March, 14 March, and 21 March.

59. Congress, Senate Internal Security Subcommittee of the Committee on the Judiciary, *Institute of Pacific Relations: Hearings before the Subcommittee of the Committee on the Judiciary,* 2927.

60. Ibid., 2999.

61. Ibid., 2947.

62. Ibid., 1012.

63. Thurman Arnold to Elizabeth Toll, 17 March 1952, Thurman Arnold Collection, American Heritage Center, University of Wyoming.

64. Thurman Arnold to Robert M. Hutchins, 25 March 1952, Thurman Arnold Collection, American Heritage Center, University of Wyoming.

65. Thurman Arnold, *Fair Fights and Foul: A Dissenting Lawyer's Life* (New York: Harcourt, Brace, and World, Inc., 1951), 215.

66. Congress, Senate Internal Security Subcommittee of the Committee on the Judiciary, *Institute of Pacific Relations: Hearings before the Subcommittee of the Committee on the Judiciary,* 3674–75.

67. Ibid., 3200–3201.

68. Congress, Senate Committee on the Judiciary, *Institute of Pacific Relations: Report of the Committee on the Judiciary,* 82d Cong., 2d sess., 2 July 1952, 214.

69. Ibid., 224. By way of example, the reason the McCarran committee felt Lattimore's relationship with Lauchlin Currie was "substantial in import" was that as administrative assistant to President Roosevelt Currie had recommended Lattimore as an advisor to Chiang Kai-shek: "Ever since our discussion on this matter I have been looking for the right man, as the position is of enormous importance, particularly at the present juncture. I think I have found the man in Owen Lattimore, the Director of the Walter Hines Page School of International Relations of Johns Hopkins University. . . .

He would be, I am convinced, an extremely able and persuasive protagonist in China of your broad political attitudes." Memorandum from Lauchlin Currie to President Franklin D. Roosevelt, 29 April 1941, Franklin D. Roosevelt Library.

70. United States v. Lattimore. 112 F. Supp. 507, 515–19, 519–20 (1953).

71. United States v. Lattimore, 215 F. 2d 847–55 (1954).

72. Affidavit of bias and prejudice filed by United States against Judge Luther W. Youngdahl, 13 October 1954.

73. United States v. Lattimore, 125 F. Supp. 295–96 (1954).

74. Abe Fortas to Owen Lattimore, 25 August 1954, personal papers of Owen Lattimore, in storage, Arnold & Porter.

75. United States v. Owen Lattimore, Official Transcript of Proceedings, Criminal Nos. 1879–52 and 1016–54, 13 December 1954.

76. United States v. Lattimore, 127 F. Supp. 405–13 (1955).

77. United States v. Lattimore, 232 F. 2d 334 (1955).

78. As quoted in Luther A. Huston, "Lattimore Perjury Case Dropped by Government," *New York Times,* 29 June 1955, sec. [1], p. 1.

79. James Rorty and Moshe Decter, *McCarthy and the Communists* (Westport, Conn.: Greenwood, 1954), vii.

80. Ibid., 13. The negative image did not fade. Years after the events, one researcher who attempted to assess the facts stated: "A fair reading of all this material [the hearing testimony] . . . reveal[s] . . . the picture of a self-assured politico and inveterate busybody whose views extended over a wider area than his knowledge and who . . . more often than not [could] be found advocating positions on Far Eastern policy with which the Communists were in accord." (Herbert L. Packer, *Ex-Communist Witnesses: Four*

Studies in Fact Finding [Stanford, Calif.: Stanford University Press, 1962], 173–74.)

Chapter Two

1. John Putnam Demos, *Entertaining Satan: Witchcraft and Culture in Early New England* (New York: Oxford University Press, 1982), 182.

2. Howard S. Becker, *Outsiders: Studies in the Sociology of Deviance* (New York: The Free Press, 1963), 148.

3. Ibid., 162–63.

4. Ibid., 122.

5. Richard Hofstadter, *Anti-intellectualism in American Life* (New York: Alfred A. Knopf, 1964), 37.

6. Richard Hofstadter, *The Paranoid Style in American Politics and Other Essays* (New York: Alfred A. Knopf, 1964), 3.

7. Ibid., 7–8, quoting McCarthy, *Congressional Record,* 82d Cong., 1st sess., 14 June 1951, 6602.

8. John Lord O'Brian, *National Security and Individual Freedom* (Cambridge, Mass.: Harvard University Press, 1955), 46.

9. Ibid., 47–48.

10. J. C. Hubbard to P. Stewart Macaulay, 24 October 1951, the Ferdinand Hamburger, Jr., Archives of the Johns Hopkins University, Record Group Number 03.001, Office of the Provost, Series 2, P. Stewart Macaulay, Subseries 2, Numerical Subject Files, File #116, Walter Hines Page School of International Relations.

11. Fulton Lewis, Jr., Washington Report, "New 'Smear' MacArthur Campaign," 14 June 1951.

12. As quoted in "J.H.U. Rapped by Kohlberg: Its Trustees Commit 'Crime against Students,' He Says," *Baltimore Sun,* 17 March 1954.

13. FBI Headquarters File 100-24628–Owen Lattimore, Espionage (R)-837.

14. Robert A. Collier, Chief Counsel to United States House of Representatives, Committee on the Judiciary, Subcommittee to Investigate the Department of Justice, to J. Edgar Hoover, Director, Federal Bureau of Investigation, 9 January 1953, FBI Headquarters File 100-24628–Owen Lattimore, Espionage (R)-4066.

15. "Investigation Johns Hopkins," Letter to the Honorable Frank L. Chelf, 5 January 1953, FBI Headquarters File 100-24628–Owen Lattimore, Espionage (R)-4066.

16. Letter from L. L. Laughlin to Mr. Fletcher, [5] February 1950, FBI Headquarters File 100-24628–Owen Lattimore, Espionage (R)-153.

17. FBI Headquarters File 100-24628–Owen Lattimore, Espionage (R)-155.

18. Letter from J. Edgar Hoover, 30 July 1954, FBI Headquarters File 100-24628–Owen Lattimore, Espionage (R)-6034.

19. Letter from J. Edgar Hoover, 3 August 1954, FBI Headquarters File 100-24628–Owen Lattimore, Espionage (R)-6049.

20. FBI Headquarters File 100-24628–Owen Lattimore, Espionage (R)-2241.

21. FBI Headquarters File 100-24628–Owen Lattimore, Espionage (R)-837.

22. Memorandum from SAC, Baltimore (100-1630), to Director, FBI (100-24628), 12 February 1953, FBI Headquarters File 100-24628–Owen Lattimore, Espionage (R)-4201.

23. FBI Headquarters File 100-24628–Owen Lattimore, Espionage (R)-2241.

24. Memorandum from SAC, Baltimore (100-1630), to Director, FBI (100-24628), 12 February 1953, FBI Headquarters File 100-24628–Owen Lattimore, Espionage (R)-4201.

25. FBI Headquarters File 100-24628–Owen Lattimore, Espionage (R)-1013a.

26. FBI Headquarters File 100-24628–Owen Lattimore, Espionage (R)-2241.

27. Senator Joe McCarthy, *McCarthyism: The Fight for America, Documented Answers to Questions Asked by Friend and Foe* (New York: Devin-Adair Company, 1952), 57–66.

28. John T. Flynn, *The Lattimore Story* (New York: Devin-Adair Company, 1953), 110.

29. Ralph de Toledano, *Spies, Dupes and Diplomats* (Boston: Little, Brown, and Company, 1952), vii.

30. Ibid., viii.

31. Ibid., 124.

32. Ibid., 186.

33. Ibid., viii.

34. Paul W. Ward, "Spokesman Calls Action Step to Keep Professor from 'Skipping' Country: State Department Move Not Merely Routine, McDermott Asserts," *Baltimore Sun,* 21 June 1952, p. 1.

35. "Officials Have No Comment: State Department Won't Confirm or Deny 'Stop Order,' " *Baltimore Sun,* 20 June 1952, p. 1.

36. "Lattimore Restricted after Soviet Trip Tip," *Houston Post,* 21 June 1952, p. 1.

37. Patrick Skene Catling, "Has No Plans to Travel, Does Not Understand Action, Says Professor: Ban Initiated by State Department, New York Port Official Avers; Request for Stopping Departures Called 'Quite Rare,' " *Baltimore Sun,* 20 June 1952, p. 1.

38. Ward, "Spokesman Calls Action Step to Keep Professor from 'Skipping' Country."

39. Catling, "Has No Plans to Travel, Does Not Understand Action, Says Professor."

40. "Plans to Visit Reds Denied by Lattimore: Professor Says He Had Considered Teaching at India University," *Baltimore Sun,* 21 June 1952, p. 1.

41. *Congressional Record,* 82d Cong., 2d sess., 4 July 1952, 98, Pt. 11: 4336.

42. Letter from H. E. Wilson to the President of the John[s] Hopkins University, 21 June 1952.

43. Editorials, "The Fortnight," *The Freeman* 2 (28 July 1952).

44. Harold Lord Varney, "Johns Hopkins Flunks Anti-Communism Test," *American Mercury* (June 1959): 5–11.

45. Ibid., 5.

46. Ibid., 6.

47. Ibid., 7.

48. Ibid., 10.

49. Ibid., 9.

50. Ibid., 5.

51. Ibid., 11.

Chapter Three

1. Edward A. Shils, *The Torment of Secrecy: The Background and Consequences of American Security Policies* (Carbondale and Edwardsville, Ill.: Southern Illinois University Press, 1956), 142.

2. Edgar P. Walls to Detlev Bronk, the Ferdinand Hamburger, Jr., Archives of the Johns Hopkins University, Record Group Number 02.001, Office of the President, Series 1, Numerical Subject Files, 1878–1963, File #902, Walter Hines Page School of International Relations.

3. Clarence P. Milligan to President, the Johns Hopkins University Archives, Office of the President Records, File #902.

4. Letter from [Oluf L. Veierk], the Johns Hopkins University Archives, Office of the President Records, File #902.

5. The Johns Hopkins University Archives, Office of the President Records, File #902.

6. A. M. Causey to President, 26 May 1950, the Johns Hopkins University Archives, Office of the President Records, File #793.7.

7. James R. Young to P. Stewart Macaulay, 1 December 1945, the Ferdinand Hamburger, Jr., Archives of the Johns Hopkins University, Record Group Number 03.001, Office of the Provost, Series 2, P. Stewart Macaulay, Subseries 2, Numerical Subject Files, File #116, Walter Hines Page School of International Relations.

8. P. Stewart Macaulay to James R. Young, 5 December 1945, the Johns Hopkins University Archives, Office of the Provost, Series 2, Subseries 2, File #116.

9. James R. Young to P. Stewart Macaulay, 9 March 1946, the Johns Hopkins University Archives, Office of the Provost, Series 2, Subseries 2, File #116.

10. Letter from Mrs. E. Webster Wanner, 2 April 1950, the Johns Hopkins University Archives, Office of the President Records, File #793.7.

11. P. Stewart Macaulay to Detlev Bronk, 25 March 1952, the Johns Hopkins University Archives, Office of the Provost, Series 2, Subseries 2, File #116.

12. V. O. Hill to Gentlemen, 28 August 1950, the Johns Hopkins University Archives, Office of the President Records, File #793.7.

13. V. O. Hill to Gentlemen, 3 October 1950, the Johns Hopkins University Archives, Office of the President Records, File #793.7.

14. George E. Stringfellow to President, 1 August 1951, the Johns Hopkins University Archives, Office of the President Records, File #902.

15. George E. Stringfellow to President, 6 August 1951, the Johns Hopkins University Archives, Office of the President Records, File #902.

16. George E. Stringfellow to President, 23 August 1951, the Johns Hopkins University Archives, Office of the President Records, File #902.

17. George E. Stringfellow to President, 17 October 1951, the Johns Hopkins University Archives, Office of the President Records, File #902.

18. George E. Stringfellow to President, March 1952, the Johns Hopkins University Archives, Office of the President Records, File #902.

19. Letter from George E. Stringfellow, the Johns Hopkins University Archives, Office of the President Records, File #902.

20. Letter from George E. Stringfellow, the Johns Hopkins University Archives, Office of the President Records, File #902.

21. Internal Memorandum, 3 April 1950, the Johns Hopkins University Archives, Office of the President Records, File #793.7.

22. Mrs. Pearl P. Stevens to President, 28 January 1953, the Johns Hopkins University Archives, Office of the President Records, File #902.

23. Letter from N. W. Wal[ker], 6 April 195?, the Johns Hopkins University Archives, Office of the President Records, File #902.

24. George A. Finch to Dr. Detlev W. Bronk, 28 March 1952, the Johns Hopkins University Archives, Office of the President Records, File #902.

25. [C.] Madsen to President, 6 April 1952, the Johns Hopkins University Archives, Office of the President Records, File #902.

26. Sam Hiram Houston to President, the Johns Hopkins University Archives, Office of the President Records, File #902.

27. Semper Paratus to Dr. Bronk, 7 August 195?, the Johns Hopkins University Archives, Office of the President Records, File #902.

28. Letter to Detlev Bronk, the Johns Hopkins University Archives, Office of the President Records, File #902.

29. [H. E. Hepner] to President, 17 [December] 1952, the Johns Hopkins University Archives, Office of the President Records, File #902.

30. Richard Lloyd Jones to Dr. Bronk, 21 June 1952, the Johns Hopkins University Archives, Office of the President Records, File #902.

31. Richard Lloyd Jones to Detlev Bronk, 17 December 1952, the Johns Hopkins University Archives, Office of the President Records, File #902.

32. Letter, 10 April 1950, the Johns Hopkins University Archives, [Office of the President Records, File #902].

33. Postcard to Dr. Detlev Bronk, postmarked 5 July 1952, the Johns Hopkins University Archives, Office of the President Records, File #902.

34. Letter to President Bronk, received 1[9] April 1952, the Johns Hopkins University Archives, Office of the President Records, File #902.

35. Letter to Detlev W. Bronk, the Johns Hopkins University Archives, Office of the President Records, File #902.

36. Letter from [Julian T. Molj] (Yale Club) to President, the Johns Hopkins University Archives, Office of the President Records, File #902.

37. Letter from John Simpson, the Johns Hopkins University Archives, Office of the President Records, File #902.

38. Letter from C. L. Thomas, the Johns Hopkins University Archives, Office of the President Records, File #902.

39. Letter to President, 21 June 1952, the Johns Hopkins University Archives, Office of the President Records, File #902.

40. The Johns Hopkins University Archives, Office of the President Records, File #902.

41. R. C. Peters to Detlev Bronk, the Johns Hopkins University Archives, Office of the President Records, File #902.

42. The Johns Hopkins University Archives, Office of the President Records, File #902.

43. Letter, 28 March 1952, the Johns Hopkins University Archives, Office of the President Records, File #902.

44. Lawrence A. Stone to President, 2 July 195?, the Johns Hopkins University Archives, Office of the President Records, File #902.

45. Postcard, the Johns Hopkins University Archives, [Office of the President Records, File #902].

46. Letter from Arnold J. H.[], 3 [July] 1952, the Johns Hopkins University Archives, Office of the President Records, File #902.

47. Letter to President, the Johns Hopkins University Archives, Office of the President Records, File #902.

48. B. K. Fox to President, 21 January 1953, the Johns Hopkins University Archives, Office of the President Records, File #902.

49. Thomas A. Bush to President, 24 September 1952, the Johns Hopkins University Archives, Office of the President Records, File #902.

50. Letter from Richard Lloyd Jones, the Johns Hopkins University Archives, [Office of the President Records, File #902].

51. Leland H. Anderson, M.D., to President, 1 August 1951, the Johns Hopkins University Archives, [Office of the President Records, File #902].

52. Letter to Doctor Bronk, received 21 April 1950, the Johns Hopkins University Archives, Office of the President Records, File #793.7.

53. The Johns Hopkins University Archives, [Office of the President Records, File #902].

54. [The Johns Hopkins University Archives, Office of the President Records, File #902].

55. Letter from Spencer Clinton, 8 May 1952, the Johns Hopkins University Archives, Office of the President Records, File #902.

56. George S. Richardson, M.D., to Chancellor, 22 March 1952, the Johns Hopkins University Archives, Office of the President Records, File #902.

57. A. M. Causey to President, 26 May 1950, the Johns Hopkins University Archives, Office of the President Records, File #793.7.

58. J. Henderson to Edward R. Murrow, 2 May 1950, the Johns Hopkins University Archives, Office of the President Records, File #793.7.

59. Letter to Honorable Herbert Brownell, Attorney General, 30 March 1953, the Johns Hopkins University Archives, Office of the President Records, File #902.

60. Mrs. Charles Clifton Moses to Senator Pat McCarran, 13 August 1951, the Johns Hopkins University Archives, [Office of the President Records, File #902].

61. Elizabeth W. McMillan to President, 10 August 1950, the Johns Hopkins University Archives, Office of the President Records, File #[902].

62. Julian T. Bishop to President, 8 July 1952, the Johns Hopkins University Archives, Office of the President Records, File #902.

63. Senator Pat McCarran to President, 20 March 1952, the Johns Hopkins University Archives, Office of the President Records, File #[902].

64. P. Stewart Macaulay to Senator Pat McCarran, 31 March 1952, the Johns Hopkins University Archives, [Office of the Provost, Series 2, Subseries 2, File #116].

65. Joseph P. Kircher to Gentlemen, 27 March 1952, the Johns Hopkins University Archives, Office of the President Records, File #902.

66. H. A. Wilson to Dean of the University, 24 March 1952, the Johns Hopkins University Archives, Office of the President Records, File #902.

67. The Johns Hopkins University Archives, Office of the President Records, File #902.

68. Letter to President, 23 April 1952, the Johns Hopkins University Archives, Office of the President Records, File #902.

69. Mr. Patrick Ha[gingblau] to Gentlemen, 23 March 1952, the Johns Hopkins University Archives, Office of the President Records, File #902.

70. The Johns Hopkins University Archives, Office of the President Records, File #902.

71. Robert W. Williams to Detlev W. Bronk, 11 April 1952, the Johns Hopkins University Archives, [Office of the President Records, File #902].

72. Harvey S. R[ussel] to President, 3 July 1952, the Johns Hopkins University Archives, Office of the President Records, File #902.

73. G. E. Nelson, Jr. to Board of Directors, 1 August 1951, [the Johns Hopkins University Archives, Office of the President Records, File #902].

74. Edward N. Squire to Detlev Bronk, 20 May 1951, the Johns Hopkins University Archives, Office of the President Records, File #902.

75. Charles L. Horn to President, 25 June 1952, the Johns Hopkins University Archives, Office of the President Records, File #902.

76. Remarks added to "Probers Link Lattimore Aid to Red Party: Demand Investigation of Prof's Defender," *Chicago Tribune* Press Service, the Johns Hopkins University Archives, [Office of the President Records, File #902].

77. Remarks from A. Buckhei[m]er, the Johns Hopkins University Archives, [Office of the President Records, File #902].

78. Remarks added to Willard Edwards, "Bare Lattimore Wiles to Win China for Reds: Propaganda Snare for Banker Lamont Fails," *Chicago Tribune* Press Service, the Johns Hopkins University Archives, [Office of the President Records, File #902].

79. Donald B. Phillips to the president, 2 August 1951, the Johns Hopkins University Archives, [Office of the President Records, File #902].

80. Remarks added to Argus, "The Political Views of Hopalong Lattimore," *The New Leader,* 24 March 1952, the Johns Hopkins University Archives, Office of the President Records, File #902.

81. Headline from newspaper, 17 December 1952, the Johns Hopkins University Archives, [Office of the President Records, File #902].

82. Remarks added to article, Fulton Lewis, Jr., "What Ever Became of Owen Lattimore?" the Johns Hopkins University Archives, Office of the President Records, File #902.

83. Mrs. H. A. Gallagher to President, 1 June 1951, the Johns Hopkins University Archives, Office of the President Records, File #902.

84. Donald B. Phillip to President, 25 August 1951, the Johns Hopkins University Archives, [Office of the President Records, File #902].

85. Postcard from Carl Schoening, M.D., to Detlev Bronk, postmarked 30 March 1952, the Johns Hopkins University Archives, Office of the President Records, File #902.

86. Mrs. Pearl P. Stevens to President, 28 January 1953, the Johns Hopkins University Archives, Office of the President Records, File #902.

87. Mrs. Jane C. [Carson] to President, 1 May 1952, the Johns Hopkins University Archives, Office of the President Records, File #902.

88. Lee Crist to President, 2 April 1953, the Johns Hopkins University Archives, Office of the President Records, File #902.

89. [Joe Brown] to President and Board of Trustees, the Johns Hopkins University Archives, [Office of the President Records, File #902].

90. P. Stewart Macaulay to Sydney M. Cone, Jr., 21 July 1952, the Johns Hopkins University Archives, [Office of the Provost, Series 2, Subseries 2, File #116].

91. Charles Edey Fay to Detlev W. Bronk, 17 December 1952, the Johns Hopkins University Archives, Office of the President Records, File #902.

92. Gerald W. Johnson to President Bronk, 21 December 1952, the Johns Hopkins University Archives, Office of the President Records, File #[902].

93. Detlev W. Bronk to Gerald W. Johnson, 14 January 1953, the Johns Hopkins University Archives, Office of the President Records, File #902.

94. Mr. and Mrs. M. S. Koch, Jr., to Detlev Bronk, 20 December 1952, the Johns Hopkins University Archives, Office of the President Records, File #902.

95. Detlev W. Bronk to Mr. and Mrs. Koch, 23 December 1952, the Johns Hopkins University Archives, Office of the President Records, File #902.

96. Maury Maverick, 23 September 1953, the Johns Hopkins University Archives, Office of the President Records, File #902.

97. Lowell J. Reed to Mr. Maverick, 30 October 1953, the Johns Hopkins University Archives, Office of the President Records, File #902.

98. Victor Johnson, M.D., to Detlev W. Bronk, 19 December 1952, the Johns Hopkins University Archives, Office of the President Records, File #902.

99. Detlev W. Bronk to Dr. Victor Johnson, 14 January 1953, the Johns Hopkins University Archives, Office of the President Records, File #902.

100. Charles Edey Fay to Detlev W. Bronk, 17 December 1952, the Johns Hopkins University Archives, Office of the President Records, File #902.

101. Lionel Heap to President, 2 December 1952, the Johns Hopkins University Archives, [Office of the President Records, File #902].

102. Jesse Beer to Detlev W. Bronk, 26 January 1953, the Johns Hopkins University Archives, Office of the President Records, File #902.

103. Detlev W. Bronk to Jesse Beer, 3 February 1953, the Johns Hopkins University Archives, Office of the President Records, File #902.

Chapter Four

1. As quoted in "Bronk Confident Lattimore Will Have Reply," *Baltimore Evening Sun,* 13 March 1950.

2. Statement by Dr. Bronk, read to the press, 16 March 1950, the Ferdinand Hamburger, Jr., Archives of the Johns Hopkins University, Record Group Number 02.001, Office of the President, Series 1, Numerically-Coded Subject Files, 1878–1963, File #793.7, Loyalty Problems. It is worth noting that in 1981 Lattimore told an interviewer that Bronk had been advised by his predecessor to "get rid" of him. (David Harvey, "Owen Lattimore: A Memoire," *Antipode* 15, 3 [1983]:6.)

3. Three days after President Bronk's formal statement, Eleanor Lattimore expressed the view that "the university didn't want more publicity till Owen could answer for himself." (Eleanor Lattimore to Wilma and John [Fairbank], 19 March 1950, the Pusey Archives, Harvard University, John K. Fairbank papers, Box 10.)

4. "Lattimore's Record Cited: Wife Denies Communist Bent, Link to State Department," *Baltimore Sun,* 14 March 1950.

5. John K. Fairbank to Senator [Millard] Tydings, 27 March 1950, the Johns Hopkins University Archives, Office of the President Records, File #793.7.

6. Letter from Frederic C. Lane, the Johns Hopkins University Archives, [Office of the President Records, File #793.7], "Excerpts from Letters and Telegrams from Scholars with a Professional Knowledge of Owen Lattimore's Work."

7. Letter from George Grassmuck, the Johns Hopkins University Archives, [Office of the President Records, File #793.7], "Excerpts from Letters and Telegrams from Scholars with a Professional Knowledge of Owen Lattimore's Work."

8. As quoted in "Hopkins Students Back Lattimore," *Baltimore Evening Sun,* 4 April 1950.

9. FBI Headquarters File 100-24628–Owen Lattimore, Espionage (R)-4769, 17 June 1952.

10. Eleanor Lattimore to President Bronk, 20 March 1950, the Johns Hopkins University Archives, [Office of the President Records, File #793.7].

11. P. Stewart Macaulay to Dr. Bronk, 21 March 1950, the Johns Hopkins University Archives, [Office of the President Records, File #793.7].

12. Detlev W. Bronk to Senator Millard Tydings, 22 March 1950, the Johns Hopkins University Archives, [Office of the President Records, File #793.7].

13. "Promises Reply in Detail upon Return Home," *Baltimore Evening Sun,* 27 March 1950, and "Lattimore Denies Being Spy: Charges Are Termed 'Pure Moonshine;' Retraction Asked," *Baltimore Evening Sun,* 27 March 1950, Enoch Pratt Free Library, Baltimore, Maryland.

14. As quoted in "Bronk Says Senator Must Present Proof," *Baltimore Evening Sun,* 27 March 1950.

15. The Johns Hopkins University Archives, Office of the President Records, File #793.7, as quoted in "Hopkins Faculty Plans Tribute to Lattimore: Professors to Honor Colleague at Dinner Tuesday, Designed to Show Opposition to Attack," *Baltimore Sun,* 13 May 1950

16. John M. Scott, M.D., to Dr. George Boas, 15 May 1950, the Johns Hopkins University Archives, Office of the President Records, File #793.7.

17. Charles A. Thierry to the president, 15 May 1950, the Johns Hopkins University Archives, Office of the President Records, File #793.7.

18. Old Timer to Doctor Bronk, 17 May 1950, the Johns Hopkins University Archives, Office of the President Records, File #793.7.

19. Memorandum, 15 May 1950, the Johns Hopkins University Archives, Office of the President Records, File #793.7.

20. As quoted in Edgar Williams, "Faculty, Students Cheer Lattimore at Hopkins," *Baltimore News-Post,* 17 May 1950.

21. E. A. Park to President Bronk, 25 April 1950, the Johns Hopkins University Archives, Office of the President Records, File #793.7.

22. "Hopkins Group Asks Decision on Lattimore: Silence Would 'Discourage Free Expression,' A.A.U.P. Chapter Says," *Baltimore Sun,* 21 May 1950.

23. Donaldson Brown to Angus B. Echols, 17 August 1950, the Johns Hopkins University Archives, [Office of the President Records, File #793.7].

24. Donaldson Brown to Detlev W. Bronk, 17 August 1950, [the Johns Hopkins University Archives, Office of the President Records, File #793.7].

25. Donaldson Brown to Detlev W. Bronk, 17 August 1950, the Johns Hopkins University Archives, [Office of the President Records, File #793.7].

26. Detlev W. Bronk to Donaldson Brown, 13 September 1950, the Johns Hopkins University Archives, Office of the President Records, File #902.

27. George O. Blome to Board of Trustees, 14 January 1952, Special Collections, the Milton S. Eisenhower Library, the Johns Hopkins University.

28. Detlev W. Bronk to Mr. White, 24 January 1952, Special Collections, the Milton S. Eisenhower Library, the Johns Hopkins University, MS194, Series 7.

29. Francis White to Detlev W. Bronk, 28 [January] 1952, Special Collections, the Milton S. Eisenhower Library, the Johns Hopkins University.

30. George O. Blome to Board of Trustees, 25 February 1952, Special Collections, the Milton S. Eisenhower Library, the Johns Hopkins University, MS194, Series 7.

31. Carlyle Barton to Francis White, 12 March 1952, Special Collections, the Milton S. Eisenhower Library, the Johns Hopkins University, MS194, Series 7.

32. [Francis White], to Carl[yle] Barton, 27 March 1952, Special Collections, the Milton S. Eisenhower Library, the Johns Hopkins University.

33. Owen Lattimore to John K. Fairbank, 20 September 1950, the Pusey Archives, Harvard University, John K. Fairbank papers, Box 15.

34. John K. Fairbank to Owen Lattimore, 25 September 1950, the Pusey Archives, Harvard University, John K. Fairbank papers, Box 15.

35. Minutes of Meeting of 13 March 1952, the Ferdinand Hamburger, Jr., Archives of the Johns Hopkins University, Record Group Number 04.010, Academic Council of Homewood Faculties, Subgroup 1, Series 1.

36. Special Collections, the Milton S. Eisenhower Library, the Johns Hopkins University, MS194, Series 7, 2d Draft.

37. Special Collections, the Milton S. Eisenhower Library, the Johns Hopkins University, MS194, Series 7, 31 March 1952.

38. Donaldson Brown to Detlev W. Bronk, 31 March 1952, Rockefeller Archive Center, Record Group 303-U, Box 5, Folder 7.

39. Minutes and Supporting Papers, Meeting of 26 May 1952, the Ferdinand Hamburger, Jr., Archives of the Johns Hopkins University, Record Group Number 01.001, Board of Trustees, Series 2.

40. Special Collections, the Milton S. Eisenhower Library, the Johns Hopkins University, MS194, Series 7, December 1952.

41. Many years later, Lattimore adduced what he believed was the true reason Carter offered testimony against him:

> There was one case of a man, a university professor, with whom I had discussed the collaboration between the Page School of International Relations and his department. He was Catholic, and it turned out that he was what is called in America a "populist," which means that he was against the rich being too rich and the poor being too poor. He came from one of the Western states where everybody hunted. In Maryland, however, the shooting of ducks, in migration seasons along the Maryland estuary, for example, was controlled by a few rich people who owned this or that section of the shore, and they acted together so that they reserved the shooting to themselves and kept outsiders out. This made this man furious. As soon as I knew that he was radical in this sense, I asked him some questions to find out how radical he was in general.
>
> Later, he used the fact that I had asked him such questions as evidence of my being a Communist agent seeking to recruit him. One bit of the testimony he gave was that when he was invited to an outdoor party at my home in Maryland, John Service, the state department man who was also one of the guests, said that he had a document that he wanted me to examine. This document was a denunciation of the United States by Mao Tse-tung, and in it he used a couple of phrases in his Hunan dialect which Service had not been able to identify in a dictionary. So, he and I went up to my study, and I got my dictionaries out, and we tried to find the correct translation for the bad language used by Mao Tse-tung, which said something like "the Americans stink like an ancient corpse." This university professor later reported to the investigation that Service and I had gone away to examine in private a classified document.

(Owen Lattimore [compiled by Fujiko Isono], *China Memoirs: Chiang Kai-shek and the War against Japan* [Tokyo: University of Tokyo Press, 1990], 234.)

42. Letter from twenty-nine faculty members to President Detlev W. Bronk, 1 April 1952, Special Collections, the Milton S. Eisenhower Library, the Johns Hopkins University, MS194, Series 7.

43. As quoted in "Trustees May Decide," *The Johns Hopkins University News Letter,* 4 April 1952.

44. Carlyle Barton to P. Stewart Macaulay, 1 April 1952, the Ferdinand Hamburger, Jr., Archives of the Johns Hopkins University, Record Group Number 03.001, Office of the Provost, Series 2, P. Stewart Macaulay, Subseries 2, Numerical Subject Files, File #[116, Walter Hines Page School of International Relations].

45. P. Stewart Macaulay to Mr. Barton, 2 April 1952, the Johns Hopkins University Archives, Office of the Provost, Series 2, Subseries 2, File #116.

46. Marjorie M. Scott to Carlyle Barton, 2 April 1952, the Johns Hopkins University Archives, Board of Trustees Supporting Papers.

47. Helen B. Taussig, M.D., to Carlyle Barton, 3 April 1952, the Johns Hopkins University Archives, Board of Trustees Supporting Papers.

48. Joseph Stokes, Jr., M.D., to Detlev Bronk, 21 April 1952, the Johns Hopkins University Archives, [Office of the President Records, File #793.7].

49. [Edwards A. Park] to Mr. Barton, 5 April 1952, the Johns Hopkins University Archives, Office of the President Records, File #902.

50. E. A. Park to President Bronk, 6 April 1952, the Johns Hopkins University Archives, Office of the President Records, File #902.

Chapter Five

1. J. D. Colman to Carlyle Barton, Detlev W. Bronk, P. Stewart Macaulay, and Lynn D. Poole, 28 March 1952, the Ferdinand Hamburger, Jr., Archives of the Johns Hopkins University, [Record Group Number 01.001, Board of Trustees, Series 2, Minutes and Supporting Papers].

2. Owen Lattimore to Detlev W. Bronk, 7 April 1952, the Johns Hopkins University Archives, Board of Trustees Supporting Papers, Special Collections, the Milton S. Eisenhower Library, the Johns Hopkins University, MS194, Series 7.

3. Board of Trustees Minutes, Meeting of 21 April 1952, Special Collections, the Milton S. Eisenhower Library, the Johns Hopkins University, MS194, Series 7.

4. Detlev W. Bronk to Owen Lattimore, 21 April 1952, the Johns Hopkins University Archives, Board of Trustees Supporting Papers.

5. Draft of statement on academic freedom, prepared 22 May 1952, the Ferdinand Hamburger, Jr., Archives of the Johns Hopkins University, Record Group Number 03.001, Office of the Provost, Series 2, P. Stewart Macaulay, Subseries 2, Numerical Subject Files, File #1, Academic Council.

6. Letter and report from Philip Bard to Detlev W. Bronk, 23 May 1952, the Johns Hopkins University Archives, [Office of the Provost, Series 2, Subseries 2, File #1].

7. Francis White to William C. Bullitt, 26 May 1952, Special Collections, the Milton S. Eisenhower Library, the Johns Hopkins University, MS194, Series 7.

8. Donaldson Brown to Charles S. Garland, 20 May 1952, the Johns Hopkins University Archives, [Board of Trustees Supporting Papers].

9. Carlyle Barton to Detlev W. Bronk, 6 August 1952, the Ferdinand Hamburger, Jr., Archives of the Johns Hopkins University, Record Group Number 02.001, Office of the President, Series 1, Numerically-Coded Subject Files, 1878–1963, File #902, Walter Hines Page School of International Relations.

10. Leo Spitzer, 1952.

11. Donaldson Brown to Charles S. Garland, 20 May 1952, the Johns Hopkins University Archives, [Board of Trustees Supporting Papers].

12. Lionel S. Lewis, *Cold War on Campus: A Study of the Politics of Organizational Control* (New Brunswick, N.J.: Transaction Books, 1988). See, esp., chaps. 2 and 4.

13. George Boas, "The New Authoritarianism," *The Johns Hopkins Magazine* (May 1952): 2–3, 27–32.

14. Rignal Baldwin to P. Stewart Macaulay, 24 March 1953, the Johns Hopkins University Archives, [Office of the Provost, Series 2, Subseries 2, File #110].

15. Remarks added to a letter soliciting funds from Detlev W. Bronk, the Johns Hopkins University Archives, [Office of the President Records, File #793.7].

16. Harry N. Baetjer to Henry S. Baker, 6 November 1952, the Johns Hopkins University Archives, [Board of Trustees Supporting Papers].

17. Carlyle Barton to Harry N. Baetjer, 10 December 1952, the Johns Hopkins University Archives, [Board of Trustees Supporting Papers].

18. Harry N. Baetjer to Carlyle Barton, 13 December 1952, the Johns Hopkins University Archives, [Board of Trustees Supporting Papers].

19. Detlev W. Bronk, the Johns Hopkins University Archives, [Office of the President Records, File #793.7].

20. Paul R. Goudy to Eli Frank, Jr., 15 December 1952, the Johns Hopkins University Archives, Office of the Provost, Series 2, Subseries 2, File #110.

21. P. Stewart Macaulay to Paul R. Goudy, 2 February 1953, the Johns Hopkins University Archives, Office of the Provost, Series 2, Subseries 2, File #110.

22. Eli Frank, Jr., to Colonel William J. Witte, 5 January 1953, the Johns Hopkins University Archives, Office of the Provost, Series 2, Subseries 2, File #116.

23. Sydney M. Cone to James R. Young, 9 February 1952, the Johns Hopkins University Archives, Office of the Provost, Series 2, Subseries 2, File #116.

24. P. Stewart Macaulay to Sydney M. Cone, Jr., 13 February 1952, the Johns Hopkins University Archives, Office of the Provost, Series 2, Subseries 2, File #116.

25. The Ferdinand Hamburger, Jr., Archives of the Johns Hopkins University, the Johns Hopkins University Financial Reports, Summaries of Income and Expenditures, from years ended 30 June 1948 to 30 June 1958.

26. Owen Lattimore, "Lattimore on the Moscow Trials," *The New Leader,* 10 November 1952, 16.

27. Sidney Hook, "Lattimore on the Moscow Trials," *The New Leader,* 10 November 1952, 17–19.

28. Arthur M. Schlesinger, Jr., "History of the Week," *New York Post,* 21 December 1952.

29. Thurman Arnold to Arthur M. Schlesinger, Jr., 9 March 1953, Thurman Arnold Collection, American Heritage Center, University of Wyoming.

30. The Johns Hopkins University Archives, Board of Trustees Minutes, Meeting of 16 December 1952.

31. The Johns Hopkins University Archives, Board of Trustees Minutes, Draft, Meeting of 16 December 1952.

32. As quoted in "Far Eastern Authority Proclaims Innocence; Arraignment Due Friday," *Baltimore Sun,* 17 December 1952.

33. Owen Lattimore to Detlev W. Bronk, 21 December 1952, the Johns Hopkins University Archives, [Office of the President Records, File #793.7].

34. Telegram from E. F. McDonald, Jr., to Detlev W. Bronk, 18 December 1952, Rockefeller Archive Center.

35. Edwin Hirschmann to Board of Trustees, 30 December 1952, the Johns Hopkins University Archives, Office of the President Records, File #902.

36. The Ferdinand Hamburger, Jr., Archives of the Johns Hopkins University, Records of Academic Council, Subgroup 2, Committees, "Lattimore Committee, 1952."

37. Memorandum from E. P. Churchill, the Johns Hopkins University Archives, Office of the Provost, Series 2, Subseries 2, File #116.

38. Vannevar Bush to Detlev W. Bronk, 22 December 1952, the Johns Hopkins University Archives, [Office of the President Records, File #793.7].

39. Donaldson Brown to Andrew T. Court, 9 January 1953, Special Collections, the Milton S. Eisenhower Library, the Johns Hopkins University, [MS194, Series 7].

40. Letter soliciting funds from George Boas, to Dear Colleague, 5 January 1953, the Johns Hopkins University Archives, [Office of the President Records, File #902].

41. Milton T. Edgerton, M.D., to George Boas, 8 January 1953, the Johns Hopkins University Archives, [Office of the President Records, File #902].

42. Letter soliciting funds from George Boas, to Dear Colleague, 5 January 1953, the Johns Hopkins University Archives, [Office of the President Records, File #902].

43. Milton T. Edgerton, M.D., to Detlev W. Bronk, 8 January 1953, the Johns Hopkins University Archives, Office of the President Records, File #902.

44. J. M. T. Finney, Jr., M.D., to Detlev W. Bronk, 9 January 1953, the Johns Hopkins University Archives, Office of the President Records, File #902.

45. Amos R. Koontz to George Boas, 29 January 1953, the Johns Hopkins University Archives, Office of the Provost, Series 2, Subseries 2, File #116.

46. Paul Hessemer to George Boas, 18 March 1953, [the Johns Hopkins University Archives, Office of the Provost, Series 2, Subseries 2, File #116].

47. Lucius C. Porter to George Boas, 16 February 1953, [the Johns Hopkins University Archives, Office of the Provost, Series 2, Subseries 2, File #116].

48. The Johns Hopkins University Archives, Board of Trustees Minutes, Meeting of 12 January 1953.

49. As quoted in "Seek $40,000 Defense Fund for Lattimore," *Worcester (Mass.) Gazette,* 10 January 1953.

50. Proposed Text of Resolution to Be Submitted to the Academic Council, January 1953, Rockefeller Archive Center.

51. "Colleagues Open $40,000 Drive in Lattimore Defense," *Boston Herald,* 11 January 1953.

52. "Boas Clarifies His Plea for Lattimore," *Baltimore Evening Sun,* 27 January 1953.

53. As quoted in "Hopkins Disavows Fund for Lattimore: Collection Called Project of Boas," *Baltimore News-Post,* 27 January 1953, the Johns Hopkins University Archives, Office of the Provost, Series 2, Subseries 2, File #116.

54. Milton T. Edgerton, M.D., to George Boas, 8 January 1953, the Johns Hopkins University Archives, [Office of the President Records, File #902].

55. Mrs. Malcom Stewart to Detlev W. Bronk, 17 February 1953, the Johns Hopkins University Archives, Office of the President Records, File #902.

56. As quoted in Edwin Hirschmann, "Not Sanctioned by Hopkins Officials; Gifts Voluntary," *The Johns Hopkins University News Letter* (16 January 1953): 1, 11.

57. Fulton Lewis, Jr., Washington Report, "The Only Issue in Lattimore Trial," Baltimore News-Post, January, 1953, [the Johns Hopkins University Archives, Office of the President Records, File #902].

58. [Elvera Thomsen] to Gentlemen of the Johns Hopkins University Administration, 21 January 1953, the Johns Hopkins University Archives, Office of the President Records, File #902.

59. Letter to the Editor, *Baltimore Evening Sun,* 27 January 1953, Special Collections, the Milton S. Eisenhower Library, the Johns Hopkins University, MS10.

60. George Boas and Harvey Wheeler, eds., *Lattimore the Scholar* (Baltimore, 1953). The letter of solicitation began: "The recent charges against our colleague, Owen Lattimore, include that of not being a reputable scholar. It is admitted that he is a clever and able journalist, but since he has no university degree and title of 'professor,' he is accused of occupying a position on the faculty under false pretenses. As a friend of Lattimore, I believe that it is important to vindicate his reputation and that vindica-

tion can come only from those of his colleagues who occupy chairs of Far Eastern thought, language, culture, history and the like." Letter from George Boas to [forty scholars], 29 August 1951, Special Collections, the Milton S. Eisenhower Library, the Johns Hopkins University, Records of the History Department, RG 04.110, Series 3, Faculty Records).

61. Reverend W. Owings Stone to Mr. J. Harvey Wheeler, 18 February 1953, [the Johns Hopkins University Archives, Office of the President Records, File #902].

62. R. Sanger to George Boas, 10 February 1953, [the Johns Hopkins University Archives, Office of the President Records, File #902].

63. As quoted in "UN Council's Invitation to Lattimore Allowed: Watson Permits Club to Schedule Speech with Reluctance," *Harvard Crimson,* 14 December 1953, p. 1.

64. As quoted in "Lattimore to Speak Despite Legion Attack," *Harvard Crimson,* 13 February 1954, p. 1.

65. As quoted in "Legion Aims to Pressure College about Lattimore: Will Try to Prevent His UN Council Talk," *Harvard Crimson,* 15 February 1954, p. 1.

66. As quoted in "Page School to Go at Johns Hopkins: Lattimore's Title of Director to Be Discontinued—Move Is Part of Reorganization," *New York Times,* 17 April 1953, p. 11.

67. The Johns Hopkins University Archives, Board of Trustees Minutes, Meeting of 2 February 1953.

68. P. Stewart Macaulay to Lynn D. Poole, 4 February 1953, the Johns Hopkins University Archives, Office of the Provost, Series 2, Subseries 2, File #66.

69. Owen Lattimore to Cyril Clemens, 11 May 1953, personal papers of Owen Lattimore, in storage, Arnold & Porter.

70. Richard Lloyd Jones, "That Johns Hopkins Professor," *Tulsa Tribune,* 2 May 1953.

71. Lewis, *Cold War on Campus,* esp. chap. 6.

Chapter Six

1. "Hopkins Is Silent on Lattimore Action," *Baltimore Sun,* 29 June 1955, p. 2.

2. Carlyle Barton to Lowell J. Reed, 28 June 1955, the Ferdinand Hamburger, Jr., Archives of the Johns Hopkins University, Record Group

Number 02.001, Office of the President, Series 1, Numerically Coded Subject Files, 1878–1963, [File #902, Walter Hines Page School of International Relations].

3. Carlyle Barton to Lowell J. Reed, 18 July 1955, the Johns Hopkins University Archives, [Office of the President Records, File #902].

4. Peter J. Kumpa, "U.S. Abandons Its Perjury Charges against Lattimore," *Baltimore Sun,* 29 June 1955, pp. 1, 2.

5. Owen Lattimore to Lowell J. Reed, 2 July 1955, [the Johns Hopkins University Archives, Office of the President Records, File #902].

6. Lowell J. Reed to Owen Lattimore, 9 July 1955, the Johns Hopkins University Archives, [Office of the President Records, File #902].

7. Lowell J. Reed to Carlyle Barton, 12 July 1955 and Lowell J. Reed to Charles S. Garland, 12 July 1955, the Johns Hopkins University Archives, [Office of the President Records, File #902].

8. Charles S. Garland to Carlyle Barton, 7 July 1955, the Ferdinand Hamburger, Jr., Archives of the Johns Hopkins University, [Record Group Number 01.001, Board of Trustees, Series 2, Minutes and Supporting Papers].

9. Telegram from R. A. Smith to President, 30 June 1955, the Johns Hopkins University Archives, [Office of the President Records, File #902].

10. Carlyle Barton to Lowell J. Reed, 6 July 1955, the Johns Hopkins University Archives, [Office of the President Records, File #902].

11. Carlyle Barton to Harvey B. Stone, 6 July 1955, the Johns Hopkins University Archives, [Board of Trustees Supporting Papers].

12. Carlyle Barton to Lowell J. Reed, 19 July 1955, the Johns Hopkins University Archives, [Office of the President Records, File #902].

13. The Johns Hopkins University Archives, Board of Trustees Minutes, Meeting of 9 September 1955.

14. Henry S. Baker to Lowell J. Reed, 25 August 1955, [the Johns Hopkins University Archives, Board of Trustees Supporting Papers].

15. Carlyle Barton to Lowell J. Reed, 18 July 1955, the Johns Hopkins University Archives, [Office of the President Records, File #902].

16. Ibid.

17. Charles S. Garland to Lowell J. Reed, 2 September 1955, the Johns Hopkins University Archives, [Office of the President Records, File #902].

18. C. Vann Woodward to Sidney Painter, 21 July 1955, [the Johns Hopkins University Archives, Office of the President Records, File #902].

19. Sidney Painter to Lowell J. Reed, 2 August 1955, [the Johns Hopkins University Archives, Office of the President Records, File #902].

20. Fritz Machlup to Lowell J. Reed, 8 August 1955, the Johns Hopkins University Archives, [Office of the President Records, File #902].

21. Arthur I. Waskow to Lowell J. Reed, 28 June 1955, the Johns Hopkins University Archives, [Office of the President Records, File #902].

22. Telegram from George Pope Shannon to Ralph F. Fuchs, 1 August 1955, personal papers of Owen Lattimore, in storage, Arnold & Porter.

23. Memorandum from George Pope Shannon to Ralph F. Fuchs, 16 August 1955, personal papers of Owen Lattimore, in storage, Arnold & Porter.

24. Harvey B. Stone to Carlyle Barton, 5 July 1955, the Johns Hopkins University Archives, [Office of the President Records, File #902].

25. The Johns Hopkins University Archives, Office of the President Records, File #902, "Lattimore Freed," *Chicago Tribune,* 30 June 1955.

26. Carlyle Barton to Lowell J. Reed, 18 July 1955, the Johns Hopkins University Archives, [Office of the President Records, File #902].

27. Robert W. Williams to Lowell J. Reed, 18 August 1955, [the Johns Hopkins University Archives, Office of the President Records, File #902].

28. Charles S. Garland to Lowell J. Reed, 2 September 1955, the Johns Hopkins University Archives, [Office of the President Records, File #902].

29. Faculty Committee to Lowell J. Reed, 8 September 1955, the Johns Hopkins University Archives, [Office of the President Records, File #902].

30. The Johns Hopkins University Archives, Board of Trustees Minutes, Meeting of 9 September 1955.

31. Carlyle Barton to Jacob France, 13 September 1955, the Johns Hopkins University Archives, [Board of Trustees Supporting Papers].

32. Carlyle Barton to Jacob France, 26 September 1955, the Johns Hopkins University Archives, [Board of Trustees Supporting Papers].

33. John Nelson to Francis White, 14 September 1955, Special Collections, the Milton S. Eisenhower Library, the Johns Hopkins University, MS194, Series 7.

34. Francis White to John Nelson, 19 September 1955, Special Collections, the Milton S. Eisenhower Library, the Johns Hopkins University, MS194, Series 7.

35. Jacob France to Carlyle Barton, 10 November 1955, the Johns Hopkins University Archives, [Board of Trustees Supporting Papers].

36. Carlyle Barton to Lowell J. Reed, 15 November 1955, the Johns Hopkins University Archives, [Office of the President Records, File #902].

37. "Lattimore Back on Job: He Returns to Active Status as Johns Hopkins Lecturer," *New York Times*, 23 September 1955.

38. "Owen Lattimore Again Lecturing at Johns Hopkins," *Baltimore Sun*, 23 September 1955.

39. Edith Dickey Moses to Lowell J. Reed, 24 January 1956, the Johns Hopkins University Archives, Office of the President Records, File #902.

40. Lowell J. Reed to Owen Lattimore, 13 September 1955, the Johns Hopkins University Archives, [Office of the President Records, File #902].

41. Owen Lattimore to Lowell J. Reed, 19 September 1955, the Johns Hopkins University Archives, [Office of the President Records, File #902].

42. Lowell J. Reed to Owen Lattimore, 29 September 1955, the Johns Hopkins University Archives, [Office of the President Records, File #902].

43. Owen Lattimore to Lowell J. Reed, 1 October 1955, the Johns Hopkins University Archives, [Office of the President Records, File #902].

44. Memorandum regarding Owen Lattimore from Lowell J. Reed to File, 10 October 1955, the Johns Hopkins University Archives, [Office of the President Records, File #902].

45. Owen Lattimore to David Lattimore, 4 October 1955, personal papers of Owen Lattimore, in storage, Arnold & Porter.

46. George W. Freeman, M.D., to President, 1 October 1955, the Johns Hopkins University Archives, [Office of the President Records, File #902].

47. Postcard from J. H. Nil[ene] to Sir, the Johns Hopkins University Archives, Office of the President Records, File #902.

48. Florence M. P. Van Kirk to President, 25 September 1955, the Johns Hopkins University Archives, Office of the President Records, File #902.

49. Postcard from L. C. MacKinney to Sir, 24 October [1955], [the Johns Hopkins University Archives, Office of the President Records, File #902].

50. [S. Hull] to Chairman of the Professorial Board, 15 October 1955, the Johns Hopkins University Archives, [Office of the President Records, File #902].

51. "Lattimore Reassumes JHU Lecturing Post: Case Closed," *The Johns Hopkins University News Letter,* 7 October 1955, the Johns Hopkins University Archives, [Office of the President Records, File #902].

52. "A University Stood Firm," *St. Louis Post-Dispatch,* 25 September 1955.

53. Lowell J. Reed to Edwards A. Park, 10 October 1955, the Johns Hopkins University Archives, Office of the President Records, File #902.

54. As quoted in "Lattimore Reassumes JHU Lecturing Post: Case Closed," 1.

55. "Lattimore Talk Shifted: Hartford Insurance Company Cancels Offer of Hall," *New York Times,* 7 December 1955, p. 78.

56. "Lattimore, in Hartford, Says He Has Stock in Company That Denied Him Auditorium," *New York Times,* [17] December 1955.

57. Memorandum from P. Stewart Macaulay to File, 18 January 1956, the Johns Hopkins University Archives, [Office of the Provost, Series 2, Subseries 2, File #110].

58. Memorandum from P. Stewart Macaulay to the President's Confidential File, 9 February 1956, the Johns Hopkins University Archives, [Office of the President Records, File #902].

59. Memorandum regarding Mr. Owen Lattimore from President Lowell J. Reed to File, 8 February 1956, the Johns Hopkins University Archives, [Office of the President Records, File #902].

60. Sidney Painter to Owen Lattimore, 10 February 1956, the Johns Hopkins University Archives, Records of the History Department, RG 04.110, Series 3, Faculty Records.

61. Memorandum from President Reed to File, 24 February 1956, the Johns Hopkins University Archives, [Office of the President Records, File #902].

62. Owen Lattimore to President Reed, 15 July 1956, the Johns Hopkins University Archives, [Office of the President Records, File #902].

63. Lowell J. Reed to Mr. Lattimore, 2 August 1956, the Johns Hopkins University Archives, [Office of the President Records, File #902].

64. Owen Lattimore to President Reed, 26 August 1956, the Johns Hopkins University Archives, [Office of the President Records, File #902].

65. Memorandum regarding Mr. Owen Lattimore from President Lowell J. Reed to File, 28 September 1956, the Johns Hopkins University Archives, [Office of the President Records, File #902].

66. Lowell J. Reed, to Mr. Lattimore, 28 September 1956, the Johns Hopkins University Archives, [Office of the President Records, File #902].

67. Adams Family to Dr. Eisenhower, 13 August [1957], the Johns Hopkins University Archives, Office of the President Records, File #902.

68. Kathryn Ellis Nowak to Dr. Milton Eisenhower, 17 November 1957, the Johns Hopkins University Archives, [Office of the President Records, File #902].

69. Keith Spalding to Mrs. Nowak, 22 November 1957, the Johns Hopkins University Archives, Office of the President Records, File #902.

70. Memorandum regarding Owen Lattimore from President Milton S. Eisenhower to File, 9 January 1957, the Johns Hopkins University Archives, [Office of the President Records, File #902].

71. Milton S. Eisenhower to Mr. Lattimore, 22 January 1957, the Johns Hopkins University Archives, [Office of the President Records, File #902].

72. The Johns Hopkins University Archives, Board of Trustees Executive Committee Minutes, Meeting of 4 February 1957.

73. Owen Lattimore to President [Milton S.] Eisenhower, 31 January 1957, the Johns Hopkins University Archives, [Office of the President Records, File #902].

74. Frederic C. Lane to Mr. Eisenhower, 11 February 1957, the Johns Hopkins University Archives, [Office of the President Records, File #902].

75. E.F. Penrose to Dr. Eisenhower, 1 March 1957, the Johns Hopkins University Archives, [Office of the President Records, File #902].

76. Sidney Painter to President Eisenhower, 27 February 1957, the Johns Hopkins University Archives, [Office of the President Records, File #902].

77. C. Vann Woodward to Mr. Eisenhower, 18 February 1957, the Johns Hopkins University Archives, [Office of the President Records, File #902].

78. Owen Lattimore to President Eisenhower, 22 March 1957, the Johns Hopkins University Archives, [Office of the President Records, File #902].

79. Milton S. Eisenhower to Owen Lattimore, 28 March 1957, the Johns Hopkins University Archives, [Office of the President Records, File #902].

80. Sidney Painter to President Milton S. Eisenhower, 17 April 1957, the Johns Hopkins University Archives, [Office of the President Records, File #902].

81. Sidney Painter to President Milton S. Eisenhower, 10 May 1957, the Johns Hopkins University Archives, [Office of the President Records, File #902].

82. Milton S. Eisenhower to Owen Lattimore, 21 May 1957, the Johns Hopkins University Archives, [Office of the President Records, File #902].

83. Eleanor Lattimore to Dearest Barretts, 17 March 1957, personal papers of Owen Lattimore, in storage, Arnold & Porter.

84. Sidney Painter to President Milton S. Eisenhower, 23 December 1957, the Johns Hopkins University Archives, [Office of the President Records, File #902].

85. P. Stewart Macaulay to Sidney Painter, 22 January 1958, the Johns Hopkins University Archives, [Office of the Provost, Series 2, Subseries 2, File #110].

86. As quoted in "Lattimore Gives Advice on Red China: Suggests Being Guided by Peiping's Neighbors on U.N. Seat," *Baltimore Sun,* 11 November 1958, Enoch Pratt Free Library, Baltimore, Maryland.

87. As quoted in "Dodd Asks Probe of Lattimore Junket," [*Baltimore Evening Sun,* 23 August 1961], the Johns Hopkins University Archives, Office of the President Records, File #902.

88. As quoted in Donald Bremner, "Traveler's Return: Lattimore for Nod to Mongolia, but Disclaims U.S. Policy Role," *Baltimore Evening Sun,* 4 October 1961, the Johns Hopkins University Archives, Office of the President Records, File #902.

89. Oliver B. Hopkins to Chairman Board of Trustees, 21 August 1961, the Johns Hopkins University Archives, Office of the President Records, File #902.

90. Letter from Isaiah Bowman to Lauchlin Currie, 2 May 1941, Franklin D. Roosevelt Library.

91. The Johns Hopkins University Archives, Board of Trustees, Executive Committee, Minutes, Meeting of 5 November 1962.

Chapter Seven

1. C. Wright Mills, *The Sociological Imagination* (New York: Grove Press, 1961), 143.

2. Paul F. Lazarsfeld and Wagner Thielens, Jr., *The Academic Mind: Social Scientists in a Time of Crisis* (Glencoe, Ill.: The Free Press, 1958), 92–93.

3. Lionel S. Lewis, *Cold War on Campus: A Study of the Politics of Organizational Control* (New Brunswick, N.J.: Transaction Books, 1988), see, esp. pp. 138–44, 222–32, 237–47, 266.

4. Fisk University, Board of Trustees Minutes, Executive Committee, Meeting of 19 November 1954.

5. Lewis, *Cold War on Campus.* (As was the case at Johns Hopkins, at Cornell University there was considerable publicity and pressure on the authorities to curtail the political activities of the physicist Philip Morrison. Although Morrison did not lose his job, the administration was far from resolute [pp. 210–22].)

6. There were few exceptions. See Charles H. McCormick, *This Nest of Vipers: McCarthyism and Higher Education in the Mundel Affairs, 1951–52* (Urbana and Chicago: University of Illinois Press, 1989).

7. Richard Hofstadter, *Academic Freedom in the Age of the College* (New York: Columbia University Press, 1961), 120.

8. Francis Wayland, *Thoughts on the Present Collegiate System in the United States* (Boston: Gould, Kendall, & Lincoln, 1842), 23.

9. Ibid., 151.

10. Hubert Park Beck, *Men Who Control Our Universities: The Economic and Social Composition of Governing Boards of Thirty Leading American Universities* (Morningside Heights, N.Y.: King's Crown Press, 1947), 6.

11. Thorstein Veblen, *The Higher Learning in America: A Memorandum on the Conduct of Universities by Business Men* (New York: Hill and Wang, 1962), 59–61.

12. John R. P. French, Jr., and Bertram Raven, "The Bases of Social Power," in Dorwin Cartwright, ed., *Studies in Social Power* (Ann Arbor: The University of Michigan, Research Center for Group Dynamics, Institute for Social Research, 1959).

13. David R. Holmes, review of *Cold War on Campus: A Study of the Politics of Organizational Control,* by Lionel S. Lewis, *Journal of Higher Education* 61 (March/April 1990): 228.

14. As quoted in "The Professor and the Police," *Harvard Magazine* (September–October 1989): 42–45.

15. Lewis, *Cold War on Campus*, passim.

16. Ibid. See, esp., pp. 137, 153–65.

17. The conventional view remains that boards are "essential to the effective functioning of American higher education," and that lay boards

have been instrumental in making it "the best system of higher education in the world." Clark Kerr and Marian L. Gade, *The Guardians: Boards of Trustees of American Colleges and Universities* (Washington, D.C.: Association of Governing Boards of Colleges and Universities, 1989), 5, 7.

18. Lewis, *Cold War on Campus*, see, esp., pps. 222–32.

19. Hugh Hawkins, *Pioneer: A History of the Johns Hopkins University, 1874–1889* (Ithaca, N.Y.: Cornell University Press, 1960). See, esp., pps. 21–23, 36–37, 91.

20. Ibid., 21.

21. Ibid., 22.

22. Ibid., 36.

23. Ibid., 37.

24. Daniel Coit Gilman, "Another Word on College Controversies," *Nation* (24 July 1884): 69.

25. Hawkins, *Pioneer: A History of the Johns Hopkins University, 1874–1889,* 91.

26. Paul Neff Garber, *John Carlisle Kilgo: President of Trinity College, 1894–1910* (Durham, N.C.: Duke University Press, 1937), 241.

27. Ibid., 261–63.

28. Walter Hines Page, "A Notable Victory for Academic Freedom," *World's Work* 7 (January 1904): 4287.

29. Eliot Freidson, *Professional Powers: A Study of the Institutionalization of Formal Knowledge* (Chicago: The University of Chicago Press, 1986), 150.

30. Reece McGee, *Academic Janus: The Private College and Its Faculty* (San Francisco: Jossey-Bass Inc., 1971), 21.

31. Freidson, *Professional Powers: A Study of the Institutionalization of Formal Knowledge,* 136.

Index